DAVID R. LIPTON received a PHD in history from the University of Toronto in 1975. He is now pursuing a career in finance.

This probing study of the career, works, and influence of Ernst Cassirer – a German-Jewish neo-Kantian who taught at the University of Hamburg until Hitler came to power – analyses his thoughts on human culture as they developed during the turbulent political and cultural conditions in the Germany of his time. The most striking characteristic of Cassirer's life and work was his belief in the freedom of the individual and in the necessary connection between individual freedom and the primacy of reason in human history. Cassirer wanted to pass on to his contemporaries the courage to use their own reason. His failure to create a lasting world view based on these ideas reflected a dilemma confronting many liberal intellectuals on the European continent.

The author examines several distinct phases in Cassirer's career. Part 1 deals with Cassirer as a philosopher of Imperial Germany and examines his early neo-Kantian writings (1899–1914). Part 2 covers the years 1914–22 and the reorientation of Cassirer's intellectual standpoint in connection with the issues arising within the German academic community and his reaction to the war of 1914–18. Part 3 covers the Weimar period, 1922–33, observing how Cassirer tried to unite all his past and contemporary intellectual activities with his liberal political ideas in order to create a durable critique of human culture. The final chapter, dealing with the period from 1933 to 1945, when he was a political refugee, presents an epilogue to Cassirer's philosophical career in Germany outlining his hesitant reappraisal of his earlier work in the light of the consequences of the rise and fall of Hitler's Third Reich.

An accomplished piece of intellectual history, this book provides a sensitive study of Cassirer's work and its context in the crisis of European civilization between 1914 and 1945.

DAVID R. LIPTON

# Ernst Cassirer: The dilemma of a liberal intellectual in Germany, 1914-1933

UNIVERSITY OF TORONTO PRESS
Toronto   Buffalo   London

© University of Toronto Press 1978
Toronto   Buffalo   London
Printed in Canada

**Library of Congress Cataloging in Publication Data**

Lipton, David R 1947 –
   Ernst Cassirer: the dilemma of a liberal intellectual in Germany, 1914 –
1933.

   Bibliography: p.
   Includes index.
   1. Cassirer, Ernst, 1874 – 1945.    2. Philosophers – Germany –
Biography.    3. Germany – Intellectual life – 20th century.
B3216.C34L56      193      78-6945
ISBN 0-8020-5408-0

Cover photo: Yale University Archives, Yale University Library

TO MY PARENTS

The kind of philosophy that one has depends upon the kind of man that one is.

Fichte

# Contents

# Preface

Despite the great volume and diversity of Cassirer's intellectual output no study exists which attempts to present a coherent overview of his lifelong activities. This volume deals with Cassirer's thought as a whole. His ideas of freedom, progress, and the role of rationality in human affairs are the themes which pervade his discussions of science, philosophy, European culture, primitive life styles, and language formation. This thematic approach makes it possible to deal with his thought in relation to his era. A connection emerges between the intellectual and political pressures of the times and the course of Cassirer's life and work, a connection which hitherto has been unsuspected or ignored by the vast majority of his critics.

When considering the secondary writings on Cassirer, one perceives the Cassirer anomaly: here is a man whose works on the history of thought, particularly those on the Renaissance and the Enlightenment, are classics in their fields, yet whose life has never been thoroughly examined. The Cassirer scholarship has been dominated by people who have approached his work with narrow philosophical problems in mind. The larger humanistic and historical dimensions of his endeavours have been pushed aside in favour of detailed analyses of his theory of concept formation or his critique of science. Consequently, a number of texts, speeches, and letters not directly related to particular philosophical issues have been ignored. Indeed, no one appears to have thought it worth while to find out if any unpublished writings of Cassirer's existed.

This study examines texts neglected by the philosophers which tie his philosophy directly to historical events and in particular his works during and immediately following the first world war. Of equal importance, unpublished speeches and letters which cast more light on Cassirer's reaction to contemporary events are presented here for the first time. Letters and papers from the following places are used: Marburg University Library, Marburg, West Germany, the Warburg Institute, London, England, and Yale University Library, New Haven, Connecticut, USA.

When these sources are used with the already well known material, Cassirer's life's work appears relevant to people not primarily concerned with philosophical issues. In fairness to his critics it should be noted that events just as much as individual interests decisively shaped the trend of Cassirer scholarship. A broader analysis of Cassirer's work was hindered by two events: his abrupt departure from Germany in 1933 and his sudden death in 1945.

In 1933 the German academic community was shaken from top to bottom. The Nazis expelled a large number of professors from the universities, and ultimately from the country. As a result, the neo-Kantian tradition was thrust aside. While the tradition itself – through the works of Cassirer, Cohen, Natorp, Windelband, and Rickert – formed an important part of German scholarship before 1933, after that date neo-Kantianism sank into oblivion because it was one of the losers to Nazism. Indeed, since he was one of the few neo-Kantians left, Cassirer's flight from Germany represented the end of neo-Kantianism in its homeland. Once the tradition lost its base in Germany, it was up to Cassirer to carry his philosophical tradition to another country. Unfortunately, just as he was succeeding in building up a following in the United States, he died of a heart attack.

The cumulative result of the 1933 and 1945 events was that the importance of neo-Kantianism in Germany from 1871 to 1933 had slipped from the purview of scholarship, and from historical memory. With the appearance of the works of Fritz Ringer, Martin Jay, Georg Iggers, and Peter Gay, the academic losers of 1933 have begun to receive a greater hearing. The old tendency to focus on the highest peaks of German culture, so to speak, has yielded to an interest in the lesser peaks and valleys – all of which are critical for a complete understanding of the whole landscape of German culture after the unification of Germany in 1871. The study of the Nietzsches, Manns, Husserls, Heideggers, and Einsteins has given way to the examination of people who might be considered the less interesting figures of the period, a judgment which in my view reflects the lack of scholarship on these men rather than any lack of quality in their work.

In spite of these new developments, a comprehensive study of Cassirer's thought is still lacking. This is lamentable for two reasons. First, his ideas are interesting in their own right, particularly for those concerned about securing an overview of European thought since the Renaissance. Secondly, Cassirer may well be the best representative of both the philosophical side of German liberalism and the dwindling number of academics who supported the Weimar Republic and voted for the German Democratic Party to the bitter end. Cassirer's thought was his life. By using his thought as a case study it is possible to understand better the plight of liberals of his kind in Germany.

Since this book is the first general survey of Ernst Cassirer's life and work I would like to note several bibliographies that may be of use to others interested in his thought. For a complete chronological list of Cassirer's published writings from 1899 to 1946 see Carl H. Hamburg and Walter Solmitz 'Bibliography of the Writings of Ernst Cassirer to 1946' *The Philosophy of Ernst Cassirer* ed. Paul A. Schilpp, pages 883–910 in volume 6 of *The Library of Living Philosophers* (Evanston, Illinois, The Library of Living Philosophers, Inc. 1949). For a list of Cassirer's writings arranged by subject matter see R. Klibansky and W. Solmitz 'Bibliography of Ernst Cassirer's Writings' pages 338–53 in R. Klibansky and H. J. Paton, eds. *Philosophy and History: Essays Presented to Ernst Cassirer* (Oxford, Clarendon Press 1936; 2nd ed., New York, Harper Torchbooks 1963). Finally, for extremely useful lists of the secondary materials on Cassirer see Donald P. Verene's 'Ernst Cassirer: A Bibliography' *Bulletin of Bibliography* 24 (1964): 104–6, 103; and 'Ernst Cassirer: Critical Work 1964–1970' *Bulletin of Bibliography* 29 (1972): 21–4.

Toronto
January 1978

# Acknowledgments

This book grew out of my doctoral dissertation for the University of Toronto. I am especially grateful to Professors Kenneth L. Schmitz and Modris Eksteins of the University of Toronto for their helpful criticism of my work. Many thanks also go to my typist, Eleanor Cowan, who faithfully typed and retyped the dissertation.

The present work uses a number of hitherto unpublished sources either written by Ernst Cassirer or written about him. I would like to express my thanks to the following institutions for permitting me to use some of their materials in this book: Marburg University Library, Marburg, West Germany; the Warburg Institute, London, England; Yale University Library, New Haven, Connecticut, USA.

Most important of all, I wish to thank my wife, Katharine Rounthwaite, for her encouragement and insightful comments while I was editing my dissertation, and her help in proofreading.

Publication of this book has been made possible by grants from the Canadian Federation for the Humanities, using funds provided by the Social Sciences and Humanities Research Council of Canada, from the University of Toronto, and from the Publications Fund of the University of Toronto Press.

ERNST CASSIRER
THE DILEMMA OF A LIBERAL INTELLECTUAL
IN GERMANY 1914-33

# 1

# Introduction

Ernst Cassirer was born to Jewish parents on 28 July 1874 in Breslau. His was an extended family from the upper middle class with commercial and publishing interests. He lived in Germany until May 1933, when he left his homeland because of the Nazi regime's anti-Semitic policies. Even though for a large part of his life Cassirer confined most of his social and intellectual activities to his family circle and a few select colleagues, the course of his life and work were clearly influenced by the events of the period from 1871 to 1933.

The most striking characteristic of Cassirer's life and work was his commitment to preserving the spiritual autonomy of the individual. Throughout his philosophical career Cassirer never doubted that humanity in general and man in particular were free. This fundamental belief was at once the beginning and the end of his intellectual endeavours. Cassirer's desire to affirm the fact of human freedom as completely and convincingly as possible reflected his deep-seated liberalism and its ethical ideal. In the tradition of Kantian ethics, he believed that each individual should be treated as a rational being and as an end in himself, rather than as a means to an end.

It was the courage to use one's own reason, together with his belief in human freedom, that Cassirer sought to pass on to his contemporaries. In pursuing this goal he found himself on the horns of a dilemma. The greater his effort to create a rationalist, liberal world view acceptable to himself, the greater his estrangement from the majority of his compatriots. Conversely, the more he tried to accommodate his contemporaries, the greater his infidelity to his rational, liberal ideals. In order to resolve this dilemma he would have had to rethink his fundamental assumptions and constantly expand the scope of his work. While he was prepared to do this to some extent from 1916 to 1926, he refused to doubt the ability of human reason to satisfy humanity's deepest needs. Instead he fell back on a dogmatic rationalism in the critical years of 1927 to 1933. His overly intellectual world outlook undermined his defence of individual autonomy. Few people found his approach to the human condition very palatable or inspiring.

One of the most remarkable features of Cassirer's work was his consistency. Throughout his life he returned to the idea that man as an individual contained within himself the principles underlying the development of all humanity. In his own words, 'in man as a microcosm all lines of the macrocosm run together.'[1] By stressing the universal significance of the individual and by conceiving each man as an agent of all humanity, Cassirer provided his reader with the theme for comprehending his wide-ranging studies. Whether he dealt with a problem in physics, the Renaissance conception of art, the evolution of language and myth, or the German idea of freedom, Cassirer always argued as if the matter under consideration were best understood through the thoughts of various individuals.

Cassirer's projection of the individual into the centre of historical and cultural developments was a reflection not only of his own bias but of that of his profession as well. German academics, particularly from 1890 to 1933, saw themselves as the bearers of German culture, as a chosen, élite group, which was endangered by the rapid industrialization of Germany.[2] The values of the emerging materialistic society were, they felt, antithetical to their own values. German intellectuals, like their counterparts in other countries, believed they owed their positions in German society to their educational qualifications, not to material or monetary considerations. Hence, they exalted the spiritual quality of a man rather than his financial situation. This view of the world was summed up in the concept of *Kultur*,[3] which sought to elevate the individual to a superior level of existence through the cultivation of his ethical, artistic, and intellectual abilities. The individual was trained to form and perfect the world within and around him. The process assumed universal significance because each individual was potentially a single manifestation of humanity's collective activities. It was this attitude towards culture and the cultivated individual that German intellectuals felt they had to protect from a hostile, rapidly indistrializing society and to transmit to future generations.

Cassirer entered the German university system in 1892 and completed his doctorate in 1899. His first years in academic life coincided with the university community's heightened awareness of its isolation from the mass society which supported it. Faced with a society increasingly uninterested in the autonomy of the cultivated man, Cassirer too adopted the German academicians' view of the individual. This kind of individualism postulated that the cultured individual could achieve a total understanding of every aspect of human activity yet preserve his identity in the faceless masses of an industrialized society.

During the first two years of his academic career Cassirer wandered from subject to subject and from university to university.[4] However, his vacillation between various subjects abruptly ceased in the summer of 1894, when, while taking a course on Kant given by Georg Simmel, Cassirer was introduced to the work of Hermann Cohen, leader of the Marburg School of neo-Kantianism. During one of his lectures, Simmel announced that 'the best books on Kant are written by Hermann Cohen; but I must confess that I do not understand them.'[5] Cassirer apparently held his teacher in such high regard that a strong recommendation by Simmel was enough to induce him to give Cohen's works serious consideration. He became convinced that Simmel's estimation of Cohen had been correct and went to Marburg in 1896 to study philosophy under Cohen.

Despite his move to Marburg and although he later became a prominent member of the neo-Kantian movement, Cassirer remained influenced by Simmel. The most important theme that Cassirer absorbed from Simmel was the idea of the unavoidable and insoluble conflict between the individual and society. Simmel's view of this conflict was not original in itself. It was a classic expression of the German academicians' anxieties about the future of the cultivated individual in a society which demanded more regimentation and standardization from its members as well as a statement of liberal credo affirming the rights of the individual. Simmel believed that the practical problem of society always revolved around the tension between societal forms (that is, institutions, laws, customs, opinions) and the individual's desire for freedom to create his own life style. Simmel envisioned this tension between freedom and form as an insoluble conflict between 'the whole, which imposes the onesidedness of partial function upon its elements, and the part, which itself strives to be a whole.'[6]

Cassirer sought to place this conflict in a wider philosophical and historical context. By placing the free and rational individual at the centrepoint of his speculations, he connected the history of humanity with each individual's struggle to establish himself as a spiritually autonomous entity. For Cassirer it was important to realize that the perpetual conflict between the individual and his society, a conflict which resulted in the quest for personal freedom, was the essential ingredient of history.

Cassirer's individualism was in effect the intellectual synthesis of three closely related ideas: a specific idea of freedom, a commitment to the use of reason, and a cosmopolitan view of history. Each of these ideas was meaning-ful only in combination with the other two. A man was free in so far as he used the dictates of reason to guide his own activities and to comprehend his place in the continuous chain of human history. The dictates of reason were those principles that made knowledge and existence intelligible to all men. On realizing that those principles were the collective, historical creation of humanity, each individual could live in accordance with them and consider himself free. For to live according to one's own rules is to be free. The univer-sal or cosmopolitan view of history was attained once the individual recog-nized that all peoples participated in the growing awareness of the role of rea-son in human history, and that this awareness itself was the condition of the possibility of individual freedom. Cassirer's concept of the individual was in effect an imperative: to be free one must have the courage to follow the dic-tates of reason in one's own life, and thereby to discover the meaning and place of reason and freedom in human history. Cassirer's *Kultur*-oriented vi-sion of history first clearly emerged in his wartime study of German thought (1916) and was to remain a permanent fixture of his philosophical specula-tions until his death. Significantly, his cosmopolitan humanism later played a very important role in his studies of the philosophies of the Renaissance (1927) and the Enlightenment (1932).

The idea of progress was another cardinal element of Cassirer's historical vision. In the intellectual sense, progress was humanity's increasing realiza-tion that all men became free through the use of reason. In political terms, progress was the actual expansion of human freedom through the increasing application of reason to political and social affairs. Ideologically speaking, this position placed Cassirer in the liberal camp. Liberals, especially in the late nineteenth and early twentieth centuries, cherished the belief that the history of mankind was in effect the story of man's achievement of freedom and of the establishment of a political order which would institutionalize and preserve human freedom.[7] A republican parliamentary system of government was considered the best way to guarantee the individual's autonomy by pro-tecting his right to be in opposition to the regime and to other members of so-ciety. Generally, Cassirer's view of politics was in the Kantian tradition of po-litical liberalism, where politics was primarily a matter of principles, not of actual ruling. The split between theory and practice, between the formula-tion of the theoretical basis of a liberal regime and the means of establishing that regime in fact, afflicted Cassirer's politics as it did all other German fol-lowers of Kant's idealist conception of liberalism.[8]

When mixed with his own neo-Kantian inclinations, Cassirer's commit-ment to individual liberty and the *Kultur* ideal resulted in a unique outlook on the world (*Weltanschauung*). While his writings went through different phases, his rationalist liberal world view remained the same. There were three distinct yet closely related levels to Cassirer's *Weltanschauung*; these provide the schematic basis for this analysis of his work. First, on the philosophical level, he remained a neo-Kantian who maintained a relational theory of knowledge. He believed that conceptual relations, that is, a priori ideas, were the basis of any comprehension of reality. Furthermore, knowledge of reality was not something that required the acceptance of immutable facts. On the contrary, such knowledge was an endless task of establishing relations between facts and values, between the particular and the whole. Second, on the cultural and historical level, Cassirer remained a cosmopolitan humanist who included all peoples, from primitive tribes to the inhabitants of industrial urban centres, in humanity's movement towards freedom and enlightenment. Third, on the political or ideological level, Cassirer remained dedicated to liberal values. The development and preservation of free and rational individuals was a task that always absorbed his energies.

Cassirer's *Weltanschauung* evolved through several distinct phases. In the first phase (1899–1914), we see him as a philosopher in Imperial Germany, dealing with the problem of knowledge as discussed in neo-Kantian circles in Germany from 1871 to 1914. The second phase, the years 1914–22, covers the reorientation of his intellectual standpoint in connection with the issues arising in the German academic community and in reaction to the war of 1914–18. In the years 1923–33, his Weimar period, Cassirer tried to unite all his past and contemporary intellectual activities with his liberal political ideas in order to create a lasting and all-encompassing spiritual synthesis – a critique of human culture.

In the first stage of his Weimar period, 1923–26, Cassirer waged a successful fight to maintain the harmony of his *Weltanschauung*. This intellectual equilibrium, which is one of my major considerations, rested on Cassirer's balancing of a specific view of humanity's progressive enlightenment, a commitment to a logical analysis of consciousness, and a respect for and interest in the totality of concrete life forms. In the second stage of the Weimar years, 1927–33, Cassirer's orientation changed, and he returned to his pre-1914 interest in epistemological problems which focused primarily on an analysis of human consciousness. This was because he felt it would be the best way to defend his rationalist outlook on the world. The political implications of this intellectual reorientation occupy the final pages of my discussion of Cassirer's Weimar period.

The last chapter of the study is an epilogue to Cassirer's philosophical career in Germany. From 1933 to 1945 he was a political refugee. After being driven from his homeland by the Nazis Cassirer moved to England, then to Sweden, and finally to the United States, where he died on 13 April 1945. In the last twelve years of his life Cassirer gradually re-examined his philosophical assumptions in the light of the events of 1933–45.

LIBERAL VALUES AND PRACTICES: THE LIBERAL DILEMMA

Although no record exists of Cassirer's political preferences prior to the first world war, he probably voted liberal. Since the Napoleonic era liberalism had championed Jewish emancipation. This circumstance and the fact that most Jews were middle class predisposed them to vote overwhelmingly for one of the liberal parties. Apparently, many of them felt that liberalism offered the best way of attaining full political and social equality for all Germans without jeopardizing the freedom of the individual. In any event, Cassirer's politics largely remained a private matter, and he deliberately avoided active party politics.[9]

However much Cassirer side-stepped political issues, he could not escape his Jewish background. He was constantly affected by the anti-Semitic feelings pervading German society in general, and more particularly the government-controlled universities. These sentiments not only delayed his acquisition of a university teaching position until 1906; they also caused the abrupt termination of his academic career in April 1933. Cassirer's interest in individual freedom and tolerance of human diversity was not only an intellectual response to his times but an emotional one as well.

Cassirer's correspondence with his fiancée in December 1901 clearly showed that his difficulties in securing a university post were due to the anti-Semitism of many university officials.[10] Statistics dealing with the religious composition of the student bodies and teaching staffs of German universities from 1890 to 1910 confirm that German Jews were both over-represented in the universities and subject to discrimination. In Prussia from 1888 to 1890 Jews constituted about 9 per cent of the university student body.[11] From 1890 to 1910 approximately 12 per cent of the university teaching assistants were Jews.[12] So far there seemed to be no evidence of discrimination. On the contrary, the Jews seemed to have more than held their own, since between 1890 to 1910 they never constituted more than 1 per cent of the German population. However, when we examine the percentage of Jews in the higher academic ranks, the bias against them becomes clear, since less than 3 per cent of the full professors were Jews.[13] One would expect that the teaching assistants would in the usual course of events rise in the ranks, so presumably Jews were promoted far less frequently than their Christian counterparts. Most Jews, like Cassirer, were never promoted at all in Imperial Germany. Despite the publication of his work on Leibniz's system in 1902 and his growing reputation as a philosopher and a scholar, Cassirer was not invited to take up a university teaching position. When he was finally appointed a *Privatdozent* at the University of Berlin in 1906, it was primarily due to the personal intervention of Wilhelm Dilthey,[14] and he remained in that position until 1919. No university in Imperial Germany ever rewarded Ernst Cassirer with the professorial position he deserved.

Cassirer's experiences would probably have embittered most people, but this apparently never happened to him. He was often described by his contemporaries as possessing an imperturbable inner serenity coupled with a gracious bearing towards others. These personal qualities did more than prevent Cassirer from becoming embittered. In his work he transformed the social and cultural disharmony surrounding him into an intellectual vision which sought and often found the deeper unity underlying the discordant world of appearances. His belief that a unity pervaded human affairs and his unrelenting efforts to give all human thoughts and actions a proper place in his philosophical speculations imbued Cassirer's work with a liberal and openended quality.

What connected Cassirer to his liberal compatriots in active politics was not so much any participation in political activities, which he abhorred, but his commitment to liberal beliefs. Cassirer's high estimation of the role of freedom in human affairs, his inclination to approach politics through the dictates of reason, and his faith in the inevitability of progress were beliefs held, in varying degrees, by all liberals.

Cassirer's politics displayed the characteristics of one of the two major tendencies of German liberal theory and practice. As with European liberalism generally, the German variant suffered from tension between its idealist and materialist tendencies, but in Germany this clash became acute.

The idealist conception of liberalism gave priority to abstract interpretations of such matters as individualism, the inalienable and natural rights of man, and the necessity of human freedom.[15] Kant became the great philosophical representative of this liberalism. It used the idea of freedom as the means of uniting ethics with politics.[16] Cassirer showed the connection between Kant and liberal values when he said that freedom was the beginning, the centrepoint, and the goal of Kant's entire philosophy.[17]

The materialist conception of liberalism focused on more practical matters. Its position may be summarized in one phrase: *laissez faire*. A government's best achievements would be those which cleared the way for a free market economy. The abolition of internal tariffs and the suppression of all organizations (for example, guilds) interfering with the free circulation of labour would be good examples of desirable state action from this liberal viewpoint. These liberals were not so much interested in the preservation of individual freedom as in the establishment of a social order that would guarantee the supremacy of the profit motive together with its economic system, the free market economy.

While the materialist-idealist dichotomy split German liberals into two opposing camps, the conflicting demands of freedom and equality further divided them. Generally speaking, liberals extolled the virtues of freedom, be it of the spiritual or free market variety, but feared equality. In social terms this fear was translated into anxiety about the masses, while in political terms it became an aversion to satisfying any substantial number of their demands for equality.[18] This attitude decisively affected the history of modern German liberalism. Since the revolution of 1848 most liberals, except for the radical democrats, had initiated a pattern of political behaviour that effectively isolated them from the majority of the German people. When the crunch came in 1848–9, and the middle classes had to choose between order or democracy, they refused to make common cause with the latter. Subsequently, the liberal movement could not, from 1848 to 1933, collectively decide on and consistently follow one course of action in relation to the radical democrats or, later, the social democrats.

With the readmission of the Social Democratic Party (SPD) into the legal political life of Germany in 1890 the principal elements of the German political spectrum were set until 1918. Those groups on the left wanted reform or revolution; those on the right favoured the status quo or a return to the past. From left to right the political groups were situated as follows: socialists, left (idealist) liberals, Catholic Centre party, right (materialist) liberals, conservatives. After 1890 socialism and democracy became equivalents in the public mind; social democracy was synonymous with the industrial masses' demands for the equalization of social and economic benefits. The rising power of social democracy demanded a response from the liberals as it did from the other political and social groups. In political terms, liberals had to ask themselves whether they were willing to co-operate with the SPD in parliamentary elections – a problem of party tactics that exacerbated the idealist-materialist tension in liberalism.

The tactical problems of the liberals were aggravated by a lack of cohesion in their supporters. Their electoral support came largely from the industrial upper class, large and small merchants, artisans, white collar workers, civil servants, and farmers. The demands of these groups were bound to conflict and create striking fluctuations in the party programs which limited the liberals' capacity to enter coalitions with other parties.[19] When left (idealist) liberals, like Theodor Barth and Friedrich Naumann, tried from 1893 to 1910 to build bridges from the liberal centre to the SPD to strengthen the forces of political reform, they were rebuffed both at the polls and within their own parties.[20] In 1910 the left liberal parties unified themselves into the Progressive Party. However, this unity was a fragile one. After the leadership of the party decided to co-operate with the socialists in the runoff federal elections of 1912, the bulk of the Progressive Party's voters preferred to cast their ballots for the conservative rather than for the agreed-upon SPD candidates.[21]

The liberals' reaction to social democracy was an important symptom of their larger problem: between 1871 and 1933 German liberalism encountered insuperable difficulties in reconciling theory and practice. In the wake of national unification in 1871, the rapid industrialization of Germany combined with the nationalist and authoritarian tradition produced a society which placed liberalism on the defensive to such an extent that its theoretical principles had little chance of being realized.[22]

While industrialization had produced an economic system where the middle classes became important in the economic life of the nation, this same economic progress undermined the political independence and social cohesion of the middle classes. The industrial revolution in Germany had created an urban working class (mostly represented by the SPD) that had, at least in theory, a unified vision of history and society, which made it the implacable enemy of the middle-class or capitalist economic system.[23] On the other hand, industrialization fragmented the middle class so that it had 'lost most of its homogeneous social character by the end of the nineteenth century.'[24] Thus, while middle-class liberal voters remained identifiable to their opponents, that is, to the socialists on the political left as well as to the anti-capitalist right-wing parties like the conservatives, they lost their own sense of identity.

The growth of nationalism in Germany also aggravated the liberals' dilemma of choosing between two courses of action, one leading to political and social reform, the other to a passive acceptance of the Imperial status quo, neither of which gave much satisfaction to liberal ideals. While the process of industrialization undermined the social basis of liberal unity, nationalism undermined its spiritual component. German liberalism expounded a system of government under law (*Rechtsstaat*). In the *Rechtsstaat* a society would be governed only by those laws which had been approved by the members of the national community. Brute force or dictatorial government had no place in this concept of the state. While this was only an ideal, it was crucial to German liberalism. Once this principle of government under law was violated or abandoned, a good portion of liberal ideology was meaningless. Between 1862 and 1866 Bismarck ruled Prussia without the consent of the Prussian parliament. The liberals led the opposition to Bismarck's policies, but after the Prussian victory over Austria in 1866, many liberals went over to Bismarck's side and voted for a bill in parliament (the indemnity law) to legalize the past four years of his de facto government. In March 1867 the liberals institutionalized this division with the formation of the National Liberal Party, which broke away from the Progressive party.

The significance of this split was clear. The desire to create a unified German nation had become more important to many liberals than the rights of the individual and the rule of law. Henceforth, a large portion of the middle classes favoured the benevolent dictatorship of the Prussian monarchy, which would not hesitate to sacrifice the rule of law for the maintenance of national unity. Bismarck had succeeded between 1867 and 1871 where the liberals failed in 1848-9; Germany had been unified by force of arms and not by the force of law. The National Liberals felt they were realistic in accepting Bismarck's *fait accompli* and that the Progressives were too idealistic in rejecting it. The Progressives sensed that their former political allies were all too willing to disregard the rule of law, the principal safeguard of individual freedom, when it suited their immediate needs. While the National Liberals became enthusiastic supporters of the Bismarckian system, the Progressives acquiesced to the new political realities. They continued to stress the importance of individual freedom within the context of a *Rechtsstaat* and attempted to build political bridges to the left, culminating in their 1912 electoral agreement with the social democrats. After the founding of the Weimar Republic in 1918, the German People's Party (DVP) took the place of the National Liberals in the liberal political spectrum, and the German Democratic Party (DDP) assumed the tasks of the Progressive Party.

The division of German liberalism into two distinct wings not only was a reaction to the pressure of events but also constituted an ideological response to the question of the relation between freedom and equality. The liberal right (the National Liberals and DVP), arguing from materialist premises, extolled the virtues of economic freedom and opposed any movement towards social equality; they tended to co-operate with the more conservative parties. The moderate and liberal democrats (the Progressives and the DDP), starting from idealist premises, tended to see individual freedom and social equality as interrelated issues and hesitantly sought to co-operate with the left. In spite of their different ways of dealing with the issues of freedom and equality, both the materialists and idealists ultimately failed to sustain the liberal's main cause – the autonomy of the individual. In their responses to the events of 1871 – 1933 all German liberals progressively, though not intentionally, undermined the very ideal they sought to preserve. While the materialists were so committed to their society that they readily sacrificed the individual to the demands of the nation and its economic system, the idealists effectively undermined their own ideals by making them too abstract and general enough to satisfy everyone. Unfortunately, such programs failed to win massive electoral support (with the exception of the elections of January 1919). Regardless of their actions liberals could not remain true to their ideals and gain widespread popular support. The failure to solve this dilemma became the tragedy of German liberalism.

## NEO-KANTIAN LIBERALISM: POLITICS TREATED ABSTRACTLY

It was the idealist component of German liberalism between 1871 and 1933 that influenced Cassirer's outlook on the world and was in turn reflected in his life and work.

Cassirer had in common with the idealist liberals a certain intellectual predisposition which may be called the formalizing tendency – the tendency to conceive concrete problems in abstract terms. Cassirer's formalizing inclination was expressed by his commitment to neo-Kantianism. He felt that this philosophical movement continued the work of Kant, whose ultimate goal had been to dissolve the facts of the natural world into the pure functions of knowledge.[25] For Cassirer these pure functions were none other than human judgments which established relations between the ideas of the mind and the data of the natural world. This 'relational' conception of knowledge and existence transformed every concrete fact into pure relations of facts and values. Thus, when considering legal and political matters, Cassirer shared Leibniz's belief that the study of law focused on definitions and logical proofs, not on historical facts and personal experiences.[26]

The formalizing tendency of neo-Kantianism appealed to many legal and political academicians whose tradition exhibited an inclination for dealing with concrete matters in abstract terms. Throughout the late nineteenth century and until 1933 a substantial part of German legal philosophy was devoted to showing that laws and rights were themselves somehow independent of existing conditions.[27] This tendency was criticized by de Ruggiero in his study of German liberalism:

The mistake of German legal science is that, wishing to make rights an autonomous reality, it makes them an abstraction, something unreal: the true reality of right [*Recht*] lies in its connexion with the activities of a nation's historical life. Hence, the 'State of Rights' [*Rechtsstaat*] ... taken by itself is only an empty form.[28]

However, we are less concerned with exposing the mistakes of German legal philosophy than with stressing the following point: the formalizing inclinations of German legal philosophy made it a willing ally of neo-Kantian philosophy. Beginning with the publication in 1900 of Georg Jellinek's *Allgemeine Staatslehre* (General theory of the state), legal scholars increasingly applied the neo-Kantian theory of knowledge to the study of law and politics. Hans Kelsen, one of the prominent neo-Kantian philosophers of law, expressly noted his intellectual debt to Hermann Cohen and the Marburg neo-Kantian philosophical school.[29] Interestingly, one of the works of Cohen's most famous student, Cassirer, was directly responsible for another legal scholar's critique of law. Siegfried Marck's *Substanz- und Funktionsbegriff in der Rechtsphilosophie* (Concepts of substance and function in legal philosophy) published in 1925, explicitly adopted the conceptual framework established by Cassirer in his study of substantial and functional concepts in mathematics and science which appeared in 1910.[30] Legal philosophy was also decisively influenced by the work of Heinrich Rickert, leader of the Baden School of neo-Kantianism.[31]

Starting with Kant's premise that an unbridgeable gulf separated thought from existence, neo-Kantian legal philosophers attempted to establish absolutely valid laws, called pure legal norms, based solely on human reason. In their minds it was not possible to have a law valid for all times and peoples which was also bound to a particular historical or social context.[32] Only a law rooted in the unchangeable realm of thought, with its pure forms, could provide the certainty the neo-Kantians desired. As Cassirer put it, true legal science dealt with definitions and logical proofs, not with experiences and historical facts.

The neo-Kantian preference for the abstract over the concrete had two consequences. One was desirable from their philosophical point of view, the other unacceptable for political reasons. The first consequence was the divorce of the study of law from its political and social environment. Law was confined to the realm of thought and pure forms. This suited the ideals of the neo-Kantian liberal philosophers because the defence of individual freedom and of the *Rechtsstaat* was safest in a realm where the hazards of worldly existence were by definition excluded. The second consequence was disastrous for the liberals because it carried them towards political isolation, which followed from their unwillingness to bring their speculations into the actual political, social, and economic context in which most Germans dwelled. Aside from making general comments about the inalienable rights of man and the equality of all free individuals under the law, the idealists were reluctant to say what ought to be done. This reluctance in dealing with everyday realities infuriated most Germans, particularly after 1919, when decisive government was needed.[33]

Once this idealist predilection for the abstract was transferred to the political arena, an abundance of declarations in favour of the rights of all citizens were made, but no consistent support ever materialized for thorough social and political reform aimed at realizing those rights. Liberal promises remained just promises. For example, from 1918 to 1919 many liberal democrats believed that their party, the DDP, was not a party only of the middle class but of the entire people.[34] However, in February 1919, when Friedrich Naumann, a committed democrat and one of the prominent DDP leaders, had the opportunity to give his party's support to the mine workers' demands for the nationalization of the mining industry, he said: 'Of course we want to maintain capitalist enterprise.'[35] Naumann's statement should be properly understood. His hasty return to the capitalist position was not voluntary; he had previously moved too close to the socialist position, and this had caused a stir in the right wing of the party. In order to assuage their fears Naumann made more conservative public statements. This episode was yet another symptom of the constant tension between the left and right wings of the party, which made it vacillate in both its promises and its policies. This ideological wavering threatened the DDP with either disintegration or loss of electoral support from 1919 to 1930.

The idealists' aversion to initiating any steps that might lead to the implementation of their claim to represent all classes was reflected in Cassirer's own work. His preference for the general statement of intentions over the formulation of steps to effectuate those intentions is understandable. After all, he was a philosopher. Whenever Cassirer did make political statements he relied on the same device as many other liberals sharing his creed. He appealed to his compatriots to be more enthusiastic in their support of the Weimar Republic because it endeavoured to instil in the body politic the liberal commitment to the preservation of human freedom in a society ruled by reason and law.[36] Like his political counterparts, he did not provide a concrete way of achieving his goal.

Even though Cassirer's work covered a wide range of subjects, he did not specifically formulate an ethical position until after his departure from Germany in 1933. This omission was critical because ethics is the application of philosophical principles to common (concrete) life situations. Cassirer's inability to formulate a way of actualizing his political ideals was no accident, but part of a more general flaw in his philosophy, namely, his formalizing tendency. Perhaps Cassirer never specifically formulated an ethics because in his mind ethics, politics, and philosophy were the same thing – the application of pure reason to human affairs. Nevertheless, his failure to say explicitly what was good or bad or right or wrong in a specific situation undoubtedly contributed to the vagueness of his writing. With few exceptions Cassirer avoided the use of specific social and political contexts in his work.

From 1871 to 1933 moderates and democrats in the liberal ranks perpetually hovered between progress and reaction.[37] They vacillated between their commitment to the achievement of freedom for all men and their fear of the masses' demands for equality, which made many liberals retreat into élitism and co-operation with the more conservative elements in German society. The conflict between the idealists' theoretical principles and the practical demands of their middle-class social and economic position had the unfortunate effect of undermining their primary goal: the preservation of human freedom. The interaction between major events in German history since 1871, especially the rising impact of nationalism and industrialization on German society, and the idealists' predilection for making general statements of intention, resulted in the inability to ground their ideal of freedom firmly in the concrete world of everyday life. The pressure of events together with the formalizing tendency inherent in the idealist liberals' philosophy maximized their inability to put their ideals into practice because the rapidly changing economic and social environment in Germany caused many problems requiring specific responses. When these were not forthcoming the idealists natually lost their attraction to many potential voters.

The more specific the liberal commitment to the status quo, as in the cases of the National Liberals and the German People's Party, the more limited was their appeal to other classes. However, when the more democratic-minded liberals in the Progressive and German Democratic Parties tried to broaden their parties' appeal by relying on general political platforms designed to attract other groups, they still could not permanently expand the social basis of their support. Indeed, the attempted expansion lost them support within the ranks of the middle classes.

While both the materialist and idealist conceptions of liberalism tended to be limited to the industrial and professional middle classes, the latter conception was tied to a particular view of man and the universe with which Cassirer identified himself. Neo-Kantianism was, in a sense, an academic version of the idealist-liberal *Weltanschauung*.

PART 1
CASSIRER AS A PHILOSOPHER IN
IMPERIAL GERMANY

# 2

# Marburg neo-Kantianism and Cassirer's pre-1914 writings

The philosophies of Kant and Hegel endowed German academic thought with a particular orientation. Kant's rigorous separation of the intelligible (ideal) world from the sensible (empirical) one and Hegel's belief that everything rational, that is, the totality of thought and existence, was a threefold unity provided both the intellectual starting points and limits for a great deal of academic theoretical speculation in Germany. Even though Kant believed the worlds of nature and spirit were distinct, he argued that man could bridge the two worlds.[1] Hegel broadened this bridge into an absolute unity. His response to Kant's dualism of ideality and reality was to synthesize the idea, nature, and spirit into a (philosophical) science of the experience of consciousness.[2]

The dissolution of the Hegelian synthesis in the 1830s and 1840s was accomplished by the rise of the mechanical and experimental sciences, whose rapid growth in the nineteenth century challenged philosophy's intellectual pre-eminence. In Germany the Kantian-Hegelian tradition was an integral part of philosophy's claim to be the paradigm of all knowledge. While the particular solutions offered by Kant and Hegel were modified or even rejected, their general conviction that all knowledge and existence was the necessary part of a rational system in which human consciousness played a central role went unchallenged. In the second half of the nineteenth century, the natural sciences set the tone for all other disciplines. Specialized knowledge in one field became the precondition for any general reflections on the human condition. Intellectuals either constructed a world view on the basis of an exact science, such as experimental psychology, that would bring all knowledge into a unified system of thought or started with philosophy, using one particular area of philosophical speculation, such as epistemology, as the foundation for unifying all knowledge.[3]

Neo-Kantianism was the most prominent of the philosophical schools and was largely responsible for the renewed vigour of philosophy in German universities from 1870 to 1900. Like most intellectual movements, this one encompassed a variety of ideas. Nevertheless all neo-Kantians distrusted the speculative naturalism of those enamoured with the practical results of the physical sciences and at the same time felt the need to make philosophy into a science by re-examining the work of Kant. For these intellectuals the main problem was to preserve the credibility of speculative philosophy in an age where people increasingly looked to the physical sciences as the fount of all lasting knowledge. No one entering university in the 1890s could fail to be influenced by neo-Kantian ideas. Since Ernst Cassirer was attracted to the neo-Kantians in that decade and eventually became a leading figure in the Marburg School, any analysis of his work must start with a discussion of the main ideas of the Marburgers.

The origin of Marburg neo-Kantianism can be traced back to the years 1865–6. Otto Liebmann's book on *Kant und die Epigonen* (Kant and his successors) published in 1865 provided all neo-Kantians with their motto: 'Return to Kant.' Liebmann's influence was due less to his philosophical prowess than to his ability to persuade others to rejuvenate the study of philosophy in the 1860s by going back to Kant's work and critically re-examining it. With the appearance of Friedrich A. Lange's *History of Materialism* in 1866 the neo-Kantian movement was set in motion. Lange attacked the materialist's view of the relation between ideas and physical facts in what was to become the standard neo-Kantian critique of materialist philosophy. The trouble with this philosophy was that it committed the grave conceptual error of treating physical concepts, such as force and matter, as if they were things in themselves, when in fact they were creations of the human mind.[4] Lange's work awakened many to the dangers of the abuse of scientific thought. This became a crucial point for the neo-Kantians. They did not attack the accomplishments of science per se; rather, they wanted to ensure that proper use was made of the scientific method by stressing the theoretical presuppositions of science itself. The naive philosophical materialism of many scientists helped perpetuate many misunderstandings by failing to distinguish adequately between facts and ideas. The Marburgers, particularly Cassirer, were to reiterate Lange's point again and again in the years to come.

Hermann Ludwig von Helmholtz was one of Germany's leading scientists in the late nineteenth century. He was professor of physics in Berlin from 1871 to 1888, and among many other accomplishments he helped establish the Faraday-Maxwell conception of electrical phenomena and published a classical work on physiological optics. For the Marburgers Helmholtz was a model scientist, for he combined empirical research with a sophisticated understanding of philosophical issues. Kant's theory that perception involves judgment played an important part in his research efforts. Furthermore, Helmholtz never tired of extolling the contribution philosophy could make to scientific investigation. In an age when most scientists felt that speculative philosophy was outdated, the Marburgers could not but be excited by Helmholtz's grandiose effort to formulate a psychology of perception by combining Kantian questions and the results of experimental research.

In 1873, on Friedrich Lange's recommendation, Hermann Cohen received a lectureship at the University of Marburg. Three years later, when Lange died, the mantle of Marburg neo-Kantianism passed to Cohen's shoulders. Cohen's basic philosophical task remained the same. He never wavered in his belief that the logical and mathematical character of thought could establish the absolute certainty as well as the unity of human knowledge. Cohen's position became known as the logistic a priori school because it attempted to derive its ideal of truth and of philosophical science from mathematics and logic. In fact, Cohen tried to make the infinitesimal and ordinal numbers the intellectual basis of any comprehension of reality.[5] He defended this mathematical perception of reality because he felt it was rooted in the nature of reason itself.[6] By demonstrating that the possibility of consciousness was dependent on both 'the unity of consciousness' and 'the unity of the synthesis of the manifold of perception,' Cohen sought to provide a lasting foundation for the transcendental method. Here he relied on Kant's basic proposition: transcendental philosophy did not concern itself with objects, but with the human mode of knowing those objects. Once it was understood that the basis of human consciousness rested on mathematical-logical foundations, it then became the goal of the transcendental method to elucidate how pure 'form was the law of content.'[7] Since how we think was no longer separated, in Cohen's mind, from what we think, he wanted to illuminate how a priori judgments determined the relations between ideas and facts. By stressing the a priori, logistic character of knowledge, Cohen in effect tried to preserve the autonomy of human reason, since reason itself was made dependent only on human consciousness and not on any empirical data.

Throughout his work Cohen devoted his major efforts to discovering what he thought were the immanent logical laws of pure reason. Since he felt the discovery of these laws was tantamount to recreating them, Cohen argued that knowledge was not something fixed or given, but a task to be fulfilled by each man as part of humanity's movement towards enlightenment. The net effect of Cohen's reinterpretation of Kant's critiques, especially on Cassirer, was to stress the dynamic and progressive character of human reason.

Paul Natorp came to Marburg in 1881 and remained there until his death in 1925. While he began as a student in psychology he was soon won over to philosophy by Lange and Cohen, and by the early 1900s he had become a leading member of the Marburg School. Natorp's basic position was that all perception was the product of the determination of thought. He supported the 'relational' view of knowledge where 'endless correlations' unified perceptions of the external world to the logic of perception.[8] Natorp was primarily interested in examining the laws that constituted the a priori conditions of knowledge. An understanding of these conditions led to transcendental knowledge, which, according to Natorp, proceeded from the assumption that the unity of all knowledge and existence could occur only when the totality of *logical* tasks was accepted as the basis of consciousness itself.

While Cohen and Natorp agreed on the dynamic 'relational' character of knowledge and on the need to conceive knowledge as an endless task, they differed on the role of mathematics and logic in philosophical analysis. Was philosophy to concentrate on the mathematical element of human thought, as Cohen argued, or was it to examine the categories of pure reason which reflected the logical element of human thought, as Natorp argued? Was reality to be understood in mathematical or in logical terms? While the debate between Cohen and Natorp may appear scholastic and trivial to us, it had a lasting effect on Cassirer's philosophical development, since it would offer Cassirer a way out of the confines of Marburg neo-Kantianism.

The Marburg neo-Kantians were not content only to expound an abstract theory of knowledge; they believed their theory needed a political basis. Beginning with Lange's support of the workers' cause in the 1860s[9] and Cohen's incessant praise of the SPD,[10] the political orientation of the Marburgers tended to be left of centre. While the connection made by the neo-Kantians between their transcendental philosophy of human knowledge and socialism may seem quite odd, Cohen in particular thought the two were inseparable.

The Marburgers generally believed that socialism provided the best means for realizing the goals of Kantian ethics and its ideal of social justice. For them socialism would establish a social order where each man, through the use of reason, would belong as an equal in a rational community, which itself was part of the larger community of humanity. In this community the autonomy of human consciousness so crucial to all neo-Kantians would go hand in hand with the autonomy of the individual. But how did the neo-Kantians justify this connection between their philosophy and politics? They believed their ethics and politics demonstrated the interdependency of individual and social behaviour. The desirable social order was one that encouraged the development of free individuals. This vision of man in harmony with his social order was the neo-Kantian contribution to politics, which they saw as the continuation of the eighteenth century's cosmopolitan humanism.[11]

The fate of the Marburg vision of politics is revealing, for it was also the fate of many neo-Kantian principles. The political philosophy of Cohen and the Marburg School remained isolated in the academic community. Its attempt to replace the materialist bias of socialism with Kantian ethics and its desire to substitute a struggle for universal humanitarian values for the Marxist idea of class struggle remained unacceptable to most people in the socialist party.[12]

Marburg neo-Kantianism, with its odd combination of idealist philosophy and politics, offered four main ideas that Cassirer was to use as the basis of his own work. First, there was the realization that knowledge was not the comprehension but the construction of an object. Knowledge was not a given but a task. Secondly, the Marburgers believed there was no human reality except that dependent upon human consciousness. Recourse to a reality independent of experience was rejected. Since objectivity and truth were considered products of human judgment, philosophical inquiry was obliged to focus on the problem of human judgment, which itself was a reflection of a priori relations. The materialist and metaphysical approaches to understanding knowledge, existence, and man were repudiated. While the former dealt exclusively with 'hard' (natural) facts, and the latter tended to subordinate an interest in human activities to discovering their suprahuman origins, both depreciated the role of man in shaping his own life. These conclusions were unacceptable to the neo-Kantians. Thirdly, the Marburg neo-Kantians believed that the essence of philosophy was to analyse the a priori conditions of knowledge and existence. Finally, the Marburg humanitarian political vision left its mark on Cassirer's thought. However, this political attitude remained dormant until the trauma of the first world war and the turbulence of the Weimar Republic's early years forced him to take a political stand.

## CASSIRER'S EARLY WRITINGS 1899–1914

Cassirer's early work clearly showed his intellectual debt to the Marburg neo-Kantians. He made their a priori rationalism his starting point, and it was to remain one of the cornerstones of his whole philosophical career. Using the standard neo-Kantian tactic of returning to Kant, Cassirer started most of his own philosophical reflections by referring to Kant's fundamental insights. While concluding (in 1906) his first major analysis of Kant's philosophy,

Cassirer admirably captured the abstract, a priori orientation that dominated his pre-first world war writings: 'The dissolution of the "given" [the data of the natural world as well as of man's spiritual activities] into the pure functions of knowledge forms the final goal and result of the critical teachings.'[13] Cassirer's attempt to dissolve knowledge and existence into the pure functions of reason was his own way of applying Kant's insights to the study of man. For Kant the critical question was: is it the function of imagination only to connect those things together which are given in consciousness, or is it possible that there is a creative element already present in the consciousness of experience itself?[14] Kant's affirmative answer to the second part of this question opened the way for the discovery of two interrelated principles fundamental to all Kantians: first, that the conditions of the possibility of experience in general were also the conditions of the possibility of the objects of experience,[15] and secondly, the recognition that the first principle rested on the assumption of the original synthetic unity of consciousness.[16]

Starting from a presupposed unity of consciousness, Cassirer advocated the Marburger view of progress: progress was measured by the extent to which humanity recognized the conceptual basis of knowledge and existence.[17] This recognition meant the rejection of materialism. Further, Cassirer envisioned the conceptual foundation of consciousness and existence as the result of synthetic a priori judgments. The judgments co-ordinated natural data (the objects of empirical intuitions) with the a priori conditions of the possibility of experience itself. Since Cassirer accepted the Kantian belief that judgments unified ideas with reality, conceptions with empirical intuitions, he argued that the study of synthetic judgments was essential for establishing a criterion for evaluating the progress of human spirit in history.

Cassirer's first major work was his doctoral dissertation at the University of Marburg in 1899 on Descartes' critique of mathematics and natural science. This study of Descartes was the first step in his attempt to create a definitive critique of man based on neo-Kantian principles. Descartes' system, according to Cassirer, had a twofold significance for the history of modern thought: first, Descartes assigned a new and important place to the problem of knowledge in regard to the totality of philosophical problems, and secondly, he prepared the ground for the science of Cassirer's own time.[18] In discussing the latter point, Cassirer revealed his own view of science. He argued that 'the concept of function' was essential to modern science because it provided the conceptual means (through mathematical equations) of uniting all data ranging from the 'logical-universal determinations of the mind' to 'the physical-substantial' facts of the natural world.[19]

Cassirer's description of modern philosophical consciousness in terms of logical determinations and concepts of function underscored his Marburg orientation. Reality was not something static to be grasped at once; rather, it had to be reconstructed. The dynamic character of consciousness had to be fully recognized. Descartes' great contribution to modern thought was that he had been the first to grasp the necessity of conceiving a general law of motion in mathematical terms.[20] By establishing the epistemological necessity of conceiving nature in lawlike terms, Cartesian physics gave solid foundation to the belief that the concept of causality dissolved itself completely into the idea of an exact quantitative law. The causality of nature was thus subordinated to mathematical concepts. Descartes had overcome the dichotomy between physical movement and mathematics – the former became a manifestation of the latter. However, these speculations, according to Cassirer, rested on the belief that the unity of all knowledge was dependent first on the unity of human consciousness and secondly on the assumption that the discovery and reaffirmation of this unity was a task to be achieved by philosophy. For the unity of knowledge in human consciousness was the fundamental presupposition of any coherent philosophical system.[21] Significantly, in making the preceding point Cassirer distorted Descartes' ideas because the latter had very little to say about the unity of human consciousness. Cassirer was making too much of a Kantian out of Descartes.

The study of Descartes became the introductory chapter of his critique of Leibniz, which was published in 1902. Cassirer's first problem was to answer this question: what was the connection between Descartes, Leibniz, and German idealism? Cassirer's response not only gave a clearcut answer to the question, it also provided the theme for understanding the remainder of his pre-1914 writings. According to Cassirer,

Progress from Descartes' thought was conditioned by an adherence to idealist conceptions. In the quest for the *scientia generalis* the young Leibniz discovered infinitesimal calculus: the search for the basis of logic opened up to him the fundamental method of mathematics and natural science. This interpenetration of logic and mathematics, of mathematics and natural knowledge, which was itself a special discovery, also dominated the systematic advance of thought – in it lay the interest and significance of Leibniz's establishment of the foundation of philosophy.[22]

Mathematics and logic again occupied the centre of Cassirer's analysis. According to him Leibniz's ideas implied that mathematics was the necessary agency for unifying ideal logical principles with the reality of nature. Descartes did not carry his speculations so far; his work largely confined itself to mathematizing movements in nature and did not delve into the logical essence of thought itself. Further, the nature of mathematics required a unity of intellectual operations, which itself presupposed the Kantian belief in an existing transcendental unity of consciousness.

Cassirer turned to Leibniz's conception of the monad as a means of finding a systematic unity to Leibniz's work as well as expressing the neo-Kantian drive towards the ideal unification of human thought with natural existence. He believed the monad was comprehensible solely as 'the activity of unification,'[23] and not as an actually existing entity. It was the methodological correlation binding the unity of consciousness to the empirical data contained within it. For Cassirer the monad represented the unity of mental operation and not the unity of its contents.[24] He converted the monad concept into a Kantian regulative principle. Monads were not things in themselves; rather they were principles for making the sensible world intelligible to man. They organized the myriad of experimental data in regard to a certain goal (*telos*) and in relation to specific ends or purposes.

Cassirer stated his general view of Leibniz's monads and their relation to reality as follows: 'The whole of reality shows itself as the essence of single subjects, which develop according to particular laws and specific series of conscious contents; with these ideas we have encountered the well-known system of monads.'[25] Leibniz's monadological conception of reality, with its emphasis on the individual, involved the idea of a pre-established harmony of all knowledge and existence. For it was only by assuming that a pre-established harmony prevailed between the individual (the particular) and the whole (the universal) that all knowledge and existence could be unified into one system of thought. By arguing through Leibniz's idea of the monad, Cassirer envisioned the major task of philosophical science as the elucidation of 'the harmony of the particular and the cosmos.'[26]

The monad was a concept which envisioned every thing in the world as being in harmony with everything else. This concept was not very precise, but Cassirer tried to make it more explicit by redefining Leibniz's terminology. For example, when discussing Leibniz's idea of politics Cassirer took two general terms, the 'particular' and the 'whole,' which Leibniz frequently used, and translated the 'particular' into the autonomous individual citizen and the 'whole' into the community.[27] He then argued that for the purpose of comprehending in a logical and systematic way the interaction of an individual with his society, Leibniz's monad concept could be used as the means of showing how the tension and conflict between the citizen and his society was essential for the preservation of human freedom. Here for the first time Cassirer applied to abstract ideas Simmel's idea of the inevitable tension between the rational individual, who wanted autonomy, and society, which demanded conformity to social norms.

Cassirer resolved this tension in a way that he was to use in all his subsequent reflections on freedom. As a neo-Kantian he saw each man as an autonomous entity and as a member of the community of reason. When the individual realized that he was a member of a universal community of rational ends, each man would see his own personality (or individuality) as part of a larger world community. Hence, there could be no real lasting tension between the two.

Cassirer extended Leibniz's philosophy to the realm of history. By uniting the idea of pre-established harmony with his own belief in the free and rational individual, Cassirer laid the groundwork for his own cosmopolitan conception of history:

No single people ... can now [after Leibniz's work] be valued more than another as the exclusive bearer and representative of the historical progression towards an end. Thus, the universalism implicit in the concept of harmony prepares the way for the comprehensive unity of the humanity concept and its application to the philosophy of history.[28]

Cassirer's conception of history permitted him to place the individual in a universal context. The development of the particular, be it a single man, a particular culture or nation, or a specific field of human activity, could be interpreted as a variation of the general development of the universal. The development of every aspect of human activity became a part of humanity's progression towards the attainment of the realm of reason. Each man and every people participated in the enlightenment of all humanity.

Cassirer now had a principle for examining the evolution of modern philosophy. He first applied this principle in a four-volume study, *Das Erkenntnisproblem in der Philosophie und Wissenschaft der neueren Zeit* (The problem of knowledge in philosophy and science in modern times). The first and second volumes appeared in 1906 and 1907 respectively. In effect, they represented the Marburger view that the history of European philosophy since the fifteenth century culminated in Kant's work, for his system of thought was the first to recognize fully that the immanent movement of consciousness carried humanity to the realization of those principles underlying its own development.[29]

The first volume of Cassirer's study covered the period from Cusanus to Bayle. The second described the development of Western thought from Bacon to Kant. In both volumes all intellectual roads culminated in Kant's critiques. Hence, Cassirer took the disparate ideas of Cusanus,[30] Leonardo,[31] Kepler,[32] and Galileo,[33] among others, and analysed their work to illustrate the common theme uniting them. To Cassirer all these thinkers expounded a new concept of the relation between man and the cosmos. This theme reflected the development of a new consciousness where science, art, and philosophy became identified with each other on the basis of mathematical and logical analyses. This identification merged the individual life of man with the rest of creation and prepared the grounds for man's mastery over the natural world. According to Cassirer, in order to understand the significance of the period from the Renaissance to the early twentieth century, it was important to grasp the relation between philosophy and science, which was the key to the content and direction of modern culture. Intellectual progress could be measured by the increasing realization of human consciousness of its own mathematical, a priori foundation.[34]

While it was true that Cassirer had a progressive view of human thought, until 1910 it was confined to the philosophical level. From 1910 onwards he began to consider the possibility of expanding his progressivism beyond philosophy and mathematics to the humanities. In the years preceding the first world war, particularly in his book *Substance and Function* (published in 1910), Cassirer's new orientation towards the humanities emerged indirectly. His move beyond Marburg neo-Kantianism began in the midst of his dispute with Cohen over the issue of whether logistic relations or infinitesimal elements should be the basis of an analysis of theoretical knowledge.

Cassirer's *Substance and Function* was not only a memorable work presenting the logistic, a priori view of the natural sciences, logic, and mathematics. It revealed the beginning of his break from the epistemological confines of the Marburg School. When the dispute erupted in the summer of 1910, Cassirer did not grasp its implication that he had already moved beyond the Marburg conception of knowledge and existence. Nevertheless, the text indicates he was embarking on his own original philosophical course.

In a letter to Cassirer dated 24 August 1910, Hermann Cohen noted that 'our unity is jeopardized' by the thesis propounded in *Substance and Function*. Cohen's criticism ran as follows:

You put the center of gravity upon the concept of relation and you believe that you have accomplished with the help of this concept the idealization of all materiality. The expression even escaped you, that the concept of relation is a category; yet it is a category only in so far as it is a function, and a function unavoidably demands the infinitesimal element in which alone the root of the ideal can be found.[35]

The split between Cohen and Cassirer can be traced back to 1906. At the time Cassirer expressed his agreement to Natorp over the latter's de-emphasis of mathematics, particularly the infinitesimal element, in his view of the nature of a priori relations. Natorp was tiring of Cohen's constant reduction of everything to mathematics. So was Cassirer. When forced to choose between Cohen's 'mathematical' bias and Natorp's 'logical' approach to achieving the unity of knowledge and existence, Cassirer moved in Natorp's direction. In making this decision Cassirer cast aside the Marburg obsession with analysing mathematical and philosophical problems while neglecting other areas of study, like myth, literature, anthropology, language, and history.

Cassirer's rejection of Cohen's reliance on mathematics was also a response to the changing philosophical situation in Germany. By 1909, life philosophy and metaphysics were inundating the German academic community. Bergson's philosophy extolling intuition and the vital life force over the intellect was in the springtime of its influence.[36] Even members of the neo-Kantian movement admitted that examinations of knowledge must also deal with their relation to being; epistemology itself must recognize its metaphysical dimensions. All the Marburg neo-Kantian efforts to reconcile knowledge and existence in primarily logical or mathematical terms, while excluding all else, were decisively rebuffed. When viewed in this context, Cassirer's break with Cohen may be interpreted as an attempt to revise the teachings of critical philosophy by broadening its 'relational foundations' to include all spheres of human activity. This is not to say that Cassirer achieved this shift of emphasis by 1910 – very far from it. Indeed, it was only to be achieved in *The Philosophy of Symbolic Forms* (1923–9). However, *Substance and Function* did reveal the direction of Cassirer's future speculations in that his downplaying of the importance of mathematics opened the way for his attempt to introduce something else (namely, the 'symbol concept') as the foundation of his analysis of human reality.

In *Substance and Function* Cassirer expounded his thesis that all theoretical thought was the construction of relational schemata. Relations in the widest sense, not infinitesimals, became the basis of reality. He thus analysed the development of concepts in modern chemistry[37] and noted their relational character. In Cassirer's analysis the atom was not an existing entity; it was merely a symbolic concept which science used for making natural processes intelligible to man. Science 'progressed' to the extent that it realized that the concept was only a series of symbolic determinations of the relations between various particles and events in space and time. Through science the a priori judgments of human reason subdued the chaos of empirical facts: 'In this progressive mastery of the empirical material, the peculiarity of the logical process

[was] revealed; through it, the concept, while obeying the facts, at the same time [gained] intellectual dominance over the facts.'[38] Philosophical progress in understanding 'substance' required that it be evaluated as a concept, and the latter as the product of a human understanding that progressively revealed the logical structure of its own development. Cassirer made no attempt to base philosophical cognition solely on mathematical configurations even though he was impressed by the progressively mathematical orientation of the natural sciences since the seventeenth century. However, he envisioned this process as part of a larger movement of thought that could not, as Cohen wished, be based ultimately on infinitesimal elements. Rather, Cassirer was interested in the logic behind the mathematizing process in so far as it revealed the ultimate autonomy of human consciousness.

Once Cassirer realized 'the more scientific thought [extended] its domain, the more it [was] forced to intellectual conceptions that [possessed] no analogue in the field of concrete sensation,'[39] he increasingly stressed the overall importance that 'relations' had received in the works of Kant.[40] These relations were interpreted as manifestations of 'an independent activity of consciousness' – in other words, as examples of human freedom.

Freedom, not mathematical relations, became the watchword for Cassirer just prior to the first world war. Cassirer's disagreement with Cohen signified his interest in conceiving the endless task of humanity in broader terms. The entire spectrum of human spiritual activities – for example, literature, art, and religion – not only scientific and philosophical developments would be treated by Cassirer on their own terms. One realm of activity would not be considered reducible to another. His future efforts would concentrate on transforming the spectrum of activities into a mosaic. It would be a schema capturing humanity's relentless drive to express itself through the creation of different forms of knowing – specifically, different conceptions of history, literature, art, and so forth – and of existing, that is, different modes of social behaviour.

The opening phase of Cassirer's interest in the humanities was discernible by 1914. In an article written that year Cassirer expressed a major reservation he had about Kant's work. To his thinking Kant's 'abstract schematism of the critique of reason' did not provide a sufficiently concrete presentation of the context and range of applicability of the regulative idea.[41] This dissatisfaction with the abstractness of Kant's philosophy and the prevailing Kantian conception of knowledge and existence resulted in Cassirer's turn to a study of the humanities.

Cassirer wanted to justify his expansion beyond the Marburg emphasis on mathematics, science, and philosophy by appealing to Kant himself. In this connection Cassirer focused on Kant's goal principle. Kant used this principle to unify the realms of nature and freedom. He did not specifically limit its use to formal, logical matters but expanded it 'to the idea of an "absolute" final goal, in which the realms of "Nature" and "Freedom" should find their ultimate coherence.'[42] By noting Kant's emphasis on the continuity between nature and freedom, Cassirer was laying the theoretical groundwork for his own future orientation. He wanted to apply the idea of freedom to the world of natural events, rather than restrict manifestations of human freedom to the realm of pure spirit.

In philosophical terms Cassirer's interest in the applicability of all thought, hence the thought of freedom, to natural existence was further revealed by his interest in Kant's notion of the schema. The schema provided 'the unity of concept and intuition';[43] in plain language, it bound ideality (mental conceptions) to reality (empirical intuitions). Kant once succinctly stated the relation between the two: 'Thoughts without content are empty, intuitions without concepts are blind.'[44] Concepts and intuitions were to become the twin pillars of Cassirer's symbol concept, which itself provided the ideal unifying point of his philosophy of freedom, that is, his philosophy of symbolic forms.

While Kant's final goal both presupposed and fostered the interdependency of knowledge and existence, Cassirer felt that Kant had not in practice extensively applied the principles of his critique of reason to fields outside the natural sciences and philosophy. He had not formulated an acceptable schema for carrying his principles into practice. Thus, by 1914 Cassirer became aware of the need to bridge the gap separating an abstract philosophy from the practical, ordinary activities of mankind. This realization became the first major step in his advance beyond neo-Kantianism.

Before 1914 Cassirer was apparently reluctant to publish any of his thoughts and research on the humanities. It was only the pressure of the war which made him publish his studies of German cultural history.[45] He was also reluctant to discuss in public the political ramifications of his philosophical speculation. Thus, in his 1912 article on Hermann Cohen's philosophical accomplishments he avoided any discussion of Cohen's political views. This omission was remarkable because Cohen attached great value to his social democratic ideals. Cassirer's hesitancy to discuss publicly the relation of politics to philosophy was not the result of a lack of personal views on politics and society. On the contrary, as early as 1903, in a letter to Natorp, Cassirer expressed his satisfaction at the need for a second edition of Natorp's *Sozialpädagogik* (Social pedagogy), in which the author discussed such practical matters as the relationship between theoretical education and community life and values.[46] However, Cassirer seemed to feel, at least in regard to his own published work, that politics was a subject for private discussion, entirely apart from philosophy.

Even though he did not explicitly take a political position before the war, all the elements of idealist liberalism were implicit in his philosophical orientation. The preservation of the spiritual autonomy of the individual was the essence of liberalism. Cassirer's attempt to create a schema for a philosophy of freedom was in effect an extension of liberalism's initial premise that individual freedom was the only goal worth seeking. The conversion of Cassirer's 'liberal' philosophical tendencies into an actual liberal political stance required the aid of an external catalyst. His reluctance to apply philosophy to politics and his unwillingness to take a stand on political issues could be overcome only by the pressure of such events as the first world war and the turmoil of the early years of the Weimar Republic.

PART 2
CASSIRER'S INTELLECTUAL REORIENTATION
INTO THE HUMANITIES

# 3

# Kant reconsidered (1914–16)

The penetration of social and political realities into a philosophical system usually presents a complex problem because the relation between thought and action is ambiguous. Social and political facts are not often translated into their 'idea-equivalents.' Instead these facts combine with other ideas, which may or may not be connected with political and social events, and gradually filter into an intellectual's thought pattern. Cassirer's reaction to his own environment is an example of the problematic connection between an intellectual's speculations and his society. He never became very active in politics, yet his entire philosophical system had a distinct ideological dimension. What started as an examination of the epistemological relation between knowledge and existence eventually became a spiritual problem confronting all humanity. Ultimately, no thoughtful person could escape answering the question: what is man? And by answering this question one either implicitly or explicitly took a political stand, for one's conception of man, as Cassirer's own fate was to show, was irrevocably bound up with a specific political vision. In Cassirer's case it was an idealized liberalism dedicated to the preservation of the spiritual autonomy of the individual within the political context of a liberal, democratic parliamentary regime.

Between 1910 and 1914 Cassirer approached a theoretical crossroads. His disputes with Cohen on the nature of 'relations' were symptomatic of his impending reinterpretation of Kant's philosophy. Since 1910 Cassirer had been organizing and directing a new edition of Kant's collected works. In 1912 the ten-volume edition was published. Cassirer's supplementary volume to the 1910 edition, *Kants Leben und Lehre* (Kant's life and teachings), containing his new interpretation of Kant, was ready for publication in early 1916. He published the basic outline of his reinterpretation in an article on the central ideas of critical philosophy which appeared in the 1914 issue of *Die Geisteswissenschaften*. In contrast to his earlier interpretation of Kant, where the thing-in-itself occupied a good part of his attention,[1] the 1914 article focused on the schema, regulative ideas, and teleology. He also stressed the role of judgment in unifying Kant's system as well as in uniting the realms of freedom (spirit) and nature (existence). Cassirer's new interest in the regulative and teleological aspect of judgment reflected his decision to carry his philosophical ideas on freedom into more down-to-earth human activities such as art, language, and myth.

In retrospect the 1914 article was significant because it presented a snapshot image of Cassirer's approach to philosophy before the war had altered the course of his work. His inclination to reduce all knowledge and existence to the pure functions of knowledge, his tendency to interpret each philosophical problem as part of a universal context, and his belief that all humanity progressed towards enlightenment had already carried him to the limits of neo-Kantianism. The war was to push him beyond these limits.

While prior to the outbreak of war Cassirer moved in the direction of a broader view of philosophy and human existence, the 1914 article gave no indication that he connected his rethinking of Kant with political theory or the humanities. Yet, by 1916 he had completed two major works, *Kants Leben und Lehre* and *Freiheit und Form* (Freedom and form), which were full of political overtones and reflections on the humanities.

Cassirer's wartime reflections on the implications of the critical philosophy (in *Kants Leben und Lehre*) and on the course and significance of German intellectual history since the Renaissance (in *Freiheit und Form*) provided an intellectual bridge connecting his pre-war literary and philosophical interests with his reaction to the impact of the war on German society. While both studies were conceived before the war, their final drafts, especially of *Freiheit und Form*, were shaped by the wartime atmosphere of Imperial Germany. Cassirer's assertion that Kant saw in the French Revolution and the democratic, liberal principles of 1789 the practical realization of his own philosophy and his belief that German history was the continuation of intellectual trends that originated in the Renaissance and Reformation may seem fairly innocuous. But in the Germany of 1914–18 these remarks were fraught with political overtones.

THE IDEAS OF 1914

The outbreak of war in August 1914 brought about the mobilization of the entire German population for the war effort. While young Germans marched off to the front, many academics who were left behind drafted themselves into the intellectual and spiritual defence of Germany. In their eyes the military confrontation between Germany and the Anglo-French forces on the fields of Belgium and northern France was only the external manifestation of the larger struggle between Anglo-French civilization and German *Kultur*. The war was to be a new beginning for Germany. All the pre-war social and political tensions that caused many anxious moments for Germany's ruling classes were buried so the nation could meet its destiny as a unified people.[2] A civil peace was declared and unanimously affirmed by most Germans. Emperor William II set the tone for the new unity: from August 1914 he knew only Germans, and not political parties.

For the educated and professional classes the new unity was summarized by J. Plenge's phrase 'the ideas of 1914':

When we celebrate this war on a future day of remembrance, that day will be the feast of the mobilization. The feast of the second of August ... That is when our new spirit was born: the spirit of the tightest integration of all economic and political powers into a new whole ... The new German state! the ideas of 1914.[3]

The 'ideas of 1914' swept through most of the academic community. Patriotic sentiments became so overpowering that even Paul Natorp[4] and Hermann Cohen[5] were caught up in the flood tide of nationalism. Both dreamt of the new 'socialism' that would reconstitute German society, and Cohen envisioned Germany as playing a central role in a new federation of nations. Significantly Cassirer made no such patriotic statements. When he finally commented on the relation between German spirit, the war, and European history, he did so in his usual scholarly manner, and not in a heated moment of patriotic fervour.

Cassirer's reluctance to take the plunge into the river of nationalism flowing through Germany after August 1914 is all the more revealing when one considers the response of German Jews to the war. As a group they were not exempt from the war enthusiasm,[6] and most felt 'German to the bones.'[7] Ernst Toller, a Jewish poet who later participated in the left-wing revolution in Munich in 1918–19, recalled his own 1914 feelings of living under the 'intoxication of emotions,' when words like *Germany, fatherland,* and *war* had magical qualities which swept people off their feet.[8] This kind of intoxication soon reached such limits of absurdity that a university student, Nahum Goldmann, could flatly state that 'the Prussian field sergeant was the personification of Kant's categorical imperative.'[9]

In these circumstances Cassirer's unenthusiastic response to the prospect of war was striking. In a letter dated 30 July 1914 he spoke of the 'very depressing atmosphere' in Berlin accompanying the expectation of full mobilization.[10] This was a confession of his own state of mind. His initial forebodings about the war apparently kept him from succumbing to what he later called 'the limited spiritual chauvinism' of the times.[11]

It is hard to avoid the impression that a certain psychological distance separated Cassirer from the society around him. Between 1903 and 1919 his social life in Berlin revolved around his immediate family and relatives.[12] His fight to gain even a minor teaching position as a *privatdozent* in 1906 at the University of Berlin had predisposed him to concentrate on his writing and teaching. Significantly, his works were published by his cousin, Bruno Cassirer, who owned his own press.[13] The insularity of Cassirer's existence was reinforced by the German academic community's marked lack of interest in his work. Moreover, in spite of his many publications, his popularity with the students, and his winning in 1914 of the Heidelberg Academy's Kuno Fischer Gold Medal, the only professorship offered to him before the advent of the Weimar Republic in 1918 was a two-year visiting professor's appointment by Harvard University.[14] It was ironic that the first country to reward Cassirer's academic achievements with a professorship was the one where he would spend his last years and that the United States, not Germany, was to provide an intellectual milieu where his ideas would ultimately flourish.

Cassirer's acquiescence in the university status quo in Imperial Germany, where as a Jew he was for the most part tolerated but not fully accepted, effectively placed him outside the mainstream of German academic social life. Probably this predisposed him to look at Germany from a certain distance. Hence, as the 'ideas of 1914' made their way through the universities, his tendency to view Germany from the outside in, rather than from the patriotic inside out, when combined with a realistic view regarding the position of Jews in Germany, resulted in his having thoughts which were out of season. Finally, his personal aloofness to the rest of society, already evident in his student days, reinforced his inclination away from nationalist passions which might distort Germany's actual situation and in favour of an objective and rational view of the war.

The net effect of the first world war on the German academic community was to politicize it. With the outbreak of war academic speculation was no longer something done primarily for theoretical purposes; the pursuit of knowledge was no longer continued only for its own sake, but was relevant to broader political and social considerations. Ways of thinking thus became associated with specific political and cultural orientations. For example, Werner Sombart, an influential sociologist, in 1915 associated the trader mentality of the English with a profit motive orientation which stressed material values and contrasted it to the hero mentality of Germans, who thought only of their duties in relation to the spiritual well-being of the whole community. The trader spoke only of the rights that society (*Gesellschaft*) owed to him, while the hero spoke only of his duties to the community (*Gemeinschaft*).[15] Sombart's gross generalization was only one among a multitude of such popular generalizations which the German academic community dutifully churned out between 1914 and 1918. During the war years many intellectuals proved their patriotism by denigrating everything that was not German.

This blind nationalism on the part of many German academics during the war must be seen against the background of pre-war attitudes. Prior to the war German intellectuals were both unfamiliar with and fearful of political and social problems, which were not considered part of the academic domain. Naturally there were some academics who were interested in politics, for example, 'armchair socialists' like Lujo Brentano and Max Weber, but generally most educated Germans were, as Mann was to put it in 1918, conservative and unpolitical.[16] Cassirer's pre-war apolitical stance was thus characteristic of the German intelligentsia.

Despite their lack of interest in politics, most academics believed their social and cultural position was bound up with the continued existence of the Imperial political system. When this system was challenged in 1914, therefore, they quickly rallied to the spiritual defence of everything they considered to be the quintessence of Germanism (*Deutschtum*), carrying their pre-war specialized interests into a defence of their version of *Deutschtum*. Following this trend, Cassirer turned to the humanities and his reflections on German intellectual history since Luther, postponing his work on a third volume of his history of modern philosophical and scientific thought in favour of two other projects. First, he would complete his biography on Kant. Secondly, using his research into art, ethics, and religion, which he had been reluctant to make public before the war, he would offer his own vision of the German spirit. *Kants Leben und Lehre* and *Freiheit und Form* were companion works.

Cassirer's reinterpretation of the critical philosophy together with his focus on Kant's liberal-democratic sentiments in *Kants Leben und Lehre* constituted the theoretical basis of his view of the course and ultimate significance of German intellectual history as expressed in *Freiheit und Form*. He had to react on the philosophical level first before he could proceed into areas such as the humanities and politics. Apparently Cassirer was able to alter his neo-Kantian predilections only by thoroughly reinterpreting the ideas of his great mentor. His look at Kant's life and work thereby became the first positive step in his advance beyond the confines of Marburg neo-Kantianism.

CASSIRER REINTERPRETS KANT

Cassirer's neo-Kantianism predisposed him to seek the continuity and unity of a man's thought. Kant's own system was no exception to Cassirer's synthesizing tendency. On the contrary, it was precisely those principles unifying Kant's system that Cassirer was to use as a basis for analysing the activities of all mankind. His interest in finding the unity in Kant's system motivated his entire analysis of Kant. The discovery of this unity was of great importance to Cassirer because without it a rational and systematic understanding of human activities was impossible – without it the relation between the free individual, the state, and mankind in general could never be correctly ascertained. It is important to remember in all this firstly, Cassirer's association of the unity of philosophical thought with a specific political stance, and secondly, that the philosophical unity was essential to his 'liberal' orientation.

The importance of Kant's *Critique of Judgement* to Cassirer's new vision of Kantianism was obvious from the space he allotted to it in *Kants Leben und Lehre*. About one-quarter of his work on Kant was devoted to an analysis of the third critique, in strong contrast to his 1907 analysis, where the third critique was virtually ignored. Arguing from Kant's own teachings Cassirer noted 'the methodological continuity' between the first two critiques, the critiques of pure and practical reason, and his third one, the critique of aesthetic and teleological judgment.[17] In Cassirer's opinion the third critique sought to preserve the unity of the entire system of reason by making the power of judgment the link between theoretical reason and practical reason. This new agency firmly bound Kant's three critiques into a systematic and unified conception of the relation between knowledge and existence. The third critique was crucial to Cassirer because it provided the basis for an overview of 'the totality of natural and spiritual life.'[18]

In his analysis of the last critique Cassirer stressed Kant's efforts to establish a connection between theory and practice and to unite ethics with politics.[19] His interest in using the critical philosophy's ideas for more than epistemological purposes illustrated not only his new attitude towards Kant but also his new inclination to link philosophical speculation to events in the everyday world.

Since he argued that the power of judgment was central to Kant's connection of theory and fact as well as the basis of the unity of Kant's philosophy, Cassirer focused on two important traits of human judgment: its regulative and teleological tendencies. First, he noted the tendency of human reason, through its faculty of judgment, to evaluate all events in the natural world in relation to a given end or purpose (*telos*).[20] He then underlined Kant's idea that human judgment possessed 'regulative significance,' that is, human judgment tended to select rather than merely accept what the senses offered it.[21] Cassirer's emphasis on this second point was important because it expressed his conviction that man tended to regulate his life and his experiences by prescribing a 'logic,' an 'order,' or a 'purpose' to the world around him.

Kant's arguments in the second part of *The Critique of Judgement* are quite refined and abstract. They deal with such matters as the unity of nature (reality) and freedom (ideality), the resolution of the fact-theory dualism, and the analysis of causality in the natural sciences. Cassirer's ability to extract from Kant's arguments the starting point of his own critique of culture indicated his new intellectual flexibility. The measure of his future success in converting the Kantian critique of reason into a Cassirer-type critique of culture lay precisely in his realization that Kant's analysis of the regulative, teleological nature of human reason contained the seeds for a new science of man. According to Cassirer the seemingly unbridgeable gulf separating the world of everyday life (the realm of natural or empirical facts) from the world of individual freedom (the spiritual realm of ideas) could be bridged by Kant's discovery of a new manner of observation.[22] This new way of observing human knowledge and behaviour, that is, the Kantian study of human judgment's application of purposefulness to nature, had established to Cassirer's satisfaction the procedure for explaining how human reason prescribed its own ends to all human activities.

The regulative, teleological character of human judgment was important to Cassirer for two reasons. First, it revealed the unity to Kant's system. Secondly, and far more important, it opened the way for demonstrating that rational man was not only potentially, but actually, free. To a Kantian, freedom meant that the individual could live his life according to self-imposed laws and goals. Once freedom was seen as dependent on the creative power of reason, and this creativeness was manifested through the ability of judgment to impose its own logic and goal on the natural world, it was possible to envision how every activity of man was in fact an expression of his freedom. For Cassirer, demonstrating that every human activity – be it political, social, artistic, religious, or intellectual – was creative became synonomous with proving that man was free. Finally, by arguing that Kant's insights could be applied to all fields of human activity, Cassirer effectively opened the way for the expansion of his own work from philosophy into areas like art, literature, myth, and language.

Since Cassirer wanted to make Kant's abstract theories relevant to the common experience of mankind, he formulated his own philosophical imperative: the self-determining activities of reason, the ability to live under self-imposed laws (freedom), and the goal principle should (ethical-imperative) apply to the full range of human activities. In the process of formulating this imperative Cassirer reiterated his commitment to an idea of freedom and a vision of history that brought him into direct conflict with the majority of his compatriots.

## CASSIRER'S IDEA OF FREEDOM

What was Cassirer's idea of history and how was it related to his vision of European history? Why did it bring him into conflict with his colleagues? The first clue to Cassirer's difficulties lay in his discussion of the political event which in Kant's mind had promised to realize the ideals of critical idealism. Kant saw in the French Revolution and in the ideals of 1789 'the promise of the realization of the pure laws of reason.'[23] Cassirer's emphasis on this point revealed Cassirer's republicanism. He argued that 'only through the medium of society [*Gesellschaft*] could the ideal task of moral self-consciousness find its factual, empirical fulfilment.'[24] Further, and most important, complete moral self-consciousness was achieved once one recognized 'that the way to the genuine ideal unity of humanity was only through conflict and opposition.'[25]

Two observations are in order here. First, Cassirer used the German word *Gesellschaft* (society) instead of *Gemeinschaft* (community) to denote a social order. Beginning with Ferdinand Tönnies' contrast, first made in the 1880s, between a strife-torn modern society (*Gesellschaft*), with its emphasis on individual rights, and the well-harmonized activities of individuals serving the national community (*Gemeinschaft*), the term *Gesellschaft* had begun to have negative connotations in Germany.[26] Particularly with the outbreak of war in August 1914, the term *community* was increasingly associated with Germanness, while *society* was identified with the Anglo-French world. In this context, Cassirer's use of the term *Gesellschaft* to describe Kant's idea of the social and political order best suited for teaching individual citizens necessary ideas of freedom and morality was clearly out of step with the nationalist current prevailing in Germany. Secondly, Cassirer's assertion that geniune moral self-consciousness required the recognition and acceptance of the importance of conflict in combining the ideals of individual autonomy and the unity of mankind into an all-inclusive 'community of reason' was basically a Western conception of freedom and depended on competition, that is, a controlled form of conflict.

The ability to sustain conflict was safeguarded in the Anglo-French world by placing a high value on the individual's legal autonomy within the state. The West attempted to preserve freedom by postulating inalienable individual rights independent of the state – an approach to freedom that was for the most part foreign to Imperial Germany. The acceptance of Prussian authoritarianism and the belief that Western civilization, with its individual-oriented society, was threatening the harmonious and organic unity of the German community inclined most German intellectuals, especially after 1914, to look askance at any positive view of social competition within society. For his part, Cassirer placed great value on a social and political order which sustained conflict, especially in the realm of ideas.

Cassirer presented his definition of freedom within the context of what can only be called a cosmopolitan view of European history. This was no small achievement in the Germany of 1916, when many intellectuals such as Thomas Mann, Ernst Troeltsch, and Werner Sombart were stressing the complete uniqueness of the German historical experience.[27] Cassirer, on the other hand, discussed German ideas on the individual, freedom, and the state as part of a larger European phenomenon.[28] The struggle to preserve individual freedom that began in the Reformation as a struggle against the state was transformed in modern times into a task which the modern state had to perform on behalf of, and in conjunction with, the individual.[29] But what kind of freedom did Cassirer have in mind? In relation to the Reformation Cassirer spoke of Luther's attempts to have the religious authorities recognize the individual's right to 'freedom of conscience.' By the time of the Enlightenment the fight for freedom of conscience was transformed into a secular struggle for the state's recognition of the 'freedom of thought.'[30]

Cassirer's conception of freedom was revealing on two counts: both for what it included and for what it excluded. On the one hand he stressed the individual's inalienable natural rights against the authorities. Freedom of conscience and thought restrained the state's power over the individual because certain natural individual rights and liberties were placed beyond the purview of the state. The implication of this position was clear: the individual ought not to be coerced into acting or thinking in a manner repugnant to him. On the other hand, while observing the individual's rights against the state, Cassirer said nothing in 1916, and in fact was never in the future to say anything, on the duties of the individual to the national community. This approach contrasted sharply with the prevalent German tendency to associate freedom with the authoritarian state, where the individual had many duties to the state but practically no rights against it. In fact, in German thought rights tended to become an attribute of the state.[31]

We have already noted Sombart's characterization of the heroic German mentality, with its emphasis on the individual's duty to the state, in contrast to the English trader mentality, which demanded the protection of individual rights. Since most German intellectuals believed that the difference between Germany and its Western enemies was so great, the latter could not really understand the motives of the former. The West's misunderstanding of Germany was a constant theme in the war literature. This motif ranged from Meinecke's defence of the German invasion of Belgium as a necessary military move[32] to Troeltsch's claim that Germany's liberalism was unique and not to be understood in Western terms, and finally to Mann's rabid defence of every aspect of German culture and society.

Troeltsch's essay on the German idea of freedom (1916) is worth noting in connection with Cassirer's beliefs because it pinpointed the differences between Cassirer and his colleagues. In this essay Troeltsch carried the German-Western dichotomy directly into reflections on freedom. He argued that there were different ideas of freedom which were rooted in the social and political development of each people.[33] While he placed the English and French ideas of freedom together, he sharply distinguished them from the German conception.[34] Where the Western view of the matter stressed individual liberties and rights and the value of the individual's independence from the state, Troeltsch stressed the duties of the individual to the national community: 'Freedom consists more in duties than in rights, or better still, in rights that are also duties. The individual does not make up the whole, but identifies himself with it.'[35] Germans sharing Troeltsch's conception of freedom, that is, the majority of them, envisioned the individual as an integral part of the national community ('the whole'). Cassirer's position, on the other hand, was far closer to what Troeltsch designated as the Anglo-French (or Western) conception of individual liberty. The lines were clearly drawn on the political issue. Cassirer associated individual liberty with the republican principles of 1789; these in turn were associated with the primacy of the pure laws of reason and conceived as the entire issue of freedom within the context of European developments since the Reformation and the Renaissance. The majority of educated Germans upheld the ideas of 1914 in opposition to the principles of 1789, preferring to stress the uniqueness of Germany in every respect, especially its idea of freedom.

CASSIRER'S WESTERN ORIENTATION: THE OTHER GERMANY SPEAKS

Cassirer's Western attitude towards freedom and conflict was not completely foreign to Germany. In fact, it was a product of the other Germany – the classical Germany of Kant, Goethe, Schiller, and Humboldt, which rested on the ideal of rationality and on the humanist view of man as a free and cultivated individual, living as a citizen in the community of humanity. In opposition to the prevailing authoritarian and militaristic vision of the German nation, Cassirer in *Freiheit und Form* gave an intellectual portrait of Germany since the Reformation and examined the German sources of his ideals of freedom and rationalism. Far from being anti-German, Cassirer was intent on telling the other side of the story; he wanted to recapture and publicize the cosmopolitan, freedom-oriented basis of German thought.

Cassirer's Western vision of history, politics, and freedom was an anomaly in that he tried to harmonize it with the German idea of freedom. However, his conception of freedom, rooted as it was in Kantianism, contained a flaw that was characteristic of the idealist liberal *Weltanschauung*: the 'ideal' unification of ethics with politics, theory with practice was accomplished in such a manner that the unity itself minimized the possibility of ever taking effective action in the actual world.[36] Interestingly, the theoretical origin of Cassirer's anomalous 'German-Western' conception of individual autonomy would also be the basis of his renewed vision of Kantianism, namely, his commitment to extending Kant's idea of freedom to the study of all human activities.

After having stressed Kant's fusion of ethics and history, Cassirer not only linked Kant's ideas with the Enlightenment but also asserted that the Enlightenment's belief that each man should have the courage to use his reason was also 'the motto of all human history.'[37] For Cassirer, the rational process of self-liberation, which began with the lifting of the individual out of 'the constraints of natural existence' and ended with the 'autonomous consciousness of the human spirit,' was the true subject matter of all human history.[38] The unacceptability to most German intellectuals of Cassirer's vigorously positive view of the Enlightenment and of his understanding that the French Revolution was the prime historical example of enlightened ideas applied to politics further revealed the politicization of German intellectual life during the war. The Enlightenment was identified with the Anglo-French world. Even before the outbreak of war there was a distinct inclination among most German intellectuals to keep the Enlightenment at arm's length. As one critic of the German academic community between 1890 and 1933 summarized the situation:

Generally, the Enlightenment appeared in an unfavourable light, and yet it was never precisely described. Kant was not criticized, though he named the *Aufklärung* [Enlightenment] ... In any case there was always the suggestion, whether explicit or not, that the Enlightenment had been a West European phenomenon ... Some of the mainstreams of the German intellectual tradition were almost invariably portrayed as reactions against the Enlightenment, presumably against its Anglo-French version.[39]

This prevalent attitude towards the Enlightenment was obviously in sharp contrast to Cassirer's enthusiastic embrace of the age of reason. Moreover, Cassirer always dealt with the Enlightenment as a European phenomenon with a single intellectual focal point and tended to minimize rather than maximize the national origins of enlightened ideas.[40]

## CASSIRER'S KANTIAN IDEA OF FREEDOM AND HIS MOVE INTO THE HUMANITIES

Cassirer's positive attitude towards the Enlightenment was associated with his re-interpretation of Kant's philosophy. According to Cassirer, the central message of the Enlightenment had been summed up by Kant's philosophy. Freedom became synonymous with the creative power of reason. Kant's and therefore Cassirer's conviction that man could unite ideals with practice for the purpose of giving a direction to all activities rested on the assumption that the regulative teleological character of human judgment constituted the basis of all human activities. Kant's emphasis on the regulative tendency of human thought provided Cassirer with the means for transforming the Enlightenment's idealized conception of freedom into concrete, empirical terms. The spiritual and natural realms of human existence were thereby made into a unity. But was this, in fact, the case?

In his book *The German Idea of Freedom*, Krieger not only made Kant the paradigm of German liberal thought, but also specifically pointed to the Kantian conception of the regulative nature of human reason as providing the theoretical preconditions of German liberalism's failure to translate its ideals into political and social reality:

An ethics separated from politics, and a politics ultimately based upon ethics; an ethics of duty and a politics of rights ... the emphasis upon the inviolable liberty and equality of all individuals, and the equal emphasis upon the necessity of a superior authority and of a measure of inequality for human progress; the necessity of popular representation as part of a genuine division of powers and the rejection of revolution or resistance against the unjust monarch: these were Kantian formulations which were to become familiar in German liberalism under the unifying concept of the sovereignty of law.[41]

The problem with the Kantian conception of freedom was that while it had indeed formulated an ideal method for making the actual world rational and therefore intelligible, it did not specifically recommend any method for guaranteeing the initiation of a particular course of action.[42]

There was a good reason why Kant's idea of freedom could not advocate a direct course of action. The belief that freedom required one to live in accordance with self-imposed rational laws was Kant's attempt to formulate a basic political principle. The principle rested on the idea that human reason could conceive of world events as leading towards certain ends that were the result of 'the combination of human conceptions.' Since this combining tendency had less to do with 'the constitution of things than with the human manner of perceiving them,' Cassirer along with Kant stressed the regulative instead of the 'constitutive' significance of the power of human judgment.[43]

Unfortunately, Kant's 'regulative' method of uniting the realm of freedom with the world of everyday life produced the impression that his philosophy, in regard to actual political and social considerations, was a mass of brilliant but nevertheless barren abstractions. For, while the regulative tendency of judgment systematized human knowledge of reality by making all events purposive, these ideas did not seem to provide the criteria for justifying one course of human behaviour over another. It did not overcome the dualism of abstract theory and actual life experiences. Even Cassirer was later to admit (in 1928) that Kant's philosophy had the unfortunate effect of restricting German philosophical reflection on politics to the realm of ideas.

Kant's negative and positive definitions of freedom were no help in bringing theory to bear on practice. Negatively speaking, freedom was defined as independence from the natural world, while in positive terms it was defined as living one's life in accordance with self-imposed laws. Neither definition was ultimately useful in truly uniting theory and practice because the foundation of that unity, the regulative, teleological tendencies of human reason, did not give equal weight to the ideal and real components of the unity. For Kant and his followers, unity rested on the a priori goal-oriented tendency of human consciousness, and not on anything in the natural world. The use of the regulative tendency of reason to establish a viable partnership of spiritual ideals and natural facts failed because the unity was based exclusively on ideas and not on facts. Kant's theory remained just a theory.

Kant had, in fact, established a pattern of behaviour that was to characterize what we have already referred to as the idealist, liberal trend in Germany. Abstract ideas stimulated a steady barrage of appeals to the inalienable natural rights of man, but when the time for action came, liberals tended to retreat into elitism and to hang on to the Imperial and Weimar regimes. Their perpetual fear of the socialists also reinforced their abstract and elitist tendencies. In any event, the net effect of this behaviour was political passiveness. While it was true, as Cassirer noted, that in his later years Kant became a political publicist,[44] it was equally true that Kant's enthusiasm for the French

Revolution, the natural and inalienable rights of man, and the primacy of reason in theory and practice did not make him into a revolutionary eager to overthrow the existing political system.[45] Following Kant's pattern, many idealist liberals, while hostile to Imperial Germany, made almost no attempt to alter the existing state of affairs. Cassirer's own hesitation to adopt an active political position, let alone a radical one, was fully revealed by his actions in November 1918. Even when the Imperial government, a regime for which Cassirer had no emotional attachment, was overthrown, he stayed in the background.[46] For better or for worse, Kantian idealist liberalism felt most at home in the ethereal realm of human spirit.

## THE SIGNIFICANCE OF CASSIRER'S REINTERPRETATION OF KANT

The reinterpretation of Kant was an intellectual milestone in Cassirer's evolution from a neo-Kantian primarily interested in mathematical and logical problems to a philosopher of humanity, to whom the manifestations of human freedom and creativity in all fields of activity became the primary concern. Cassirer's study of Kant's life and work was an example of how a politically retiring liberal academic hesitantly moved towards applying his philosophical insights to the events occurring around him. After this theoretical reorientation, Cassirer was ready to expand the scope of his philosophical inquiries to a broader range of human activities. This he attempted to do for the first time in *Freiheit und Form*.

Cassirer's movement towards a historical position with a cosmopolitan orientation occurred within an isolated social context. From his wife's memoirs one gets the image of a man basically untouched by the nationalism of the day, except in the negative sense of worrying about the ill effects of blind nationalism on the fate of Germany.[47] After being rejected for military service for medical reasons, Cassirer spent the first two years of the war teaching at a Berlin *Gymnasium*. From 1914 to 1916 his teaching duties, his work on the Kant biography, and his occasional walks with university colleagues like Riehl, Meinecke, and Troeltsch[48] apparently constituted the major portion of Cassirer's activities. In a certain sense he seemed to have been suspended in time. Even the academic community's split in July 1915 over the question of the Imperial government's war aims, when the majority of German academics aligned themselves with the ultra-annexationist petition circulated by Professors Seeberg and Schäfer, apparently left Cassirer unmoved, in spite of the fact that his academic friends, like Meinecke and Troeltsch, signed the moderate war aims petition. However, Cassirer was not as uninvolved as he appeared to be on the surface. He privately harboured grave misgivings about the true nature of the German war effort and was very concerned that the nationalist fanaticism penetrating society might leave Germany a spiritual ruin. But these thoughts needed some concrete confirmation before they could provide Cassirer with the emotional and intellectual stimulus to carry his philosophical work into the realms of history, politics, and the humanities. When Cassirer entered the German war bureaucracy in 1916 he received the pressure necessary to launch his career as the philosopher of symbolic forms and the champion of an enlightened and free humanity.

# 4

# A cosmopolitan view
# of history (1916–18)

Cassirer's position on the political and social controversies affecting Imperial Germany in its last three years (1915–18) cannot be precisely ascertained since there is no record of his signing any petition. However, his general stance on the war and related issues is found in *Freiheit und Form*, his wife's memoirs, and the comments of several of his personal acquaintances. His initial negative reaction to the war was strengthened by the insights he gained while serving with the government bureaucracy from 1916 to 1918. His bureaucratic duties shattered whatever illusions he might have had about the war and alerted him to the danger of distorting the truth in the national interest. While most Germans believed that victory was just around the corner, Cassirer realized by 1916, 'that this war was lost for Germany.'[1]

Cassirer wrote and completed *Freiheit und Form* a study of German intellectual history from Luther to Hegel, while working for the propaganda ministry. His task was to read all the French newspapers' reports of the war and then edit them to give the impression that even the French realized the war was going badly for the Allies. This reconstructed image of the French newspapers was then released to the German public as evidence confirming the Imperial government's claim that Germany had only to keep up the pressure on the battlefield in order to win the war. From his readings of the French newspapers it was obvious that the war was not going as well as the German government claimed. Even while Cassirer helped to mislead public opinion, he could see that chauvinism led people to distort the truth for others and lose sight of reality themselves.

Even before the war Cassirer felt increasingly compelled to look beyond philosophy proper to the humanities for answers to his philosophical questions. It was at this intellectual point that the unpleasant realities of the war required a total rethinking of the nature of German thought itself. It was a time when Cassirer's inclination to break out of the Marburg mould merged with the larger demands of Germany. Many Germans never examined the lessons to be learned from the events of 1914–18, but Cassirer did. He saw the ill effects of an insidious nationalism on German society and on government policy and realized that a supranational standpoint must be the basis of any viable approach to Germany, its history, and its contemporary problems. He therefore advocated a cosmopolitan view of German history, which envisioned the evolution of German spirit within the context of European developments. He was in a favourable position to learn the lesson of how fanatical nationalism led to a dead end because his position in the war bureaucracy enabled him to see through the smoke screen of the lies and self-delusions of the Imperial government. The connection between Cassirer's motive for writing *Freiheit und Form*, the war situation, and his view of German intellectual history was made clear by his wife. In writing this work he tried simultaneously to present the rationalist view of Germany, the view which came out of the tradition of Kant, Goethe, Humboldt, and Schiller,[2] and to create for himself an indestructable and unchangeable portrait of Germany which would survive the turmoil and the aftermath of the war.[3]

Cassirer's attempt to produce an intellectual portrait of German thought before 1914 and thereby 'preserve' it from the spiritual ruin that would follow in the wake of a probable German defeat was a prime example of his method of dealing with national problems. He responded to current political and social issues on a high and somewhat rarified intellectual level – a response characteristic of German intellectuals. The net effect of such an intellectual stance was an acquiescence in the political and social status quo.[4] Cassirer was never able to free himself completely of this political passivity so typical of the majority of the German intellectuals; even when he became more involved in the social and political affairs of the government he maintained a certain aloofness from the mainstream of activity. Instead of attempting to publicize his misgivings about the direction of the war effort, Cassirer contented himself with noting in the introduction to his *Freiheit und Form* that the German spirit was being forced from its true path by a 'limited spiritual chauvinism.'[5] While this assertion may have been true, its chance of ever having any effect on a war-weary population was nil. This was a striking example of Cassirer's response to a concrete problem. The problem was elucidated in intellectual terms but nothing was done to change the situation.

Admittedly it was next to impossible for anyone in wartime Germany to change the policy of the Imperial government until the governing elite lost its nerve. Only military defeat could bring about that result. Indeed, when the tide of battle shifted against Germany in the late summer of 1918, this loss of nerve occurred, and within three months the Hohenzollern monarchy collapsed and was replaced by the Weimar Republic. Until this time all one could do was to bide one's time. Cassirer was not the only one in this position. Max Weber, a prominent economist and sociologist of Imperial Germany, and later one of the founders of the DDP, was also very worried about the lack of military and political realism in Germany.

Weber's initial enthusiasm for the war had quickly waned. In a letter to Ferdinand Tönnies dated 15 October 1914 he noted that the rigidity of German diplomacy had caused the deaths of thousands of men. Even in the event of a successful ending to the war, Weber could not see a permanent peace for Germany.[6] He attributed this diplomatic narrow-mindedness to an apparent loss of realism in high government circles. German leaders constantly miscalculated the true relation between the strength of Germany and that of its opponents. Perhaps Weber had Bethmann Hollweg, the German chancellor from 1909 to 1917, specifically in mind when he criticized the government. In any event, the chancellor later gave indirect support to Weber's position when he ruefully admitted that 'our people had developed so amazingly in the last twenty years that wide circles [that is, government, military leaders, industrialists] succumbed to the temptation of overestimating our enormous forces in relation to those of the rest of the world.'[7]

Cassirer's and Weber's criticisms of the German war effort were examples of how a moderate liberalism emerged in the crucible of wartime conditions. What united them was an obligation to the truth, which became one of the hallmarks of the idealist liberalism of the Weimar Republic's early years. While Weber increasingly directed his criticism of Imperial Germany at concrete policy issues, Cassirer kept his comments on the philosophical and cultural level. In June 1916 Cassirer castigated those whose nationalist sentiments were pushing German *Kultur* from its original course. For him the original course of German spirit, as set by the classical period of Kant and Goethe, was towards enlightened rationalism and individual freedom; recent events seemed to alter that course towards a mystical, metaphysical devotion to Germanism. On two different levels, Cassirer and Weber saw that patriotic delusions, about either the course of the war or the nature of German spirit, would ultimately lead to a dead end. In this regard, Cassirer's and Weber's wartime reflections may be seen as part of the rising chorus of moderate liberal intellectuals. Their appeals to reason and open mindedness became more emphatic as the military situation became worse for Germany and as the nationalism of the majority of educated Germans reached an hysterical pitch.[8]

CASSIRER AND ANTI-SEMITISM

As the war progressed, the strain of the war effort began to take its toll of the German population. The disputes within the academic community were only intellectual manifestations of the more general malaise affecting German society. Even by 1915 the new-found unity of the German nation as expressed by 'the ideas of 1914' seemed to be at an end. The old pre-war divisions of Wilhelmian Germany resurfaced. Especially after the circulation of annexationist and anti-annexationist petitions in July 1915, Germany more than ever seemed to be a house divided against itself. While the war-aims controversy did not affect Cassirer, the rise of anti-Semitism did. At the beginning of the war anti-Semitism had vanished from public sight. Most German Jews were more than happy to forget their pre-war situation, where they were increasingly isolated from, and discriminated against by, the vast majority of their compatriots.[9] However, as Germany came closer to defeat in 1918, anti-Semitism emerged again with renewed force and eventually culminated in the 'stab-in-the-back' legend, which listed the Jews as one of the enemies within Germany whose home front activities had undermined the war effort.[10]

Since the war inflicted many hardships on the Germans and ended in their defeat, it was unfortunate for the Jews that they had an unusually high public profile from 1914 to 1918. This public visibility came in part from their over-representation in the War Office. A survey conducted in early 1918 revealed that 9.6 per cent of the directors in the war bureaucracy were Jews;[11] yet they constituted less than 1 per cent of the Reich's population. The war career of Walther Rathenau, the Jewish director of the largest electrical company in Germany, was symptomatic of the conspicuous home front service of the Jews. Indeed, Rathenau performed a great service to his country by making the government aware in the war's opening days of the need for total state control of all strategic resources. Throughout the war Rathenau ran the War Materials Department and through it indirectly a great deal of German heavy industry.

Cassirer's wartime service, though not nearly as prominent as Rathenau's, exhibited the same pattern. He fought the war from a desk rather than on the battlefield. There were many understandable reasons for the large presence of Jews in the war bureaucracy. Jews tended to be better educated than the average German, and the War Office needed well-educated people. Nevertheless, the Jews' public image was discomforting. They were accused of cowardice, of being afraid to die for Germany; when the food shortages worsened after 1917, the Jews were blamed for the shortages; they were also charged with getting rich while Germans died. Even though all of these charges were grossly untrue, a war-weary population eagerly accepted them.

For Cassirer the resurgence of anti-Semitism was one specific example of the spiritually ruinous nationalism gripping Germany. In a letter dated 26 November 1916 he had to remind Paul Natorp that everyone in Germany, Jew or not, was sensitive to the reproach of lacking the appropriate national sentiments.[12] This reflected the uneasy feelings of most German Jews. In spite of his doubts about the wisdom of the Imperial government's war policies, Cassirer, like most Jews, felt every bit as German as the non-Jews did.

Cassirer came from an established upper-middle-class family in Berlin and had no background of traditional Jewish religious teachings.[13] He adopted a modified integrationist position on the relation between Jews and Germans. On the one hand, he realized and acquiesced in the limitations of his own social position in Germany;[14] on the other hand, he considered himself to be a Jewish German rather than a German Jew.[15] For him being a German was of primary importance and his religion merely modified the type of German he was. Cassirer's problem, indeed the problem of practically all the Jews in Germany, was that while they considered themselves to be Jewish Germans, the non-Jews considered them as German Jews, for whom religion was most important and nationality secondary.

As if to underline his awareness that the increasingly uneasy position of the Jews in Germany after 1916 was only a symptom of the larger problem, alongside his reminder to Natorp of the sensitivity of the Jews to the nationalist issue, Cassirer expressed his concern about the possible negative effects of nationalism on German political and spiritual life as well as on science, scholarship, and philosophy.[16] For Cassirer the potential damage that a virulent nationalism could inflict on German society in the broadest sense necessitated a total philosophical effort to help mitigate the extent of that damage to German spiritual life. He therefore dedicated his study of German history to the task of preserving the best part of the nation's intellectual heritage, namely, its idea of freedom.

CASSIRER INTRODUCES *FREIHEIT UND FORM*

In order to emphasize the connection between his cosmopolitan interpretation of German history, his conception of freedom, and the contemporary war situation, Cassirer deliberately outlined these basic issues in the foreword and introductory sections to *Freiheit und Form*. He noted that preliminary studies for the work had been done many years before, but a final plan had not materialized because he had to absorb the increased volume of contemporary scholarship on the classical period of German thought (1770–1830). Cassirer's procrastination in publishing his ideas on the subject might have gone on for several more years had not the war intervened and swept away many of his reservations:

Even at this time [June 1916] I would hardly have found the resolution and courage to publish [my preliminary studies] if the experiences and events of the last two years had not repeatedly impressed upon me the resolution that what I had originally conceived of only in abstract philosophical terms had now acquired an immediate and lively interest with regard to our contemporary situation.[17]

The war clearly enabled Cassirer to transform an abstract philosophical exercise into an existential problem concerning the entire German nation. He felt it his duty to examine the 'spiritual nature' and the 'world historical disposition' of German thought while 'the political and material existence of the German people' was engaged in a difficult struggle. Thus, for Cassirer, the essence of German spirit was not to be examined solely in abstract philosophical terms, but rather through 'the deeds and sufferings' of German spiritual history itself.[18]

With his portrayal of the historical struggle of German spirit Cassirer felt he was fulfilling his patriotic duty; he was defending the true nature of German spirit by describing its modern development as objectively as possible. Cassirer's conception of his patriotic duty was indeed interesting, especially in relation to what his peers were doing. The general procedure was to exalt German thought, especially its metaphysical and irrational tendencies, at the expense of the rationalist attitude towards existence and knowledge. In strong contrast to his compatriots, Cassirer's discussion of German spirit had no emotional or polemical side to it; his approach to the subject was cool, rational, and scholarly. For him, 'the metaphysical tendency of German spirit was neither to be praised nor denigrated, admired nor rejected'; it was merely a factor of German thought requiring consideration.[19]

Modern German thought, according to Cassirer, first emerged in the realm of religious consciousness. This newly found religious self-consciousness resulted in a new intellectual standpoint for considering the ideas of freedom,[20] which then spread into other fields of German spiritual and intellectual activity and developed within them. According to Cassirer, Luther performed the historically important task of transforming the mystical, religious individualism of the Middle Ages, with its belief in the existence of a bond that irrevocably tied the individual to the community, into the modern enlightened conception of freedom,[21] in which the individual was an autonomous unit with inalienable natural rights protecting him from the limitation of his freedom by society in general.

Cassirer's conception of Luther's historical role was itself very significant because behind it loomed a cosmopolitan view of German history. He saw Luther's work and the German Reformation as individual moments of a European Renaissance. This new movement of thought transcended all national limitations and provided European man with a new common goal – the preservation of the spiritual autonomy of the individual; and all national members of the community (Germany included) contributed to the fulfilment of that goal. Cassirer's cosmopolitan view of German history, his belief that developments in Germany were comprehensible only when envisioned as an integral part of a European cultural community, was to remain with him throughout his life.[22] While his idea that the German Reformation was part of a more general European Renaissance placed him in a minority position within the academic community, the cosmopolitan standpoint itself was characteristic of a Kantian view of history. German academics were generally not inclined to subordinate one of their own great intellectual revolutions, the Reformation, to European developments. However, neo-Kantians were generally prone to adopt the internationalist position, as was exemplified by the following statement of the relation between the German Reformation and the Renaissance: 'What one is accustomed to designate as religious reformation or simply as Reformation is a partial phenomenon of the general Renaissance, which certainly occupied a large part therein, but which did not ... form its weightiest or most potent motive.'[23]

THE NATIONALIST-COSMOPOLITAN SPLIT IN THE ACADEMIC
COMMUNITY

During the war years, according to Cassirer, intellectual and spiritual events had taken a turn for the worse because the wrong kind of attitude prevailed in Germany: a purely inward-looking nationalism displaced the classical cosmopolitan view of Germany. Cassirer's *Freiheit und Form* may be understood as part of the larger intellectual and political debate that divided the German academic community. On the one hand, the nationalist pole, the majority of educated Germans maintained an essentially inward-looking nationalism, which stressed Germany's uniqueness and superiority over other nations. On the other hand, the internationalist or cosmopolitan pole, there were those who held a view of human affairs which emphasized Germany's place within the European cultural context. Thomas Mann's *Betrachtungen Eines Unpolitischen* (Reflections of a non-political man) represents the nationalist extreme of the debate and Cassirer's *Freiheit und Form* exemplified the cosmopolitan side of the dispute, and between their works fell the ideas of Ernst Troeltsch and Friedrich Meinecke. The debate was both direct and indirect. It was direct in the sense that Troeltsch criticized the historical perspective of Cassirer's *Freiheit und Form*. It was indirect because these men often did not specifically address each other; rather their ideas were parts of the nationalist and internationalist views of the world which periodically collided with one another throughout the war.

The controversial nature of Cassirer's interpretation of the course, content, and goal of German spirit becomes clear when one reads Troeltsch's criticism of his work. In an essay entitled 'Humanism and Nationalism in Our Cultural Heritage' (1916), Troeltsch attacked the entire philosophical orientation of Cassirer's *Freiheit und Form*. Cassirer took the standard rationalist view of the dark Middle Ages: it was a time when the concept of freedom did not exist. The Reformation was envisioned as an era of progress in the movement towards individual freedom. Cassirer quite consciously applied this view to Luther. In fact, one critic has noted that Cassirer approached Luther with the attitude of a philosopher who wished to read his own philosophical values into the ideas of another thinker.[24] It was Cassirer's interpretation of Luther, the Reformation, and the Middle Ages that Troeltsch attacked.

Troeltsch cited *Freiheit und Form* as an example of contemporary scholarship which used Western ideas of reason and freedom as the standard for evaluating German thought. Cassirer's work was not able to grasp the reality of German life because German spiritual life was, according to Troeltsch, irrational in the Western sense because it was steeped in mystical medieval sentiments and values. These sentiments were foreign to the Anglo-French world precisely because the Western European mind was formed in the Renaissance-Enlightenment world of thought. Thus Troeltsch argued that Cassirer's idea of German spirit was in general a German spirit without the Middle Ages and his concept of freedom was rooted in the Renaissance of Western Europe.[25] Since Cassirer's ideas of human autonomy had their origin not in the Reformation but in Renaissance thought, which according to Troeltsch was postmedieval and therefore non-German, Cassirer's conception of Luther as the man who converted medieval spiritualism into modern individualism was wrong. Cassirer looked at the Middle Ages, Luther, and the Reformation with the eyes of a Renaissance-Enlightenment man and was therefore seeing in Luther's work and in German thought something that did not exist, namely, a Western idea of individual freedom. If Luther sought to do anything, it was to justify faith rather than defend the autonomy of the rational individual.

For Troeltsch the source of Cassirer's error was clear. He had assumed a

continuity between the Renaissance, the Reformation, and the Enlightenment when in fact these were separate movements with distinctly different
ideals of human knowledge and of human social behaviour. Because of
Cassirer's misunderstanding of the nature and relation of historical periods
and his tendency to confuse German and Western ideas of man and society,
he missed the main feature of German thought – obligation (*Bindung*) to the
community (*Gemeinschaft*), not individual autonomy within a society
(*Gesellschaft*). Troeltsch believed there was a distinct idea of freedom in German thought, but it was not one which Cassirer or any other Westerner could
grasp. Troeltsch criticized Cassirer's misconception of the medieval spirit as
follows: 'Modern [Western] man sees in the Middle Ages only bondage and
not the endless individualized freedom so characteristic of the epoch, and on
the contrary sees freedom as solely the modern product of the Renaissance.'[26]
Troeltsch was here stressing the difference between the German-medieval
and the Western Renaissance-Enlightenment conceptions of freedom. Cassirer, however, argued as if the latter idea of freedom was *the* valid idea; he further compounded his error by downplaying the uniqueness of the German
approach to the subject.

Troeltsch's criticism of Cassirer was consistent with his other wartime writings. Earlier we noted Troeltsch's distinction between the German and Anglo-French conceptions of freedom in regard to political matters. In connection with Cassirer's wartime work he explicitly extended this difference to
include the evaluation of national historical epochs. The disagreement between Troeltsch and Cassirer was indeed remarkable for what it suggested
about Germany and Cassirer's relation to it. As the majority of educated Germans shared Troeltsch's belief that Germany was distinct from the West and
must therefore be judged by its own standards, Cassirer's conception of German spiritual life was to most Germans an anomaly at best and the work of
an outsider at worst. He was a German philosopher who used German thinkers to come to an 'un-German' conclusion. Since Cassirer did not accept the
essential division between German culture and Anglo-French civilization and
even argued that Kant's ideas were realized in the principles of 1789, he
could very easily be considered one of the ideological enemies within
Germany's frontiers that Thomas Mann so vehemently polemicized against
in his *Betrachtungen Eines Unpolitischen*.

The controversial nature of Cassirer's cosmopolitan conception of German
spirit comes into sharper focus when seen in relation to Mann's book. While
Troeltsch's criticisms were the result of a scholarly, informed, and moderate
nationalism,[27] they were nevertheless part of the nationalist world view prevailing among the German academics and professional élite. Mann's

reflections on German culture more faithfully expressed the limited spiritual chauvinism gripping the German intellegentsia. The works of Cassirer and Mann are interesting on two counts. Firstly, despite the fact that their visions of Germany are worlds apart, they both purport to address the same subject and to render an accurate account of the essence of German spirit. Secondly, they part company from one another in the tone of their discussions. Whereas Mann's reflections are punctuated by polemical and emotional diatribes against the enemy, Cassirer's arguments have a detached and scholarly quality about them. Cassirer, in effect, wanted to challenge Germany without condemning it. He wanted to incite the nation to think critically about its spiritual heritage and to realize its shortcomings in the hope of overcoming them.

In the wartime reflections of Cassirer and Mann we have, in a sense, the archetypes of two conflicting *Weltanschauungen*: Cassirer represented the spirit of Weimar, namely, the liberal and cosmopolitan side of Germany while Mann represented the spirit of Potsdam, namely, the anxieties of a militaristic, anti-liberal, and inward-looking Germany. Mann and Cassirer disagreed with one another on virtually every point. The disagreement had ominous implications for Cassirer. While Mann renounced his wartime book within several years of its publication and indeed came over to Cassirer's side, his work nevertheless provided the nationalist elements in Germany with a treasure chest of ideological ammunition for use against the Weimar regime. Cassirer's *Freiheit und Form* was in effect his first attempt to preserve the liberal ideals he felt were endemic to the German spirit. Ultimately, his opposition to German illiberalism,[28] that is, his opposition to a course of action that resisted any major concession to liberal and democratic practices even at the cost of one's political independence and personal integrity, was a losing cause, but that was not at all obvious in 1916.

Mann's *Betrachtungen* was a passionate, chauvinistic defence of German *Kultur* and its war effort. His aim was to provide Germany with a new faith – a cultural nationalism that praised everything German and denigrated all that was Western. His willingness to publish a rambling, blatantly biased, and largely disorganized essay was an indication of the chauvinistic syndrome afflicting Germany. The broad outline of Mann's argument was contained in the following sentences: 'Spirit is *not* political ... the distinction between spirit and politics embodies the separation of culture and civilisation, soul and society, freedom and suffrage, art and literature; the essence of Germanism is culture, soul, freedom, art and *not* civilisation, society, suffrage and literature.'[29] Mann interpreted everything using this basic separation of Germany from the West as his starting point. Germany was seen as the protesting

nation, a protest that originated with Luther and the Reformation. This original protest against the Western-Roman world was, according to Mann, a
constant theme in German and Western European history, and the present
war against the West was merely the continuation of Germany's traditional
historical protest.[30]

Viewed in these apocalyptical terms, the war became a life-and-death
struggle between the German and Anglo-French worlds. Mann did, however,
confess that the situation was not actually so clear cut; national battle lines
did not coincide with the ideological struggle. 'Germany,' he said, 'had enemies within its own walls' – those who favoured world democracy.[31] Mann
clearly displayed his anti-liberal bias when he approvingly cited Lagarde's
contention that the principles of 1789, which were another variant of un-German thought, were firmly entrenched in Germany and sustained by German
liberals.[32] In Mann's eyes Germany was fighting not only against the West
but against itself as well. In order for Germany to win its final victory over itself and others, it was necessary to recognize that 'German spirit was essentially conservative.'[33] Mann saw the essence of this conservatism as culminating in an unreserved support for the culture of the middle class, whose
political loyalties lay with the Kaiser and the Empire.

The most outstanding feature of Mann's war effort was its extremism. In
this respect his work reproduced on the ideological and cultural level the nationalist sentiments which were sapping Germany's ability to formulate a realistic picture of contemporary events. Mann's distortions on the level of ideas
were more than matched by the delusions of the German government and
people regarding the possible outcome of the war. As the spiritual chauvinism
penetrated deeper into German minds, the nation's collective ability to
maintain a realistic view of the situation declined. Cassirer received confirmation of this when he participated in the Imperial war bureaucracy's manu-
facture of facts for home consumption. The line between reality and fantasy
was blurred; by the end of the war it had disappeared altogether. It was no
longer necessary deliberately to lie since the military government was not capable of distinguishing a false expectation from the truth. Cassirer's *Freiheit
und Form* was essentially an intellectual protest against what the war was doing to Germany. And just as Mann's *Betrachtungen* embodied the emotional
extremism of the present government, so Cassirer's work represented a detached and rational attempt to see the German nation for what it was, without any illusions.

CASSIRER'S PORTRAIT OF THE TRUE GERMANY

Cassirer's appeal to reason took the form of an application of his reinterpretation of Kant to German intellectual history. The war gave a new impetus to Cassirer's view that German history was an integral part of European history, especially in regard to the idea of individual freedom. *Freiheit und Form* was the scholarly reaffirmation of his internationalist orientation.

The tension between 'the principle of freedom' and 'the principle of form' became the central idea for his analysis of the direction and historical significance of German thought. Not surprisingly, he would use the freedom-form conflict to argue that the ultimate goal of German cultural history was to demonstrate that man was an autonomous, rational being. Cassirer also stressed the tentative quality of his own work and cautioned his readers to see the historical tension in German thought as a 'continuous *problem*' and not as a 'definitive *result*.'[34]

After beginning with Luther's reflections on spiritual freedom in Western terms, Cassirer saw Leibniz's ideal of a new logic as continuing the movement towards individual autonomy begun by Luther. Leibniz expanded the primarily theological insights of Luther into a less religious ethical theory. For Leibniz, the concept of self-consciousness completed itself in the concept of the moral individual. Moreover, he believed that moral precepts must be rooted and preserved in the morally conscious individual.[35] Leibniz's system of a cosmic pre-established harmony, where the individual and the cosmos are in sympathetic vibration with one another, rested on the above ethical position. However, the new ethical position took on a new power and significance because from it emerged the grounds of a new view of science and the world.

The new world view presupposed a novel conception of the relation holding between reason, the soul, and the cosmos. Having already placed the morally self-conscious individual into the framework of an harmonious universe, Leibniz postulated an original relation between reason and the soul: 'The sovereignty of the "soul" is essentially and originally asserted in the form of the sovereignty of "reason." '[36] Cassirer was here portraying the initial stages of the movement in German consciousness towards the realization that the autonomy of the individual was identical with the complete sovereignty of human reason.

The autonomy of the individual and human reason was more than an abstract, philosophical affair; it also encompassed the 'infinite totality of individual *life forms*.'[37] Further, this totality of life forms revealed 'the creative power of consciousness.'[38] Cassirer's interest in discussing the relation between the creative power of human judgment and activities like art and literature was indicative of his post-1914 turning to the humanities in order to find answers to philosophical questions. The pre-1914 Kantian interest in examining the pure functions of knowledge in philosophy, science, and mathematics yielded to a broader concern with the universe of life forms.

On the historical level, Cassirer wanted to elucidate how the history of German spirit revealed the principle of its own development: the belief that the 'spiritual value of the individual' could be fully elucidated only if it itself possessed a truth of 'universal significance.'[39] However, this revelation was not Germany's alone, rather it was the revelation of European humanity. Germany was but one component of the general drive of European culture towards an adequate conception of individual freedom. The more clearly German thought grasped this truth, the more thoroughly it would have understood the principle that its own historical development manifested. Cassirer's internationalist orientation permeated practically every aspect of his analysis of German cultural history. Thus, he traced the evolution of the idea of freedom from the Reformation to Leibniz and into the Enlightenment[40] and the idea of natural law, which he considered to be the legal counterpart to the idea of freedom, from Cusanus to Leibniz and finally to such Enlightenment thinkers as Wolff, Montesquieu, Rousseau, Locke, Blackstone, and Kant.[41]

Cassirer's approach to human history revolved around a single principle which yielded a series of relations linking the individual to his society to his culture and to all humanity. Starting with the belief in the creative power of human reason, he applied this idea to every form of human activity. Before the war his reasoning was largely confined to the sciences and philosophy. In those pre-war years (1899–1914) the creative power of the mind was analysed into the pure functions of theoretical knowledge. Hence, a number was described in terms of its position in the series of numbers to which it belonged, and chemical concepts (for example, the atom) were analysed in terms of their relations to a series of conceptual determinations of space, time, and number.[42] During the war (1914–16) he shifted his reflections on human creativity to more worldly problems. Each individual was considered as part of a given society, which itself was part of a given culture; finally, the society and culture along with the individual were envisioned as integral parts of a universal human order. Thus, when Cassirer spoke of European humanity's movement towards freedom, he referred to the necessity of understanding the universal significance of every individual deed. The history of mankind was for ever moving towards its goal: the realization that a liberated humanity was the ultimate purpose of history.[43]

Significantly, when dealing in humanistic terms with the relation between the individual and the whole, Cassirer hinted at his future philosophy of symbolic forms. According to Cassirer, German thought implicitly understood that any *form* of human activity (for example, linguistic activity) could be interpreted as a *symbolic* creation of the mind in accordance with the laws constituting human reality. His new inclination to think of cultural activities as part of a universal system of symbolic forms was further disclosed when he made a statement that was destined to become the principle theme of *Language*, the first volume of *The Philosophy of Symbolic Forms*. As with art, 'language in general is to be understood not as a copy and reprint of something already existing, but as the unfolding and expression of the energy of the soul.'[44] The attempt to use language and art as the starting point for a philosophical analysis of the relation between the creative power of human spirit and its cultural products (symbolic forms like language, art, myth, science) was not original with Cassirer. His interest in the relation between language, art, and philosophy was an example of an increasing tendency of German scholarship that originated in the pre-war years.[45] In an article written in 1911 on the relation between linguistic and literary history, Karl Vossler connected linguistic analysis to a broader history of literature.[46] Fritz Medicus in 1913 made an even more explicit connection between philosophy and poetry, when he interpreted them as complementary spiritual activities; art was the revelation, and philosophy the knowledge, of life.[47] Medicus' view of the relation between philosophy, art, and life becomes all the more interesting when we realize that he was to provide the initial stimulus for Cassirer's future analysis of the Enlightenment.[48]

The variety of interpretations of Goethe's life and works in academic circles illustrated dramatically the division between Cassirer's humanist world outlook and the often extreme nationalist views of his compatriots. While Mann's *Betrachtungen* contained relatively few references to Kant and Goethe (when references were made, their principle purpose was to denigrate liberal ideals and the principles of 1789),[49] Cassirer placed these men at the centre of his analysis of German cultural history. This was true literally as well as conceptually. The middle third of *Freiheit und Form* was devoted to examining the work of Kant and Goethe. When Mann was opposed to liberal, republican, and Western ideas he cited Kant, Goethe, and any number of other German thinkers to support his claims. After his conversion to the Weimar Republic, he began to see Goethe as the symbol of a worldly, humanitarian liberalism.[50] Cassirer, on the other hand, had always admired Goethe[51] and constantly quoted the poet in his own works. In a sense, the Weimar Republic's subsequent adulation of Goethe[52] was foreshadowed by Cassirer's personal inclination to identify him with the essence of German thought.

Using Goethe's own words, Cassirer expressed the anthropological ideal of human history that guided his analysis of German thought. All human philosophizing remained for Goethe

an anthropomorphism, i.e., man at one with himself prescribes his own internal unity to everything that he is not, and draws all else into this unity, thereby making all other things a part of him ... We may observe, measure, calculate and weigh nature as much as we like, it is nevertheless our measure since man is the measure of all things.[53]

For Cassirer, Goethe's anthropomorphism was another version of the insight expressed by Kant in his critique of judgment that all we experience is the product of the creativity of human reason.

Cassirer began his discussion of the Kant-Goethe cultural milieu by noting the remarkable 'pre-established harmony' prevailing at the time of Kant and Goethe.[54] Largely independent of one another, these two men reached similar conclusions; Kant's philosophy was paralleled by the artistic activities of Goethe. Cassirer believed that in the lives and ideas of these exemplary German thinkers the dialectic between freedom and form had attained its classical expression.

He then summarized the insights he had gained from his reinterpretation of Kant's system. To underline the importance of this reinterpretation for his own understanding of classical German thought, Cassirer referred the reader to his book *Kants Leben und Lehre* and again stressed Kant's assumption that the teleological and purposive character of human nature was an adequate basis for unifying nature and spirit. In his efforts to unite the world of appearance (nature) and the realm of spiritual ends (human freedom) Kant had expressed in theoretical terms the world view of his contemporaries as well as the tensions characteristic of German thought. Cassirer described the historical significance of Kant's philosophy as follows:

The world of appearance [nature] and the realm of ends now stands for us as the objectively developing context of reason itself – in this twofold manner, freedom gave itself its rules as well as its form. The synthesis of freedom and form, which German intellectual history had sought and demanded, attained its deepest philosophical grounding [in Kant's thought].[55]

Kant's attempted resolution of the tension between freedom and form, between the ruler and the ruled was vitally important to Cassirer's view of German intellectual history. For Kant's *Critique of Judgement* not only pointed to art, hence to Goethe, as a possible means of resolving the tension, but it also dramatized the paradox of German thought. As the legislator of his various life forms (like art and philosophy) man demonstrated his autonomy, but as a consequence he was entangled in these freely created life forms.

Since Goethe's work had, according to Cassirer, embodied 'the spiritual content of the national past of his people,'[56] it now remained to explain how the life of Goethe merged with the development of German thought since the

Reformation. To Cassirer the significance of Goethe's achievements went far beyond the literary and artistic domains. In his usual indirect way of making historical and political observations, Cassirer noted that Goethe saw himself as the spiritual liberator of the Germans: 'Whoever has learned to understand the general import of my writings and my nature must therefore admit that he has won a certain inner freedom.'[57] Cassirer's selection of this passage to focus on the central meaning of Goethe's work was particularly interesting because it harmonized with Kant's idea that his philosophy was a philosophy of freedom. Moreover, it was precisely the purpose of *Freiheit und Form* to show that the quest for individual freedom was the driving force of German thought. It was a freedom where the individual forever strove for total autonomy, not one of the Troeltsch variety where the individual became free by binding himself more resolutely to the whole.

Goethe's view of man received its most memorable expression in the drama *Faust*, which for Cassirer symbolically summed up the course of Goethe's life. He wrote the first part of *Faust* early in his life; the second and concluding part was completed just before he died. Every nuance and shift in Goethe's ideas and activities found its way into the whole of Faust's poetic life, which was represented as pure striving and pure motion. In the drama 'the endless [human] endeavour [to create new forms] does not confine itself to a finite object or a finite form, but it finds its inner true measure in the pure law of activity, under which it places itself.'[58] Goethe's hero completely embodied the pathos and tragedy of the striving, creative being. His fate was to create, destroy, and re-create life forms; in the full life everything was experienced yet all ended in death. There was an eternal tension in the free man who for ever tried to be independent of all forms of existence yet had to live through each of them in order to be liberated from them. Through *Faust*, Goethe dramatically illustrated the tension between freedom and form that was so characteristic of the history of German spirit.

In Kant and Goethe the major philosophical and artistic tendencies of German thought met and became a unity, a cultural milieu. The Kantian idea of freedom achieved its artistic expression in the character of Faust. The Kant-Goethe pure man hovered between the world of nature, where there was little human freedom, and the realm of ends, where human freedom reigned; he was the sovereign creator of laws, yet he was bound by them. Nevertheless, this ideal being for ever strove to be free, and in the process proved that he was indeed free.

After examining the movement towards freedom in German philosophy and culture, Cassirer extended his idea of freedom to political theory. He introduced his discussion of the relation between the ideas of freedom and the state with a reference to Friedrich Meinecke's *Cosmopolitanism and the National State*. He was not concerned, as Meinecke was, with analysing only the German conception of the state, rather he would attempt to describe the evolution of the idea of the state as such within the context of the development of German spiritual life.[59] Cassirer's decision to discuss all conceptions of the nation-state, not only the German ones, was interesting because it revealed why his ideas were so much of an anomaly during the years 1914–18. While he rejected the prevailing inclination to discuss and exalt German ideas of the state, freedom, community, and so on, and opted for a broader, international view of German history, he nevertheless followed a procedure very popular in Germany: in his historical analysis he gave primacy to ideas over matters of fact – precisely as Meinecke did in his analysis of the development of German nationalism.

Cassirer's internationalist position was clear in that he was determined to discuss German history in the context of European culture. Yet, his format for discussing the state, his inclination to unify physical realities with a conception of politics and history on the basis of spiritual values and abstract ideas reflected an idealistic attitude towards man, history and politics that was consistent with many of the ideas of his more nationalist colleagues. He readily admitted that in Germany the conception of the state was very different from the one prevailing in France and England. Whereas the French and English emphasized the 'force of events' and the 'power of facts' in the formation of their respective nations, the Germans stressed the overwhelming importance of the power of thought in German political and historical events – an idea that became one of the basic ideas of German philosophy. In Cassirer's words, 'The justification of the State in and through thought, its elevation not to a physical reality, but to a specific spiritual value henceforth became one of the basic and important themes of German philosophy.'[60] With this admission he placed himself in a difficult situation because his 'spiritual' view of the state was very Germanic.

Cassirer was in fact torn between the German and Anglo-French worlds of thought, which he wanted to unite by stressing the cosmopolitan roots of German intellectual history since the Reformation. Instead of surrendering to the wartime inclination to extol the uniqueness and self-sufficiency of German culture, he returned to an idea which prior to 1914 had had many supporters, including Meinecke, but had been forgotten during the war years – the idea that 'the best German national feeling also included the cosmopolitan ideal of a humanity beyond nationality and that it "was un-German to be merely German." '[61] In other words, it was only half true that Cassirer's approach was 'Western.' His discourse on freedom and form was his response to those people who had rendered a disservice to German thought by neglecting its cosmopolitan and humanistic character.

Ironically, Cassirer's classical German standpoint was not recognized by his compatriots. Although he used many of the same conceptions of history and philosophy as everyone else, his starting point was different. Instead of starting with German history as the basic unit, Cassirer began with European history. His anomalous position rested on this paradox: while the logic of his analysis placed *Freiheit und Form* well within the German historical and philosophical traditions, the *conclusion* of his study differed so greatly from what many Germans wanted to believe that he put himself outside the mainstream of German wartime opinion. This difference of opinion was a foretaste of future developments. Throughout the years of the Weimar Republic he was to uphold consistently his internationalist view of German history and philosophy, in spite of his colleagues' overwhelming preference for the 'ideas of 1914' approach to German culture.

Cassirer's liberalism and his Western conception of the link between the autonomous individual and the state clearly emerged in the concluding chapter of *Freiheit und Form*. He explicitly connected the idea of natural rights to the French Revolution and to the mutual interaction between the concepts of the state and freedom.[62] Cassirer defined natural law in such a way as to illuminate the ideological dimension implicit in his philosophy. His views on law were obviously based on neo-Kantian legal philosophy. The first view dealt with law in general, the second with natural law:

The permanence of law does not proceed from the *existence* of various reasonable subjects, rather the recognition of the necessary validity of a legal norm is itself the *condition* for legality.[63]

Natural law is nothing other than the application of the general methodology of rationalism to the special domains of moral and legal problems.[64]

The most prominent feature of Cassirer's approach to this question was his abstract, rationalistic conception of legal matters. Legality was based on ideas emanating from the mind rather than on hard facts. In true Kantian fashion Cassirer envisioned *Recht* as the extension of man's rational ability to impose rules and laws on all his activities.

Like Kant, Cassirer attempted to fuse ethics with politics. To live under a *Rechtsstaat* one was obliged (ethical imperative) to use one's reason to create law. Cassirer's identification of the *Rechtsstaat* with *Naturrecht* (natural law) was all the more revealing from an ideological point of view because by the twentieth century, natural law had lost its wide spread appeal in Germany and was no longer considered by most German intellectuals as a valid foundation for constructing social and legal norms. First, it was too abstract in that it did not consider the specific social and political determinants of law and secondly, it was associated with Anglo-French conceptions of man and society.[65] As with his conception of freedom Cassirer was at loggerheads with the majority of his compatriots. This result was no surprise because, as Cassirer himself realized, the concept of natural law was the complement to a conception of freedom that stressed the rights of the individual against the encroachments of state power. These twin conceptions of freedom and natural law were themselves grounded in the cosmopolitan conception of history which had become quite unacceptable to Cassirer's peers.

Perhaps the most fascinating revelation concerning Cassirer's attempt to formulate a liberal humanistic *Weltanschauung* in response to the nationalist hysteria of the time came in one passage in *Freiheit und Form* in which he reaffirmed his support of the ideals of 1789. In this passage Cassirer not only reaffirmed the connection between German reflection on the inalienable rights of the individual and the liberal, democratic ideals of the French Revolution, but also foreshadowed the type of argument he would use to defend the Weimar Republic.[66] In a speech delivered in 1928, at the ninth anniversary of the promulgation of the Weimar constitution, he used the very same thoughts expressed in this passage from *Freiheit und Form* to explain why the liberal, republican conception of government – hence the Weimar Republic itself – was not foreign to Germany.[67]

*Freiheit und Form* was Cassirer's call to Germany to come to know itself again and to see itself as an inseparable component of European civilization. Cassirer believed that once the German people recognized their contribution to the larger European task, once Germany had realized that the tension in its own thought, between freedom and form, was part of the larger European cultural context, only then would Germany have realized that its own historical task was the struggle for man's self-liberation and that its end was freedom.

Cassirer's message fell on deaf ears. Perhaps the occasion of Hermann Cohen's burial in Berlin on 7 April 1918 best reflected Cassirer's and the Marburg School's isolation from the bulk of the academic community. When Cohen died the academic community generally ignored his passing. No official representative of the Universities of Marburg or Berlin attended the funeral. The academy's delegation, a polite formality which was usually accorded to most eminent intellectuals at their burials, was noticeable only by its absence. This callous refusal of the academic world to pay its last respects to Cohen, one of Imperial Germany's foremost interpreters of Kant, underscored the alienation of Cohen and Marburg neo-Kantianism from the academic community.[68] In his funeral oration for Cohen, Cassirer used Schiller's words 'Determine yourself from your own self' to make the point that the idea of freedom was the key to Cohen's and Kant's conception of philosophy.[69] This belief summarized not only Cohen's and Kant's works but Cassirer's as well. Unfortunately, in 1918 as few people in Germany were willing to listen to Cassirer's words as had been willing to acknowledge Cohen's achievements.

# 5

# Cassirer's synthesis of
# Kant and Hegel (1918–19)

## CASSIRER AND THE EVENTS OF 1918–19

Much had changed in Germany between the time of Hermann Cohen's death in April 1918 and Cassirer's move to Hamburg in October 1919. Cassirer had found himself a niche in the German academic community and a permanent task to occupy his new intellectual endeavours. In the same period Germany changed from an aristocratic empire to a republican regime. As Cassirer became increasingly satisfied with his lot in life, Germany seethed with discontent. Cassirer's improved personal situation and Germany's novel experience of internal disorder were not unrelated. While Cassirer felt that the new government fulfilled his own political ideals and in addition provided him with a respectable place in the academic world, most Germans despised the Weimar Republic.

In the spring of 1918 Germany had resumed its offensive on the Western front, but after initial success German troops were not able to overcome the stiffened resistance of the Western allies. The tide of battle turned against Germany in the early summer. By August-September 1918 Germany's Western front was caving in; morale on the battle and home fronts was ebbing. These events behind German lines coincided with the collapse of Germany's allies – Turkey, Bulgaria, and, most important of all, the Austro-Hungarian Empire. Germany sought an armistice in October and finally agreed to one effective as of 11 November 1918. Before the armistice went into effect the sailors' mutiny at the Kiel naval base on 28 October gave the initial impetus to a chain of events that resulted in the abdication of the Kaiser and the declaration of the Republic on 9 November 1918.

As political events were taking their new course the German military command withdrew from the political arena, leaving the civilian government with the odious task of requesting and then signing an armistice. This was a terrible shock to most Germans because for years they had been expecting victory. German armies stood on foreign soil, yet it was Germany that sued for peace. Germany felt cheated. The new civilian government's request for an armistice gave rise to the 'stab-in-the-back' legend. The army had not failed; it was the home front that had collapsed under the strain of war.

In spite of the confusion and the seemingly incessant street battles between government troops and various left-wing revolutionary groups, the Weimar Republic received a strong endorsement from the German people in the election of 19 January 1919. The Weimar Coalition of moderate socialists, liberal democrats, and the Catholic Centre Party came into existence, but its hegemony did not last more than fifteen months. In the election of 6 June 1920 the coalition lost its majority in the Reichstag. However, in its brief period of power, especially up to October 1919, the republican regime made peace with the Allies and promulgated a new constitution on 11 August 1919. While the achievements of the new republic were not impressive, or even acceptable to a large segment of the German population, they were good enough for Cassirer.

Ever since Cassirer had worked for the Imperial government he had lost his illusions about the governing élite in Germany. The armistice was no surprise to him. He was well aware that Germany's military and diplomatic situation was deteriorating. Thus, he was not at all confused by the quick succession of events from March to November 1918.

Cassirer's detached, rational approach to the political turmoil in Germany throughout 1918–19 complemented his personal moderation; he was not the kind of person who permitted wild emotions to dictate his course of action. Just as he resisted 'the ideas of 1914,' he avoided being caught up in the excitement and revolutionary fervour spreading in Germany from 1918 to 1919. Cassirer's wife stressed the moderation of his reaction to the revolutionary events of November and December 1918. His natural instincts tended to drive him forward; his way of thinking was progressive, but never tinged with revolutionary impetuousness. He adopted a 'wait and see' attitude during the revolution, and remained in the background.[1]

Even though Cassirer remained outside the active political arena, his understanding of events in Germany was remarkably perceptive. Some time in December 1918 or January 1919 he had a discussion with Dimitry Gawronsky, who had been an active supporter of the Kerensky government in Russia and came to Germany after the Bolsheviks overthrew that regime to warn his friends of the danger of communism. He was afraid that the revolution in Germany would result, as it had in Russia, in an extreme left-wing regime.

Cassirer replied that the situations in Germany and Russia were not compa-
rable. The power and courage of the German reaction was and would continue to be formidable, unlike the feeble response of the Imperial Russians.
He concluded his argument by saying that the revolution in Germany had already run its course.[2]

Cassirer's thoughts about the future of Germany, especially the power of
the German reaction, were entirely borne out by future developments. In retrospect, the incessant erosion of the social and political basis of the Weimar
Republic by the nationalist and conservative right-wing forces in Germany
constituted one of the main themes of the republic's unhappy and short-lived
existence. From 1919 until 1930, the pro-republican parties were to fight a
losing battle against the reactivated right-wing social groups and forces (the
army, big industrialists, the bureaucracy, and the judiciary) upon which Imperial Germany had been erected.

Cassirer had in fact participated in one of the early battles on behalf of republican ideals and had encountered and reacted vehemently against the
transparent 'political justice' of a reactionary and anti-republican judiciary.[3]
In May 1919 Eugen Leviné was put on trial for treason for the part he played
in the ill-fated Bavarian Soviet of March-April 1919. The trial was part of
the bloody repression of the Bavarian Soviet by right wing military forces.[4]
With the Free Corps' orgy of counter-revolutionary terror in full swing, many
liberal democrats and socialists felt that a fair trial for Leviné was impossible.
Accordingly, on 19 May 1919 Cassirer signed a telegram, along with people
like Hugo Haase, Maximilian Harden, and Adolph Grabowsky, all of whom
held centre-left (liberal democratic) or left-wing (socialist) political views, requesting that Leviné's trial be postponed to another time when the political
atmosphere would permit a fairer trial.[5] Their action was in vain. The reactionary judges condemned Leviné to death on 3 June 1919 and he was executed three days later.

While Cassirer was still being ignored by the old Imperial social groups, be
they judges who ignored his plea for justice or Berlin academics who refused
to reward his intellectual achievements by promoting him to a professorship,
republican Germany gave him a warm welcome as a professor at one of the
newly founded pro-republican universities. In June 1919 the University of
Hamburg eagerly sought Cassirer's appointment to their teaching faculty. He
accepted the university's offer and in October 1919 moved to Hamburg.

Both his protest on Leviné's behalf and his joining of a pro-republican university faculty underscored Cassirer's commitment to the liberal-republican
cause, which fitted into the general pattern of German Jewish behaviour after
the war. Once the Imperial government fell and the new democratic republic

was announced on 9 November 1918, many Jews looked forward to a new era in German history. The liberal dream of 1848, the establishment of a democratic republic, finally was within reach. The connection between German liberalism and the Jews was further solidified on 6 November 1918 when Theodor Wolff, a Jew and chief editor of the *Berliner Tageblatt*, published in his paper the announcement that a great democratic party (the DDP) had been formed to appeal to the entire country.[6] The proclamation contained the names of an impressive array of prominent liberals whom Wolff and Max and Alfred Weber had gathered together to organize the DDP. Significantly, a number of the liberal papers that backed the organization effort, particularly the *Berliner Tageblatt*, the *Frankfurter Zeitung*, and the *Vossische Zeitung*, were controlled by Jews. For better or for worse, the liberal press, especially the left wing of the German Democratic Party, became synonymous with the Jews. The major difference between Germans and German Jews was the latters' politics. Jews as a social group overwhelmingly voted for the liberals, although a few voted for the socialists. Germans, on the other hand, spread their votes from the conservative right to the socialist left. This was the political context in which Cassirer pursued his new intellectual task.

KANT AND HEGEL COMPARED

In the academic world Cassirer was known as a Marburg neo-Kantian. While this was true, it was not the whole truth. Far too many critics in Germany conceived of his work *only* within a Marburg context, and this half-truth distorted their perception of his ideas. Between 1917 and 1922 he ceased to be a Marburg neo-Kantian; in fact, between his reorienting insight in the summer of 1917 and his move to Hamburg in the autumn of 1919, an important process of intellectual reconsolidation took place. Beginning with the summer of 1917, when he realized that the whole human being – his passion, emotions, and practical activities – and not only his rational thought process opened the way for an understanding of the human condition,[7] Cassirer sought to provide a philosophical and cultural foundation for his new insight. If the study of man's rational thought process was insufficient for comprehending the entire man, he reasoned, it was also likely that the study of man's rational activities (for example, philosophy) was inadequate for comprehending non-rational activities such as myth, language, art, or religion. In short, Cassirer's new interest in the whole man and all his activities predisposed him to breaking out of the Marburg mould.

Cassirer's philosophical readjustment led him to become a Kantian with a distinct Hegelian bent. The recognition of his original and very personal blending of the Kantian and Hegelian systems is crucial to an accurate understanding of his philosophical position. In order to make sense of Cassirer's new orientation it is necessary to define Kantianism. All Kantians believe a/ that the conditions of the possibility of experience in general are also the conditions of the possibility of the objects of experience. And this insight rests on b/ the belief in an original transcendental unity of human consciousness. These two beliefs were the fundamental tenets that all Kantians took from Kant's critique of reason and placed beyond dispute. For Cassirer they were the starting point for his reflections on German idealism.[8]

While Marburg neo-Kantians, as one variant of Kantianism, may have taken either a mathematical approach to these fundamental Kantian principles (like Cohen) or a logistic one (like Natorp), Cassirer attempted to synthesize these orientations into one philosophy, the philosophy of symbolic forms. While his method of accomplishing this synthesis was to turn to a study of the humanities, in order to justify this turn Cassirer apparently reconsidered Hegel's philosophy in relation to a Kantian orientation. His major problem was to work out how a study of the humanities could be made relevant to Kantian philosophical concerns. To do this Cassirer felt obliged to strike a new balance between what we will call a Kantian logistic (or a priori) analysis of consciousness, an Hegelian interest in the totality of spiritual life forms, and a Kantian-Hegelian view of humanity's progressive enlightenment.

It is important to stress the political impulse guiding Cassirer's reflections. In the tradition of Kantian liberalism he believed that each individual had to be treated as an end in himself rather than a means to an end. The Imperial government's inclination to manipulate Germans for its own ends had to give way to a manner of thinking about politics and people that placed a very high value on individual initiative, regardless of how much that initiative placed the individual in opposition to his society and his government. The renewal of intellectual integrity would occur in Germany only if all Germans could be convinced that behind the multitude of viewpoints lay a deeper unity – the desire of all men to be free. To convert the dissonance of life in post-war Germany into a harmony should be the goal of all Germans. With this goal in mind Cassirer returned to the ideas of Kant and Hegel.

German philosophical idealism assumed that the principles underlying knowledge and existence are reflected by human consciousness. While all idealists accepted the validity of this tenet, its implications were open to two main courses of interpretation: the Kantian and the Hegelian alternatives. Whereas Kantians tended to see 'pure reason' as the core of human reality and seek the necessity of knowledge within the limits of human experience itself, Hegelians tended to put 'concrete spiritual life' at the centre of reality (all reality not only the human one) and sought the necessity of all knowledge and existence as a whole. While Kantians were content to confine human knowledge to man's system of perception and thought, Hegelians carried their philosophical efforts into the whole of existence.

The Kantian and Hegelian philosophies were primarily separated from each other by their respective views on the relation between knowledge and existence. For Kant, knowledge and existence were necessarily separate; for Hegel they were a necessary unity. Underlying their respective conceptions were radically different approaches to philosophy. Kant's entire philosophy, which hoped to answer the question 'How is synthetic a priori knowledge possible?' presupposed the transcendental unity of human consciousness. Hegel's philosophy, on the other hand, tried to answer this question 'How does absolute knowledge develop?' In response to this question Hegel's philosophy presupposed a 'dialectical teleological process' which consciousness necessarily executed on itself. This process would, according to Hegel, inevitably give rise to the science of the experience of consciousness. While both Kant and Hegel assumed that knowledge possessed a rational structure, they differed in that Kant approached his task through an epistemological analysis of fixed categories while Hegel examined knowledge through the various stages of its development and tended to emphasize questions of ontological importance.

The differences separating Kant and Hegel notwithstanding their respective philosophical systems formed an intellectual continuum, with Kant's critical idealism at one end of the intellectual spectrum and Hegel's absolute idealism at the other end.[9] Their systems had set the outer theoretical limits of post-1830 German philosophical thought and in a sense predetermined the theoretical basis of Cassirer's own response to the Germany of 1914–33. When considering the relation between values (spirit) and facts (nature), Cassirer adopted the standard Kantian-Hegelian presupposition that all knowledge and existence constituted a unity. After 1919 he tried to give that his personal stamp.

CASSIRER'S HEGELIAN CORRECTION OF KANT

Cassirer wanted to change the critique of pure reason into a critique of culture, transforming Kant's work into a concrete, empirical analysis of man's cultural activities. This transformation did not take place without Cassirer's Hegelian correction of Kant's system. What Cassirer was able to use most effectively from Hegel was his general dialectical orientation – his evolutionary view of human knowledge and existence, together with his understanding that an interest in the totality of human activities was the essential precondition for a true understanding of mankind. When Cassirer mixed Hegel's evolutionary and holistic vision with Kant's logistic analysis of knowledge and existence he at once realized that a complete grasp of the various life forms (for example, language and myth) required a transcendental study (Kantian) of the gradual unfolding (Hegelian) of each of those forms. Once Cassirer finally saw how Kant's and Hegel's methods could be made to complement each other, he was well on the way to transforming the 'life forms' into 'symbolic forms.'

Hegel's *Phenomenology of Spirit* was the work that convinced Cassirer of the validity of Hegel's insight that all life and thought had to be understood as constituting a unified and dynamic whole. In Cassirer's eyes the *Phenomenology* was the complete unfolding and representation of the problem of objectivity in a new frame; it wanted to capture and portray the 'essence of spirit' in all its differing and opposing forms.[10] Hegel, according to Cassirer, was the first to perceive that 'All life demands a unity which is not to be conceived in static terms, but is to be grasped as a dynamic process: a unity which thereby reconstitutes itself from an original disunity. Therein lies the concept of objectivity which is suited solely to spirit.'[11] Life demands a unity which unfolds itself in a process, and from this process emerged a concept of objectivity. Hegel saw that objectivity was given for spirit 'in the form of a general obligation, whose power he conceived as an integral part of an all-inclusive living totality.'[12] In this connection Cassirer readily accepted Hegel's dictum that the truth was identifiable with the whole of spiritual reality, that is, the truth was completely realized only when it unfolded itself in all its diverse life forms. And these forms constituted the continuous spiritual totality which was *eo ipso* the realization of the idea of freedom in time (history) and in space (nature).[13]

The dialectic was central to Hegel's conception of the totality of spiritual life forms. Hegel called 'dialectic' the dynamic process that consciousness necessarily executed on itself. Through dialectic human consciousness could transcend its own determinateness. In fact, this determinateness provided consciousness with a criterion for judging its own cognitions and hence actively participated in its necessary movement towards absolute knowledge.[14] But Hegel's dialectic was not limited only to human consciousness but was implicit in all forms of existence: 'Wherever there is movement, wherever there is life, wherever anything is carried into effect in the actual world, there Dialectic is at work.'[15] Most important of all for Cassirer, Hegel's dialectic could be discerned in actual events as 'moments of the whole.' In dialectical fashion the moments of truth could be examined 'not as abstract pure moments, but as they are for consciousness ... in virtue of which they are moments of the whole.'[16]

As early as 1916, in *Freiheit und Form*, Cassirer started to incorporate Hegel's dialectical vision into his own historical vision. Here it should be remembered that Cassirer's movement towards the formulation of the philosophy of symbolic forms between 1916 and 1919 was not direct. His path was circuitous; the various turning points in his ideas were turned only with a great deal of reluctance and caution.

Cassirer's cosmopolitan view of German intellectual history was permeated with Hegelian overtones; the dialectical moments of Hegel's idealism, with its interest in the totality of spiritual life forms, was repeatedly used by Cassirer. He duly emphasized the point that for Hegel the realization of reason lay in 'the totality of history' because 'the *whole* [of history] was the truth.'[17] Once the natures of history and of reason were made identical to one another, Hegel equated human history with the progressive unfolding of the idea of freedom.[18] Each element in the historical process was interpreted as being a moment in humanity's progressive enlightenment. In *Freiheit und Form* Cassirer seemed to apply the general Hegelian framework, with its belief that all the diverse life activities of an epoch can be characterized by a single idea, to German history since Luther.

Cassirer's conviction that there was one fundamental tendency permeating all German spiritual life, that is, the tension between freedom and form, and that this was *the truth* of German spirit was essentially an Hegelian idea. The clash between freedom and form was exhibited in Luther's religious principles, in Leibniz's pre-established harmony of monads, in Kant's belief in the spontaneity and self-imposed lawfulness of spirit, and in Goethe's artistic world view.[19] All these men were considered as living moments in the historical unfolding of German spirit. In their individual lives and works they were microcosms of the German spiritual macrocosm; they represented individually the basic tendency of German culture in general.[20] For Cassirer individual achievements were not isolated events. On the contrary, the spiritual value of the individual had to be presented as a unique moment which in spite of its uniqueness possessed universal significance.[21]

Cassirer used the harmony between the individual (particular) and the whole (complex) to unify the following: particular concepts into a coherent system, and individual person to his culture, and a single culture to human culture.[22] His inclination towards the universal or cosmopolitan standpoint, with the idea of freedom at its centre, was yet another example of how he fused the Kantian and Hegelian analyses of thought and being. For he analysed each concept, person, and culture and their respective relations to a larger totality in epistemological (Kantian) terms, but his apparent drive to understand everything as either a life form or a living totality was distinctly Hegelian.

After completing *Freiheit und Form* Cassirer continued his interest in living totalities and in life forms. Between 1917 and 1919 Cassirer carried on further research to support the cultural and intellectual position he had reached by 1916. In these years he published three essays that he later designated as 'supplementary studies' to *Freiheit und Form*. These studies of Hölderlin, Goethe, and Kleist represented a further consolidation of his new interest in the humanities and his attempt to formulate an all-inclusive critique of culture.

Cassirer's essay on Hölderlin and German idealism was an example of his new interest in human emotions as well as of his eagerness to discern a living dialectic to German cultural history. He viewed Hölderlin's poetry as embodying the tension between freedom and form that was characteristic of German thought in general. However, instead of a 'dialectic of concepts,' Hölderlin's works expressed a 'dialectic of emotions.'[23] In his poetry he brooded over the immanent rhythm of world events;[24] it was a rhythm which manifested in lyrical terms the dialectic between moments of freedom and form. Moreover, it was precisely through the lyrical dialectic of poetry that Hölderlin was capable of simultaneously grasping the deeper unity and harmony behind all life and expressing one of the innermost thoughts of German idealism: through his poetry Hölderlin was able to express how the 'moments of life' reflected 'the objective harmony of existence.'[25]

Cassirer's article 'Heinrich von Kleist und die Kantische Philosophie' (1919) further underscored his Hegelian turning to an interest in the living side of culture. He stressed the vital force connecting the ideas of Kant to the romantic literati. Kant's philosophy was seen to possess a living relevance to its time and to succeeding epochs; it was no longer just an abstract, conceptual system of thought. Accordingly, he interpreted the relation between Kant's philosophy and poets like Schiller and Kleist as follows: 'They all approached it [Kantian philosophy] not primarily as an abstract conceptual doctrine; rather they experienced it as an immediate life force.'[26]

Cassirer's inclination to read a specific meaning and logic into the lives and works of German poets was not only a result of his reflections on Kant and Hegel but was also a symptom of a new trend in German scholarship. The predisposition of some German scholars to see a logical position implicit in the romantic poets has its roots in the revival of romanticism begun in the first decade of the twentieth century. Poetry was no longer escapist and irrational; it offered 'a new mode of knowledge.'

In addition to refining and broadening his analysis of the Kant-Goethe era, Cassirer gave hints of his future orientation in his supplementary studies to *Freiheit und Form*. In the Hölderlin essay he noted: 'Myth was not for Hölderlin a bare, external sign ... but it signified for him an original ... spiritual life form.'[27] Cassirer's treatment of myth as a life form reached its climax in *Mythical Thought*, volume two of his *Philosophy of Symbolic Forms*. Similarly, in his article entitled 'Goethes Pandora' (1918), he foreshadowed the expansion of the cosmopolitan humanism elucidated in *Freiheit und Form*. In the essay Cassirer basically reworked ideas already expressed in the Goethe section of *Freiheit und Form*. However, in the process of rethinking his ideas Cassirer converted the dialectic between freedom and form into a confrontation between the 'social' and 'individualist' ideals of German idealism: 'The demand of the totality of human powers which ought to reach complete fruition in the individual is opposed to the demand of an all-inclusive communal life order, which seeks to relegate each individual to a specific place within the life order and to limit its accomplishments.'[28] When Cassirer discussed the tension between the individual and the particular as a confrontation between German idealism's individuality ('the demand for achievement of all human powers') and social ('all-inclusive communal life order') ideals, he in effect prepared the way for a more general treatment of culture.

Two observations are in order. First, Cassirer was here applying Simmel's view of the inevitability, and even the desirability, of conflict between the individual and the socio-cultural order. Secondly, the cosmopolitan standpoint was an integral part of his analysis of the clash between the individual and society. Cassirer was no longer content to examine culture only from within (that is, as a German analysing German culture), rather he was suggesting that any study of the social and individual demands within each culture must adopt the broadest possible viewpoint, that of one who was both an insider and an outsider. For as each man belonged to one particular socio-cultural life order and was therefore outside all others, he was nevertheless an insider to all cultures in so far as he was a member of the larger human cultural life order. In *The Philosophy of Symbolic Forms*, the inside-outside relation would be transformed into a pure correlation between the particular and the complex that would be applicable to all cultures.

CASSIRER'S POST-WAR REFLECTIONS ON THE PROBLEM OF KNOWLEDGE

While an analysis of Cassirer's wartime and early post-war reflections on culture displays a continuous line of development towards a unified concept of culture, the third volume of *Das Erkenntnisproblem in der Philosophie und Wissenschaft der neueren Zeit* revealed a man who was not at all certain about the ultimate direction of his own thought. In this volume Cassirer vacillated between two apparently contradictory interpretations of nineteenth-century German philosophy, reflecting the fact that his new course was still not completely clear even to himself.

In the first two volumes of *Das Erkenntnisproblem* Cassirer had already given an historical account of how Western ideas since the Renaissance culminated in the insights of Kant's philosophy. But in the third he was confronted with an entirely different situation. In the first two volumes he could use Kant's system as the goal of all previous European thought. The volume dealing with post-Kantian thought obviously had to adopt another method for unifying the historical material because there could be no Kant at the chronological end of this volume. Cassirer's interest in showing the unity behind the progression of post-Kantian thought exposed the paradoxical point that his own speculations had reached. On the one hand he wanted to weld the development of European and German thought into a coherent scheme; on the other hand he was unable to prove his point. The result was that the third volume of *Das Erkenntnisproblem* provided a snapshot of an intellectual in the midst of making up his mind.

In late October 1919, Cassirer completed the introduction to the third volume. In it he discussed the problem involved in his survey of post-Kantian thought, freely admitting both the arbitrariness and the indecisiveness of his conclusion.[29] The fact that Cassirer concluded this volume with the insignificant Friesian School underscored the inconclusive nature of his study. His omissions were even more striking. He did not mention Nietzsche at all, which was remarkable because interest in Nietzsche's philosophy had been steadily increasing in Germany since the 1890s.[30] In spite of his extensive studies Cassirer was unable to see clearly the direction of his present trend of thought. He went on to say that he would be very satisfied if all his previous writings related to the subject (*The Problem of Knowledge* volumes 1–2) could give someone else the incentive to write a more complete study of the development of the problem of knowledge in the nineteenth century.[31]

SUMMARY OF CASSIRER'S INTELLECTUAL POSITION 1916-19

Between 1916 and 1919 Cassirer's embryonic philosophy of human culture consisted chiefly of two apparent contradictory mental inclinations. One pushed him towards an abstract and primarily philosophical analysis of the relation between knowledge and existence. Hence in *Substance and Function* and in the three volumes of *Das Erkenntnisproblem* he tried to show how human (theoretical) knowledge grew more self-conscious of its own autonomy. However, from this abstract tendency emerged an idea of freedom that propelled Cassirer towards a dynamic and more empirical examination of how the autonomy of theoretical (or pure) reason made possible the autonomy of the individual *in concreto*, that is, in the common world of experience.

By 1919 Cassirer's thought was ready to crystallize into a scientific, cosmopolitan critique of human culture. In the wartime and post-war German situation what began as reflections on Kant's conception of human judgment, on the significance of German intellectual history, and on the relation between the Kantian and Hegelian modes of analysis became a spiritual reorientation which carried Cassirer into a multilevelled critique of a wide range of human activities. Cassirer subsequently used this critique as his response to the malaise afflicting the professional classes in Germany in the wake of their nation's military defeat and subservience to the Treaty of Versailles, which most considered to be a humiliating conclusion to a hard-fought war. As in 1916, Cassirer offered a rational and cosmopolitan view of man and his cultural history at a time when many intellectuals had surrendered to the virulent and frustration-fed nationalism spreading in Germany.[32]

Politics and philosophy were clearly associated with one another in Cassirer's mind. In the last pages of the third volume of *Das Erkenntnisproblem*, while commenting on the contemporary Friesian school, he approvingly cited a statement that metaphysical knowledge was incapable of shedding light on the nature of reason because metaphysics itself originated in darkness.[33] This veiled attack on contemporary inclinations towards a metaphysics which surrendered itself to the murky process of a spontaneous and direct experience of life, without the use of reason, was to come to full flower in the introduction to *The Philosophy of Symbolic Forms*. In that instance Cassirer strongly criticized the metaphysical currents of thought as capitulations to the paradise of mysticism. Worse still, for Cassirer these metaphysical currents severely hindered the rise of a scientific, objective conception of human existence.

Cassirer was also wary of letting any system of thought become a philosophy justifying a political status quo or a philosophy of political reaction.[34] For him, philosophy's sole task was to grasp the truth of all human existence. And this truth was to have a liberating effect on man, not a constricting one. The truth of human existence, for Cassirer if not for most of his peers, was that each man was free. To ensure this freedom, each man was entitled to certain natural rights. On the philosophical level these rights were metamorphosed into an intellectual imperative: that the truth had to be pursued in as many ways as possible and that each man ought to pursue the truth in his own way, even if it meant being in intellectual isolation. On the political level, these rights were to ensure the representation in the body politic of the broadest possible range of political ideals and practices. In the context of the political turmoil of 1919, Cassirer had good cause to worry, both intellectually and politically, over the ill effects of any philosophy permitting itself to be used as a crude political tool.

# 6

# The origin of the philosophy of symbolic forms (1919–22)

In the wake of the bitterness following the armistice of November 1918, German nationalists lashed out in all directions, seeking to place the blame for defeat on everyone's shoulders save their own. Jews in particular were singled out for blame: they had undermined the war effort at home, and after the defeat had set up their own government in Germany – the Weimar Republic.[1] To right-wing political groups like the conservatives and nationalists, the republic was a haven for Jews. It accorded them positions in German society and politics they had never held before. Popular anti-Semitism reached a high point between the signing of the Versailles Treaty in 1919 and the end of the disastrous inflation in 1923.[2]

Nowhere was anti-Semitism stronger than in the academic community. Most German academics were no longer willing to tolerate a government which had ruined their financial status through inflation and further undermined their social cohesion by promoting Jews in the universities. It is significant that Cassirer was granted a professorship by newly founded pro-republican universities; the old state universities, especially the ones in Prussia, retained the usual double standard with respect to the Jews; they were the last to be hired and almost never advanced up the professorial ranks.

Even after the demise of the old political order in 1918 the academic community did not welcome Jews into their ranks. The community's relations with Cassirer were a case in point. Like Cohen, who was isolated in Marburg and never called to another German university, Cassirer was not able to find a place for himself in the traditional university community. The only professorship he held in Germany was the one at the University of Hamburg. No other university except Frankfurt, another institution founded by the Weimar Republic, ever invited him to join its faculty.

Before Cassirer moved to take up his post at the University of Hamburg, the psychologist William Stern sent him a letter in early October 1919 warning him that a recently established union of right-wing students was demanding a boycott of all Jewish professors.[3] Fortunately this clamour soon died down. But less than two years later, in the summer of 1921, Cassirer clashed with anti-Semitism in the person of Siegfried Passarge, a professor of geography at the University of Hamburg. Passarge was very active in supporting the policies of the nationalist, anti-Semitic, and anti-republican German People's Protective and Offensive Alliance.[4] He was particularly fond of mouthing theories which 'proved' that Jews and Germans originated from different racial groups. When Passarge tried to expound this point of view to Cassirer in person, Cassirer responded by branding his theories as 'complete nonsense.'[5]

Passarge's racial ideas might be considered as the ranting of one half-baked intellectual had his attitude not indicated the changed nature of German anti-Semitism after 1918. Prior to 1914 blatant anti-Jewish feelings tended to be spontaneous and poorly organized. In polite society, the public expression of such sentiments was regarded as vulgar. After the war, anti-Semitism became organized nation-wide and was virulent and even respectable. Organizations like the German People's Protective and Offensive Alliance and the National Germanic Union of Clerks (DHV), the largest non-Marxist employees' association, joined together to make anti-Semitism an important factor in German national politics.[6] The support of professors of Passarge's type added even more prestige to such groups.

Cassirer's encounters with anti-Semitism were by no means ended in 1921. Anti-Semitism reached a new high point in June 1922 with the assassination of Walther Rathenau, the German Foreign Minister. The identification of the Jews with the Weimar Republic, the hatred of many ultranationalists for the Jews, and the republic's policy of fulfilling treaty obligations to the Western powers intersected in the person of Rathenau. In the minds of the nationalists, he was the living embodiment of the Jews' political attitudes as well as of their rise to political prominence in the Republic. He had to be removed. The nationalists' anti-Semitic slogans against Rathenau had the desired effect. The words 'Bump off Rathenau, that damned Jewish swine' were very much on the minds of the men who assassinated him on 24 June 1922.

Approximately two weeks before Rathenau's assassination, the Cassirer family had its own encounter with anti-Semitism. Although their experience was not nearly so tragic or newsworthy as Rathenau's murder, the Cassirer episode may be more representative of the daily experience of Jews in Germany at the time. In the process of an argument between Mrs Cassirer and a non-Jewish neighbour, the latter said to the Cassirer family: 'You all belong back in Palestine.' Cassirer was so incensed at this comment that he sent a curt note (dated 10 June 1922) to the neighbour reprimanding him.[7] This incident underscores the general situation of the German Jews. They tended to live together in the urban centres and therefore had a high social profile. In a survey taken in 1925 it was found that while Jews constituted less than 2 per cent of Hamburg's population, yet 48 per cent of them were concentrated in two of the city's districts.[8] In any event, incidents of the kind described could only serve to strengthen Cassirer's commitment to a government which, at least officially, attempted to integrate Jews into the social and institutional structure of Weimar Germany.

By early 1919, therefore, Cassirer had clearly aligned himself with the fledgling republic. First, he voted for and consistently supported the German Democratic Party,[9] the party which in everyone's mind, along with the Social Democratic Party, was synonymous with the new government. Secondly, he joined with other republicans in condemning the Leviné trial in Bavaria. And thirdly, he accepted a professorship at the pro-republican University of Hamburg. From 1919 to 1933, Cassirer's fate, like the fate of the German Jews, was bound up with the survival of the Weimar Republic.[10]

## THE WARBURG LIBRARY

In spite of the disappointment over the outcome of the war and the alarm concerning the political and economic turmoil within Germany from 1918 to 1922, many idealistic Germans felt that the new government could mark a new beginning for Germany. The revolution and the republican regime could signify a victory of German spirit, a first step towards self-redemption.[11] In a memoir on Cassirer, Fritz Saxl described the atmosphere in Hamburg around 1920, particularly the hopes of the intellectuals who began to gather around the University of Hamburg and the Warburg Library, and the relation of Cassirer to those hopes:

It must have been in 1920 that I first met Ernst Cassirer. Although the war had been lost by Germany, the air was full of hope. The collapse of material power had produced a strong and favourable reaction in the intellectual field, and one of the symptoms of this was the foundation, in Hamburg ... of a new university ... He lent a peculiar dignity to the young arts faculty, and an ever growing number of students came to his courses, eager for the truth and for learning, after the many deceptions of the war years.[12]

It was Saxl, as chief librarian and custodian of the Warburg Library, who first initiated Cassirer into the Warburg intellectual circle of scholars by giving him a thorough tour of the library facilities and explaining to him Warburg's purposes and aims regarding the library.

Aby Warburg was the scion of a prominent family of bankers from Hamburg. He was independently wealthy and devoted to scholarly research. Warburg spent most of his time travelling, writing ingenious essays on the Renaissance and Reformation, and amassing an enormous collection of books on a wide range of subjects from magic to science, from primeval to modern art, and from primitive religions to contemporary philosophy. From 1918 to 1920 Warburg's physical and mental health declined to the point where he was committed to a sanatorium in 1920. His collection of books, known as the Warburg Library, was left in Saxl's hands.

The library's major goal, according to Saxl, was to provide the student of civilization with a collection of books uniting the various branches of the history of human civilization. In order to find the key that would unlock all the secrets of the human spirit, Warburg followed the evidence into all fields of human cultural activity. The key to understanding man was to be sought everywhere and anywhere; no thought, no pictorial detail, no mythical belief was to be overlooked. As a result of this approach the Warburg Library had a very unorthodox classification system. Books and articles were arranged according to themes so that writings on philosophy, magical rites, folklore, literature, and religion were mixed with each other rather than segregated according to the usual subject classifications.

One of Warburg's main problems was to find a location in Germany where the intellectual atmosphere would be congenial to the unorthodox arrangement and purpose of the library. He decided to locate it in Hamburg, the city that had been so favourable to the Warburg family's past endeavours. In this strongly independent merchant town, with an established tradition of learning but without a university and its hierachy of professors until 1919, Warburg felt his library had a chance to survive and prosper. Hamburg's independence could provide the right environment for his unorthodox thematic approach to the study of civilization.[13]

The evolution of Cassirer's work made him look favourably on Warburg's search for the key to human culture. However, there was a political dimension to Cassirer's interest in the humanities and in the Warburg project. The renewal of German spirit, especially its rationalist element, and the refounding of a national and intellectual unity for Germany became a pressing concern during the years 1918 to 1923. Widespread disappointment over the military defeat and later the bitter resentment over the peace terms permanently poisoned the political situation of Weimar Germany. The republic's inability to deal adequately with the nation's political, social, and economic problems provoked contempt of republican ideals and practices. Political assassinations and attempted *coups d'etat* made up the political background of the period when Cassirer started to formulate both his defence of science and his first principles of the philosophy of symbolic forms. Even more ominously, violent political practices in Germany penetrated the academic world. In 1918 Max Weber warned about the danger of opening the universities to people who craved for leaders, not for teachers.[14] Several years later Meinecke noted that after the events of 1918–19 a 'new irrationalism' began to develop in Germany, especially in the younger generation.[15]

Cassirer continued on two fronts to reconstruct and revitalize the rationalist tendencies of German spirit. First, he vigorously defended the modern scientific method in his essay on 'Einstein's theory of relativity' (1921). Here Cassirer countered the irrationalist and relativist philosophical claims that sought to undermine the basis of science, which for him was the foundation of objective truth. Secondly, he attempted to incorporate the claims of contemporary intuitionism, life philosophy, and irrationalism into a rationalist critique of culture, where the a priori, universally valid laws of pure reason held the last word. In this connection Cassirer began to formulate some of the main postulates of his philosohy of symbolic forms in two other essays written between 1921 and 1922. Significantly, both essays, 'Die Begriffsform im mythischen Denken' (The form of concepts in mythical thought) and 'Der Begriff der symbolischen Form im Aufbau der Geisteswissenschaften' (The concept of symbolic form in the construction of the humanities), appeared in the first publication of the Warburg Library (1921–2). In these essays Cassirer not only permanently joined forces with the Warburg group but also updated his lifelong interest in formulating a methodology for relating knowledge to existence.

CASSIRER'S DEFENCE OF SCIENCE

The Warburg group was part of a larger number of German intellectuals who saw the scientific, scholarly attitude as the essential precondition for an objective and truthful understanding of man.[16] It was therefore not surprising that many of these people in the early post-war years (1919–22), when anti-scientific and irrationalist sentiments were gaining ground in Germany, spent a great deal of effort in elaboration and defending their views of science. Generally, they believed that science required the creation of a logical structure of laws and concepts, which were then subjected to empirical verification.

Two related developments after 1919 went a long way in undermining the general acceptability of the scientific ideal as espoused by men like Cassirer. Both developments had their origins in the pre-war years, yet both were aggravated by the bitterness following the war. The first set of events led to the politicization of academic opinion. This politicization involved the specific linking of ideas to nations, and nations to political ideals – a process that warped the exchange of ideas in Germany after 1919. While this process started well before the war, it was only in the post-1919 period that the politicization of thought culminated in what one historian called 'the politics of cultural despair.'[17] Mechanistic science, cultural decay, and liberalism were all lumped together and identified as Western and non-German by popular writers like Paul de Lagarde, Julius Langbehn, and Moeller van den Bruck. Even sophisticated thinkers like Troeltsch after 1919 ruefully accepted that a dichotomy existed between Anglo-French and German thought. Mechanistic Anglo-French positivism, with its commitment to natural law and liberalism was seen in opposition to a German dialectical, historical materialism, with its denigration of natural law and adherence to an authoritarian political system.[18] In this connection Troeltsch characterized Cassirer's work as a surrender to a one-sided logistic, mathematical conception of human experience which had its roots in the Anglo-French world.[19]

The second development adversely affecting the viability of the scientific standpoint originated with the work of the scientists themselves. The emergence of Einstein's theory of relativity and Planck's quantum theory had three interrelated results: classical Newtonian physics were overthrown; in the popular mind the eternal verities of science and the validity of scientific procedure were open to doubt; and relativism and anti-intellectualism in the broadest ethical and philosophical senses were given new impetus. The first result largely revolved around a series of experimental and conceptual problems within modern physics. Classical Newtonian mechanics seemed incapable of resolving discrepancies between its own theories and the empirical data it was supposed to explain. The theories of Einstein and Planck, taking account of the new information gained in the nineteenth century, were more successful in meshing physical concepts with physical realities. Consequently, these theories were gradually accepted as true; in the process the Newtonian framework was discarded. However, this first result of the new physics is of far less interest to us than the spiritual effects of this revolution in science on the minds of non-scientists.

The overthrow of Newtonian science in the public mind had the effect of dissolving all the certainties of the universe. As H.S. Hughes has shown in his study of European thought from 1890 to 1930, where he emphasized developments in psychology, political science, history, and sociology, the revolt against the rational and mathematical understanding of reality permeated all these fields. Edmund Wilson's examination of literature and Werner Haftmann's discussion of the pictorial arts since the 1880s pointedly connected literary and artistic developments to the disillusionment with science. In order to understand the extent of what happened and why Cassirer felt obliged to use Einstein's work as a means of defending the validity of science, it is useful to see what general ideas of the universe prevailed before and after the first world war.

Before 1914 the classical Newtonian conception of the universe prevailed in Western Europe. Essentially, this view, held by physicists and laymen alike, assumed that 'absolute determinism was ... the fundamental dogma of practical physics.'[20] An infinite accumulation of empirical evidence could, in theory, enable mankind to create a system of physical knowledge where every conceivable kind of matter and energy, every existing entity in the cosmos, could be completely determined by mathematical equations. Thus, Ernst Haeckel, one of the most successful popularizers of scientific thought in the late nineteenth and early twentieth centuries, could say that the great law of causality, linking matter and energy, could solve the riddle of the universe. By the advent of the first world war, the ideal of ultimate truth and the truths of classical physics were widely accepted as being identical.

When in the light of Einstein's and Planck's theories a complete reversal in scientific thought began to occur and the determinist concept of inevitable effect gave way to the indeterminate ideas of relative observations and probable trends,[21] all order and meaning seemed to leave the universe. Since the Enlightenment science had sought to replace religion as the fount of truth and to a large extent had succeeded in doing so, principally because of the ability of scientific knowledge to improve the living conditions of the masses of people. However, once science admitted that it could no longer hold out the hope of establishing truths of universal and eternal validity, and given that the fruits of scientific knowledge were used during the war to destroy people in massive numbers hitherto unrecorded in human history, the backlash against science became severe. It was in this demoralized intellectual atmosphere that Cassirer defended science by analysing what he considered to be the true implications of Einstein's theories.

Cassirer's 1921 essay on Einstein's theory of relativity was ostensibly an examination of relativity theory from an epistemological standpoint. However, this essay was far more than a narrow philosophical examination of a given theory. Cassirer defended the scientific, rational pursuit of truth and clarified for himself the basic theme that was to become the foundation of his own critique of culture, namely, man's symbolic conception of reality.

In the opening section of the essay Cassirer suggested to his contemporaries that physics should not be asked for what it could not give: a definitive explanation. Physics used concepts such as mass, force, magnetic potential, and so on, which were not in themselves reproductions of sensations or objects in the external world. They were merely our theoretical assumptions and constructions.[22] These concepts were merely schemata that we imposed on the world in order to make sense of it:

Each creative epoch of physics discovers and formulates new characteristic measures for the totality of being and natural process, but each stands in danger of taking these preliminary and relative measures, these temporarily ultimate intellectual instruments of measurement as definitive expressions of the ontologically real.[23]

Clearly, for Cassirer physics and any other natural or humanistic science carried the stamp of its human creator. Science could tell us something about ourselves and how the world may appear to us, but never about the world in itself.

Having circumscribed the explanatory range of science by limiting it to the conceptual activities of man, Cassirer went on to stress the evolutionary rather than the revolutionary character of Einstein's corrections of Newtonian physics:

The criticism made by the theory of relativity of the physical *concepts* of objects springs ... from the same method of scientific thought, which led to the establishment of these concepts, and only carries this method a step further by freeing it still more from the presuppositions of the naively sensuous and substantialistic view of the world.[24]

It is interesting that Cassirer focused on the method of science and on its progressive character. He employed two Kantian premises in his analysis of relativity theory. First, there are no pre-existing or given objects in the world; human reason creates conceptual relations through which we come to know the universe of objects. Secondly, the evolution of the scientific method, applicable to both the natural sciences and to the humanities is *eo ipso* man's progressive liberation from the naive and substantialistic (materialist) view of the world. However, Cassirer was not interested only in elucidating Einstein's theory from a Kantian standpoint. Hidden behind his interest in methodology was his conviction that an examination of the scientific method itself could lead mankind to the truth of human existence. And the truth for Cassirer was that Einstein's work reaffirmed the *method* of science, a method whose goal was to show the symbolic nature of all human knowledge and in the process reveal that the symbols were none other than the expressions of a free and creative human spirit.

One gets the impression from reading the Einstein essay that Cassirer was less concerned with the scientist's ideas per se than in using them as a jump-off point for his own new philosophy. Science must realize, he argued, that its task is to transform the 'given of perception' and replace it with a conceptual symbol: 'We must never measure mere sensations, and we never measure with mere sensations, but in general to gain any sort of relations of measurement *we must transcend the 'given' of perception and replace it by a conceptual symbol* which possesses no copy in what is immediately sensed.'[25] Admittedly, Cassirer's version of the scientific imperative was a bit one-sided. Instead of stressing the correspondence and verifiability of conceptual symbols in relation to empirical facts, he directed his attention primarily to the transforming of the empirical data of perception into a symbol which had no correspondence to the actual world. How could science lead to the truth if it weakened its links to the physical world surrounding man? How was mankind to check the veracity of its own self-proclaimed truths?

In responding to such questions Cassirer sought to refute the claims that developments in modern science led to a relativity of values and truths and to propose a philosophical system which could provide the criterion for judging all the activities of man. In his discussion of Einstein, Cassirer for the first time used an epistemological discussion of a particular form of human activity (physics) as the starting point for a broader analysis of all human cultural activities. This aim was signaled by his use of the term 'symbolic form.' Physical science could be interpreted as one among a number of symbolic forms (for example, language or myth) which were part of a total system of cultural forms. Cassirer reformulated the scientific imperative into a philosophical imperative which sought to transcend all cultural 'givens' by a system of symbolic forms: 'It is the task of systematic philosophy, which extends far beyond the theory of knowledge ... to grasp the *whole system* of symbolic forms, the application of which produces for us the concept of an ordered reality.'[26]

Once it was recognized that reality was 'ordered' by man himself, every particular of human existence could be related and thereby placed within the larger context of human activity in general. This all-inclusive context, with its rules for relating the particular to the whole, would, according to Cassirer, provide the criterion for a universal standard of truth. Each particular form would be 'relativized' with regard to the others. Since this 'relativization' was reciprocal throughout the entire context, that is, it held for all individuals in their relations to each other and to the whole, only the systematic totality, and not the individual form, could serve as the expression of truth.[27] To Cassirer, we either accept all individual cultural activities as being valid in so far as they belong to a larger human context, or we deny the validity of the entire context and leave ourselves with no standard at all by which to judge anything.

## TOWARDS A CRITIQUE OF CULTURE

In 1917 Cassirer realized that a complete understanding of the human condition necessitated not only the examination of man's intellectual activities, but also an analysis of his feelings and impulses. In the Einstein essay he used this new insight to suggest a broader study of man's symbolic cultural activities. The symbol concept would be the key to the entire study because the symbol, according to Cassirer, could emcompass all theoretical, practical, and emotional levels of man's 'ordered reality.' By holding that all human activities were manifestations of a single logically ordered system of symbolic forms, Cassirer was in effect claiming that what appeared *prima facie* to be a non-rational activity (for example, myth) could be included in a rational critique of all human cultural activity. Henceforth, Cassirer would devote himself to formulating a methodology for a critique of culture.

The two essays written for the Warburg Library between 1921 and 1922 contained the basic themes of his philosophy of symbolic forms. The elaboration of this philosophy would remain Cassirer's main task until his departure from Germany in May 1933. These essays, 'Der Begriff der symbolischen Form im Aufbau der Geisteswissenschaften' and 'Die Begriffsform im mythischen Denken' were an intellectual unit.[28] In them, Cassirer connected individual symbolic forms to the general historical evolution of human spiritual acts, and in the process revealed how he was going to combine Kant's and Hegel's ideas into his own vision of man. These essays reflect Cassirer's attempt to strike a balance between his post-1917 philosophical position, his new interest in the historical evolution of the humanities, and his desire to contribute to the Warburg group's multifaceted studies of human civilization. Since they were exploratory works, it will be helpful to indicate here the general principles that Cassirer was later to use in the philosophy of symbolic forms and reserve a systematic analysis of the symbolic forms for the next section.

In the opening pages of his 'mythical thought' essay Cassirer stated the task of philosophy as he saw it in 1921: logic was the true task of philosophical consciousness. The development of logic was simultaneous with the attainment of scientific thought and thereafter the two were mutually dependent.[29] This view was essentially a restatement of a conception of philosophy that Cassirer first expressed in his Leibniz study of 1902.[30] However, his developmental view of philosophy took on more of a Hegelian flavour when he introduced the relation between theoretical knowledge and existence. 'Spiritual being,' 'form of becoming,' 'spiritual becoming,' and 'form of being' were standard Hegelian phrases. Their dynamic qualities were underscored by the fact that 'becoming' (a key Hegelian word) was the intermediary concept between spiritual being and progressively unfolding forms of existence: 'As *spiritual being* can not be understood other than as the *form of becoming*, so on the other hand, all *spiritual becoming*, so far as it is grasped philosophically, i.e. in a penetrating manner, is transformed into the *form of being*.'[31]

Cassirer's Hegelian view of the dynamic and historical unfolding of the structure of spirit was then given a distinctive Kantian twist. The focal point of his analysis of spirit was the concept of the symbol. The concept was 'not so much the *product* of the similarity of things, as it was the *precondition* for the conscious determining of a similarity between things.'[32] To this Kantian definition of the concept Cassirer added the idea of the symbol; here again, his newly acquired Hegelian bent was obvious. His symbol concept closed the gap between thought and existence because it embodied the 'activity of spirit' itself. This activity of the spirit provided the spiritual midpoint where the particular and the universal qualities of thought and existence respectively were united. This unity was possible because the symbol concept demonstrated 'that the general encounters itself in the particular as, so to speak, a *spiritual* mean, in which the general and the particular mutually penetrate one another to the extent that they become a *concrete unity*.'[33]

Language, myth, religion, and art possessed, according to Cassirer, a characteristic structure which distinguished them from one another. They each had a unique mode of 'spiritual conception' and of 'spiritual formation.'[34] Cassirer spent most of his time in the essays of 1921–22 analysing language and myth. In retrospect this is not surprising in view of the fact that the first two volumes of *The Philosophy of Symbolic Forms* were to deal with language and myth respectively. Language was not a haphazard construction. It possessed an inner logic which revealed its secrets to critical analysis. The starting point of the critical examination of language, and of other symbolic forms as well, rested on the realization that a thing (for example, a specific use of a verb) was not merely a 'bare individual' but had a more general significance as 'the representation of a class' (the principles of verb usage of the entire language).[35] After stressing this insight about the development of language as a whole, Cassirer proceeded to outline the three essential stages of its development. The mimetic, analogical, and symbolic stages of the historical evolution of language were posited.[36] Here for the first time Cassirer revealed his belief in a threefold development of at least one of man's symbol-creating activities.

Cassirer's analysis of myth reinforced his view of language. As in the latter case, he tried to demonstrate that the basis of mythical thought consisted in a law of its own mode of formation.[37] Language and myth were regulated by a law which embodied a particular set of relations and gave each of them a unique mode of spiritual development and formation. But what was the significance of this law? Does it tell us about man himself? In Cassirer's view the posited relations in mythical thought were not simple and accidental products of human existence; rather they represented a 'specific achievement, a unique *creation* of [human] thought.'[38] Mythical relations were created by man himself. They were concrete, historical examples of man's dealing with the world around him. This was also the case with language.[39] The three-stage development of language represented man's progressive realization that his symbolic creations stood at the centre of creation. It was through the 'activity of spirit' itself that man simultaneously created a vision of the world and a concrete unity by which the world could be systematically perceived.

Cassirer had now reached the threshold of the philosophy of symbolic forms. Language, myth, and art were not to be analysed solely as cultural activities that were distinct from one another and therefore relegated to different academic departments for detailed examination. On the contrary, 'language as a *whole*,' 'myth as a *whole*' and 'art as a *whole*' must be interpreted as possessing 'a common character of symbolic formation.'[40] For by taking language only *as a whole*, and by similarly treating myth and art, Cassirer hoped to demonstrate that all human activities possessed a unity. This 'unity of different spiritual regions' was never a unity of objects but of the relation of these regions as a whole in relation to one another. Thus, for Cassirer the common philosophical task was clear: the philosopher must work towards the formulation of a general and all-inclusive system of symbolic forms.[41] For only a systematic overview of humanity's symbolic and cultural activities could provide the basis for decisively demonstrating man's ultimate freedom.

CASSIRER'S DEFENCE OF SCIENCE AND CRITIQUE OF CULTURE
AS A RESPONSE TO HIS TIMES

Cassirer's essays of 1921–2 closed his 'reorientation period.' By using these essays to express the main elements of the philosophy of symbolic forms, he at once accomplished a unique blending of the old and the new in German thought and provided himself with a program of research that enabled him to produce his most enduring and important works. In his response to the demoralization of the academic community after the war, Cassirer attempted to revitalize German spirit by rethinking its two main philosophical components: the Kantian and Hegelian alternatives. His new philosophy would rest on the Hegelian assumption that the totality of life and spirit constitutes an indissoluble unity. Yet his Kantianism would emerge in the manner in which his philosophy of symbolic forms would be executed. He would use the symbol to mediate between the developmental Hegelian view of the totality of spiritual life forms and the static, structural Kantian view of knowledge. In the symbol, life and knowledge would find, according to Cassirer, a new point of departure, a new means of demonstrating that man was free.

While Cassirer's defence of science and his preliminary outline for a rationalist critique of culture provided him with a program for future research, an important tension remained within his system. This revolved around his regulative, teleological method of uniting knowledge to existence, the concrete to the universal, the individual to his society, and the national or cultural unit to the world community. Cassirer's assumption that the world and man could be made intelligible only if the particular (an individual man) and the universal (humanity) were understood to constitute an *ideal* unity had two important and contradictory consequences. First, he sustained a universalist orientation which sought to comprehend all concrete human activities as an integral element of an overall unity of human existence and development. But, and this is my second point, Cassirer's commitment to a regulative, teleological *ideal* unity, grounded as it was on *ideas* rather than on empirical facts, increased his inclination towards an abstract, rather than a concrete, analysis of man. So long as Cassirer maintained the tension between the conflicting demands of the individual and of the whole, the concrete and the abstract, as he did from 1921 to 1926, he was able to balance his Kantian-Hegelian theory of human spirit with an interest in providing the empirical verification to his theory.

The two conflicting results of Cassirer's work were not only the consequences of his own ideas but were also symptomatic of his times. Indeed, the intellectual consequences of his own thought were inseparable from the events in Germany between 1919 and 1922. In regard to his inclination towards the abstract, Cassirer did try to respond to the often-voiced reproach that the neo-Kantians were too idealistic and far too abstruse for their own good and for the well-being of Germany.[42] Since his war revelations of 1916–18 he became less inclined to philosophize in a political and social vacuum. The two essays written for the Warburg Library between 1921 and 1922 provided further evidence of his increasingly 'realistic' orientation. By 1921 he recognized the social and cultural dimension to symbolic activities. Language and mythical and philosophical thought were not treated as though they arose, so to speak, in pure intellectual space independent of all historical and social grounding. These activities reflected the organization of the societies in which they occurred. Prior to 1921 Cassirer had paid scant attention to historical and social considerations. Now he asked how it could be shown that human concepts of classes and types were to a large extent reflections of specific societal life practices.[43] In one case Cassirer tried to answer this general query by referring to an anthropological study of the Zũni Indians in which the author found a parallel between the Zũnis' mythical beliefs and their everyday practices: they varied the colours of their crops in accordance with their mythological beliefs about the organization of the cosmos.[44]

While Cassirer became increasingly interested in providing a factual basis for his cosmopolitan view of human spiritual activities, his predilection for the abstract pulled him away from the concrete and pushed him towards an analysis of the universal a priori conditions of the possibility of any particular experience. Instead of undertaking a detailed examination of the Zũnis' actual living conditions, Cassirer sought to demonstrate the unity of theory and practice in the life of the Zũnis by discussing various logical classification systems. Here again Cassirer focused his interest on the ideal unity behind particular human events. And the unity itself rested on the regulative idea that all deeds had to be understood in relation to a given ideal end if they were to be rationally intelligible.

The weakness of Cassirer's regulative idea of human existence is fully understandable in relation to the political and legal disputes of the time. He was considered as one of the philosophical contributors to the neo-Kantian school of legal science.[45] The 'a priori logicism' of the Marburg School provided the philosphical foundation for such neo-Kantian legal philosophers as Kelsen,[46] Stammler, and Radbruch.[47] The most important and controversial aspect of legal neo-Kantianism was its claim that pure norms, that is, abstract and logical ideas could provide the basis for the legal and juridical structure of the state. The neo-Kantians' emphasis on pure norms and their neglect of concrete social and political facts in regard to judging the legal basis of the state was so extreme that it invited an equally extreme response.

In his critique of neo-Kantian legal philosophy, Erich Kaufmann bitterly assailed the 'formal apriorism' of the neo-Kantians that left Germany leaderless in a time when reality demanded decisive political leadership.[48] He went

on to complain that the formal, contentless rationalism of neo-Kantian epistemology offered Germany 'barren schema' and 'faded shadows' instead of
concrete solutions, 'precious stones' instead of bread.[49] The bitterness of this
attack indicated that far more than philosophical issues was at stake. The reference to bread indicated his political disenchantment. Kaufman's attack on
the neo-Kantians was published in 1921, so the book itself was written in the
midst of the political and social chaos of the first years of the Weimar regime.
The shame of defeat, the miseries of the German people, and especially the
Republic's inability to ensure an adequate supply of food for Germany were
the other conditions influencing his violent attack on a philosophy identified
with the existing government.

The interesting point to notice about Kaufmann's criticism of the neo-
Kantians was the connection he made between their rational, formalistic conception of politics and the apparent inability of the Weimar Republic to solve
Germany's problems. Kaufmann's position was, in fact, representative of that
of many German intellectuals who identified the principles underlying the
Republic and its constitution with the rationalist arguments of the neo-Kantian legal philosophers.[50] The association of liberal, democratic ideals and
practices as enunciated by the neo-Kantians with the ineffective national
government of 1921 had unfortunate results: rationalist views of man and
politics were discredited.[51]

In view of the war and post-war events more people tended to doubt the rationality of man, which the neo-Kantians held so dear. To most people it was
not at all apparent that man was rational and that human rationality could
provide the best means for achieving the most favourable results for all humanity. The irony of Cassirer's new version of the rationalist critique of human spirit was that while it provided a means of unifying all the specific
deeds of mankind into a coherent account of human progress towards enlightenment, his assumption that a unity of knowledge and existence was possible
on the basis of the pure forms of reason tended to pull him into a more abstract, and hence unpopular, treatment of mankind. However, for the next
five years (1921–6) the tension between the concrete and the abstract, between the individual and the universal, helped Cassirer to create a memorable vision of human spirit in its movement towards the realization of freedom.

PART 3
CASSIRER'S WEIMAR PERIOD

# 7

# Intellectual equilibrium (1923–6): ideological background

INTRODUCTION

Cassirer's Weimar period corresponded roughly to the period of German history which began with the economic stabilization of the Weimar Republic in December 1923 and ended with its demise in January 1933. In this decade Cassirer not only reached the high and low points of his identification with German society and politics, he also produced his most memorable works, the three volumes of *The Philosophy of Symbolic Forms* and his studies on the Renaissance and the Enlightenment. Cassirer's work did not evolve in a political and cultural vacuum. His cosmopolitan and humanistic outlook on the world was influenced by events in Germany.

Even though a definite shift of emphasis occurred in Cassirer's work several years (1926–7) before the end of effective parliamentary government in Germany (September 1930), his return to an abstract, logistic analysis of human activity and the destabilization of the German republican political system were two symptoms of one basic fact: the increasing untenability of German liberal ideology both in theory and in practice.

Cassirer's philosophy of symbolic forms was an intellectual complement to German liberalism. Cassirer's Weimar period is divided into two distinct phases. In the first phase (1923–6) he achieved a remarkable balance between his epistemological inclinations, his cosmopolitan overview of human history and culture, and his liberal republican political ideas. In the second phase (1927–33), the abstract tendency of Cassirer's early work began to reassert itself. This tendency led him to refocus his work on the realm of pure thought and to formulate his insights in a general and abstruse manner. In fact, he became more of a dogmatic rationalist.

## THE POLITICIZATION OF *WISSENSCHAFT*

In Weimar Germany there was a high correlation between particular theoretical arguments and those intellectuals who opposed the Weimar Republic or supported it, or who wanted a more radically democratic government. The split in the German intelligentsia between 'orthodox' and 'modernist' intellectuals, which extended back to the controversy over war aims in July 1915, had, since the defeat of Germany, hardened into two competing world views.[1] The orthodox and modernist positions were not so much logical alternatives as associations of ideas and feelings, and the dispute between these positions was a symptom of the general political and social divisions in Germany from 1918 to 1933.

The orthodox intellectuals (like Oswald Spengler), who formed the majority of the academic community, tended to rely on ambiguous concepts for their own research and avoided any systematic verification of their concepts with the relevant facts. They were strongly anti-Western and extolled the uniqueness of the German national experience. Naturally they despised the Republic, which they associated with the German defeat of 1918 and viewed as an imposition of an un-German republican form of government on the German people. Finally, these individuals always adopted the gloomiest view of the decline of German culture and society, and lauded the 'good old days' when Germany was a pre-industrial, monarchical society. Politically, they supported the conservative and nationalist parties.

The modernist intellectuals such as Weber and Cassirer were inclined to accept the empiricist methodology and the testing procedures associated with it. Hence when forming general concepts of knowledge and existence they tended to restrict the application of their general concepts. They were generally pro-Western and cosmopolitan. While recognizing the uniqueness of German history these academics nevertheless felt that Germany was an integral part of Western civilization. Politically, they tended to support the Weimar Republic and adopt, in some cases very reluctantly, bourgeois liberal ideals.

The political dimension of the orthodox-modernist dispute clearly emerged in Spengler's comment on left-wing political programs; he argued that these rested on the intellectual rationalists' conviction that reality could be thoroughly mastered and understood by the use of abstraction.[2] This comment is remarkable because it not only pinpointed the line dividing liberal and cosmopolitan intellectuals from conservative and nationalist ones, but also indicated the link made in right-wing circles between a particular mode of thought and a political orientation. Spengler's definition of the left was so far to the political right that the DDP in general and liberals like Cassirer and Weber in particular were classified as left-wing simply because they gave rational and abstract ideas a central role in politics. The significance of Spengler's comment is all the greater when one realizes that his ideas were very popular in Weimar Germany, especially among right-wing groups.[3]

Spengler's views were representative of a broad segment of German opinion which exalted an intuitionist, mystical, and anti-rational conception of man and society. His identification of left-wing political thought with a tendency to formulate universally valid abstract laws, a tendency characteristic of scientific thought, had the effect of throwing the latter on the defensive. In an era where many considered the uniqueness of personal experience to be superior to an objective, scientific grasp of human and social reality, the defence of the scientific and scholarly attitude was a heavy burden, but modernist intellectuals, especially Cassirer and Weber, did not shrink from making this defence.

In 1918 Weber argued that science needed the quiet, sheltered atmosphere that academic life could offer. People's values had to be left outside the classroom if scientific truth were to emerge from patient, scholarly activity. Politics had no place in the university. If the university and the pursuit of scientific truth were to survive, political disputes had to be set aside in favour of the pursuit of objective scientific truth.[4] Weber wanted to minimize the links between the tumult of contemporary politics, where values were disputed, and the quietude of science, where value-free knowledge was at stake. This is not to suggest that there were no specific values motivating his work, but only that Weber believed these values should interfere as little as possible in the objective presentation of one's own ideas and research.

Cassirer deliberately converted his commitment to a rational, scientific view of man and culture into a specific scholarly life style. While erecting his philosophy of symbolic forms Cassirer followed Weber's suggestion of not mixing contemporary politics with scientific study.Within the peaceful and politically obscure atmosphere of the Warburg Library, Cassirer patiently unfolded his new critique of culture. Any reference to contemporary events was scrupulously avoided.

Two instances are noteworthy in relation to the years 1923–5. In the second volume of *The Philosophy of Symbolic Forms* Cassirer dealt with the swastika in a very academic manner.[5] His discussion treated the swastika as an example of one of the oldest religious symbols, 'the earliest form of a four-pronged cross,' and rested on several other academic articles on the subject. Despite his unpleasant encounters with people at the University of Hamburg, like Siegfried Passarge, who were affiliated with the swastika through the Nazi movement, this contemporary political dimension to the swastika was entirely omitted from his discussion. Another example of Cassirer's separation of politics from academic activity was his memorial article of 1925 on the work of his former teacher, the leading neo-Kantian, Paul Natorp. In his last years Natorp devoted much effort to applying neo-Kantian ideals to politics,[6] but Cassirer omitted a discussion of this political phase of Natorp's work, as if it were not relevant to his philosophical activities.

There was, however, a positive side to Cassirer's efforts to keep contemporary events at arm's length and maintain the apolitical character of his sicentific critique of culture. His commitment to science and to the formulation of universal a priori laws of culture predisposed him to keep his laws as general as possible. While it was true that in the first two volumes of *The Philosophy of Symbolic Forms* and in his essay *Language and Myth* Cassirer provided numerous factual examples to support his transcendental theory of the development of human consciousness from primeval times to the present day (1925), he nevertheless believed his critique to be generalized enough to explain systematically all human activities. In this sense it was objective and scientific, for his critique could dissolve a multitude of human activities into the universally valid laws of human spirit. A distinctly progressive quality was also apparent in his philosophy of symbolic forms. Since in his critique no one category of human values, political, social, ethical, cultural, or aesthetic, would prevail over the others, Cassirer believed he could objectively show the evolution of human spirit from primeval to modern times, from naive to scientific consciousness,[7] because each stage of that evolutionary process would be examined on its own terms.

## LIBERALS AND ACADEMICS IN GERMANY: CASSIRER'S IDEOLOGICAL ORIENTATION

Cassirer's political affiliation exposed the ideological background to his intellectual orientation. His consistent support of the progressive DDP was tangible proof of his commitment to political ideals and practices many Germans despised. But what was the nature of his support for the DDP and the Weimar Republic? Was his manner of supporting liberal ideals and practices peculiar to himself, or was it representative of a large number of academics who were favourably inclined towards the Republic?

Cassirer remained aloof from political events, as did many prominent intellectuals who rallied to the Republic. They were cautious liberals who supported the Republic but were opposed to making major concessions to the social democrats.[8]

Cassirer's attitude towards the continued existence of the Republic is at once expected and surprising. It is to be expected because his incessant encounters with anti-Semitism in the academic community before the war and the rising tide of anti-Jewish sentiment in Germany after 1918 militated against active participation in politics. On the other hand, his political passivity is surprising because of the general identification of Jews with liberal ideals.[9] The rights of the Jews were intimately bound up with the fortunes of the Weimar Republic.[10] If it fell, the Jews were bound to suffer. The logic of the situation necessitated that Cassirer as a Jew should have actively participated in politics. Yet he did next to nothing. Here his individual political stance merged into the general insecurity of liberalism in Germany, and his political passivity was symptomatic of the political malaise of the Weimar Republic.

Because the Weimar Republic was initially established as the consequence of German military defeat in 1918 and of the political unrest in the nation, very few people were ever really satisfied with it. It was founded on too many compromises and contained too many contradictions.[11] When the political and economic situation finally stabilized in late 1923, the government's series of ad hoc alliances with bureaucratic and para-military organizations had both disheartened its sincerest supporters and earned it the contempt of anti-republican groups.

Even during the relatively quiescent period of 1924–8, the parliamentary government did not function well. Minority government was the rule. Political parties tended to be inflexible on major issues. All conditions were 'compromises on a very limited scale between vested interests, and alliances over specific issues.'[12] But on more general issues there was little or no compromise. Between 1918 and 1933 no combination of political parties and social groups had a philosophy that could be turned into a long-term and effective governing policy that would have received the enthusiastic endorsement of the majority of Germans. An example is the issue of defining the nature of denominational schools and their relation to state schools. In spite of the Weimar constitution's mandate to the Reichstag to legislate on this matter, repeated attempts by the federal legislature between 1919 and 1927 to pass such legislation foundered on the inability of the liberals (mostly Protestants), the centrists (Catholics), and the socialists to compromise on basic issues. Even though each group had a clear philosophy of education, no possible combination of compromises could get the approval of the majority. This impasse on the educational matter was but one example of the political failure to turn some of each party's ideals into permanent government policy. As a consequence of this, the Weimar political situation was inherently unstable, and the desire to prevent this instability from becoming political and social chaos resulted in a political stalemate; this resulted in a general disillusion with the government and ultimately to a widespread indifference to the entire governing system.

The liberal parties, primarily the DDP and DVP, were singularly prone to political inactivity and ineffectiveness in a mass democracy. True, they were capable enough of defending their interests within the parliamentary system itself. In fact, the most constructive leader of the Weimar Republic was Gustav Stresemann, the leader of the DVP. Nevertheless, the liberals in general were unsuccessful in providing their parties with a good voter base. Except for the elections of 1919 and 1920, when the DDP and the DVP received about 22 per cent of the vote, German liberalism never appealed to more than one-fifth of the population. As early as 1920 the DDP began the electoral slide from which it was never to recover. While in 1919 the party had amassed 5,641,800 votes and elected seventy-five deputies, by November 1932, despite its formal reorganization as the German State Party in 1930, it had retained only 336,500 votes (1 per cent of the total vote) and elected only two deputies to the Reichstag. The DDP's decline was remarkable because of all the parties it was the one most strongly identified with the Weimar Republic.

The conflict between ideological inclinations and organizational realities undermined the liberals' efforts to establish themselves permanently as a popular political party.[13] German liberalism was ideologically élitist and anti-authoritarian. While it enthusiastically endorsed the principle of universal suffrage, it nevertheless feared both the authoritarian and collectivist tendencies of the left and the direct participation of the masses in governing the nation. Many liberals from 1919 to 1920 refused to endorse the SPD's proposal for greater participation of the unions in directing the economy. The anti-individualist character of social democracy was unacceptable to the liberals on basic philosophical terms. The liberal parties were not organized properly for mass politics. They did not possess a widely dispersed, constantly functioning political organization like the catholics, socialists, and communists. Their political party rested on small cliques, professional associations, and small, honorary organizations. Little effort was made to encourage large numbers of people to participate in the party, beyond voting for it. Thus, the élitist organizational structure of the party paralleled the liberals' aversion to participatory democracy.

The history of German liberalism since the Revolution of 1848 reflected the irreconcilable conflict between principles that advocated equality on the basis of merit and a reluctance to put equality into effect because of the middle-class fear of the working masses. This wavering between theory and practice culminated in the inability of Weimar liberals as a whole (that is, the DDP and DVP) to make fundamental compromises either among themselves of with those to their political left or right.[14] Their incapacity to establish a popular political following also weakened their ability to compromise with other parties. Liberals stuck to their principles in Weimar Germany at the cost of broad-based support.

Liberal politicians were not the only ones reluctant to chose between their ideals and the realities of politics. Many of the intellectuals who favoured the DDP fluctuated between a fatalistic acquiescence to political events and a half-hearted defence of the government. For many pro-Weimar intellectuals the shortsighted and disastrous chauvinism of the former Imperial system had to be avoided. Many of them realized all too well the limits of a one-sided nationalist approach to politics. A few of them, Thomas Mann for one, had been victims of this approach, but the war had opened their eyes as it had opened Cassirer's. Nevertheless, a certain enthusiasm for a liberal, democratic government seemed lacking. Many conservative liberals seemed to support the Republic on the basis of good political sense rather than from personal conviction. They were perpetually worried about the threat from the masses,[15] and this coloured their political vision. For Thomas Mann, republican democracy was Germany's destiny, something that had to be accepted regardless of what one felt.[16] Meinecke said in 1918, 'I am no lover of democracy, but a democracy cannot be avoided.'[17] Troeltsch felt that whoever wanted to democratize Germany also wanted to disorganize it.[18] Yet these men were counted among the prominent intellectuals who supported the Republic and the DDP.

It is now possible to see Cassirer's intellectual activity in a new light. He maintained a certain emotional distance from the Republic as well as from the masses of people. This hesitancy to think of politics in positive terms was representative of many academics who rallied to the Republic and placed Cassirer well within the academic liberal camp. As with his colleagues, Cassirer's aversion to active politics was reinforced by liberal ideological inclinations. It was precisely the liberals' inability to come to grips with the necessities of mass democratic parliamentary politics that helped undermine liberalism in Germany.[19]

LIBERALISM AND LEGAL THEORY

The idealist liberal view of man and society rested on a conception of law that combined abstract legal principles (legal norms) with a commitment to natural law. Coming from a tradition of jurisprudence that tended to make legal rights autonomous by envisioning them as abstractions, neo-Kantian legal philosophers extended the excessive formalism of German legal science. In this conception of law, legal relations were formalized in that they were conceived of as being independent of contemporary socio-political realities.[20] For neo-Kantians the ultimate justification of all law proceeded from the eternally valid a priori rules of reason and not from contemporary practices.

The inclination to let pure reason provide the basis of law was by the early twentieth century associated with a defence of natural law. Proponents of natural law argued that a comprehensive legal system could be established solely by the force of thought. Their belief in an immutable, universally valid law of nature, which could be discovered only through the analysis of human reason, received a decisive institutional and legal setback in Germany on 1 January 1900, when the new German civil code went into effect. The promulgation of this new code was widely interpreted as a defeat for the proponents of natural law and a victory for the historical school of law of Savigny,[21] who argued that all law should be derived from age-old customs and traditional social relationships.

The group of legal scholars inclined towards a defence of natural law and of the a priori basis of all law remained undaunted. With the appearance of Hans Kelsen's work on the major problems of law in 1911, the natural law movement was deliberately linked to the Marburg School.[22] The affiliation of Marburg neo-Kantianism with logistic a priori jurisprudence, which in turn was linked to idealist liberalism, continued to the end of the Weimar Republic. Significantly, many of the defenders of the Weimar constitution and government were decisively influenced by neo-Kantian jurisprudence. Thus, in the minds of most German intellectuals, the principles justifying the republican regime were identified with the abstract legalisms of the neo-Kantian school of law.

The association of liberal ideals and practices with an abstract and a priori conception of legal and political relationships had unfortunate results. It became the tragedy of constitutional law and political theory during the Weimar Republic that the struggle against liberal conceptions of law and politics became synonymous with the struggle against the Weimar political system.[23] Many intellectuals, like Wilhelm Sauer, tended to blame neo-Kantians for the destruction of German jurisprudence. Its formalism and its distance from real-life situations helped undermine the credibility of German legal science and its abstract philosophical basis. A vivid example of the inability or unwillingness of German liberal theorists to deal with concrete issues was Rudolf Stammler's statement that law was an integral part of a system of pure principles for ordering consciousness and that '*absolute* validity ... in *legal* questions

... [can] ... be attributed only to the *pure forms*, in which we arrange *legal* experience according to a fixed and uniform plan.'[24] Not one word was said about the role of existing institutions or current practices in deciding the absolute validity of legal matters.

The broader implications of the limited appeal of neo-Kantian jurisprudence in Germany were clearly drawn by Ernst Troeltsch in a lecture delivered in 1922. According to him the concepts of 'natural law' and 'humanity' had become incomprehensible in Germany.[25] Building on the dichotomy of German and Western European thought that he had developed during the war, Troeltsch argued that since the early nineteenth century Germany had repudiated the West's mechanistic conception of science, with its reliance on human reason, and its political counterpart, a conception of (natural) law based upon a cosmopolitan and humanistic *Weltanschauung*.[26] Most educated Germans were unable to accept the final goal of natural law, which sought to preserve the autonomy of the individual and in the process reaffirm those inalienable natural rights essential to the dignity of all men. In effect, most Germans had already rejected the Western European vision of a world state, where 'the bare abstraction of a universal and equal Humanity' would become a reality.[27]

With the rejection of the Western ideals of humanity, cosmopolitanism, and natural law in Germany, those still upholding the West's ideals had an uphill battle. While Cassirer specifically endorsed the conception of natural law only in 1932[28] long before that year he used the philosophical principles underlying the cosmopolitan and humanistic ideals of German liberalism as the basis of his critique of culture. If the idealist liberal conception of law is interpreted as an example of neo-Kantian apriorism applied to legal and political relationships, then Cassirer's vision of humanity may be understood as the application of those same a priori laws of reason to *all* human activities. Indeed, Cassirer's entire critique of culture sought to demonstrate precisely how the a priori laws of reason could be the foundation for a systematic understanding of all mankind. On the basis of pure reason, and in conjunction with its most refined theoretical product, scientific cognition, Cassirer sought to conceive of human freedom from the widest possible vantage point.

Cassirer's highly idealized vision of human history and of contemporary society required, needless to say, a great deal of optimism to sustain it. Whereas many of his colleagues, like Meinecke and Mann, tended to fluctuate between pessimism and optimism regarding the long-term outlook for the survival of liberalism and humanism in Germany, Cassirer persistently maintained the cheerful outlook, at least until 1933. Further, his optimism seemed to be reinforced by his level-headed temperament. Even in the midst of Germany's catastrophic inflation of 1923 Cassirer was 'full of optimism' regarding the government's ability to end the monetary madness.[29] There was no trace of bitterness in his attitude towards the Republic. Perhaps Cassirer was naive about political and social realities. On the other hand, he might have been realistic enough to realize that any kind of central government in Berlin was not going to be very popular, regardless of what it did or did not do. In any event, Cassirer's guarded optimism and his faith in the ultimate triumph of reason in human affairs engendered a frame of mind that enabled him to construct quietly his philosophy of symbolic forms.

# 8

# Intellectual equilibrium (1923–6): the philosophy of symbolic forms

INTRODUCTION: BASIC ASSUMPTIONS

Cassirer first got the idea for the philosophy of symbolic forms when he comprehended the basic flaw in Kant's system. For Cassirer, Kant's system operated as if a philosophy of human spirit required only an abstract theory of knowledge that focused primarily on science and philosophy. By concentrating his analyses on these two logically structured fields of human creativity, Kant had neglected to observe the synthesizing activities of human reason in fields of more 'common experience,'[1] like language, myth, and art. Accordingly, Cassirer formulated his own critique of human spirit on the assumption that any philosophy of mind required 'a theory of prelogical conception and expression, and their final culmination in reason and factual knowledge.'[2]

Cassirer's desire to create a system of symbolic forms capable of evaluating all phases of human behaviour from ordinary perception (naive consciousness) to theoretical physics (scientific cognition) and of explaining human history from primeval to modern times was well received. With the appearance of the first two volumes of *The Philosophy of Symbolic Forms* in 1923 and 1925, a number of academics, including Max Scheler, M. Frischeisen-Kohler, and Ernst von Aster, applauded Cassirer's move beyond Marburg neo-Kantianism and immediately recognized the importance of his new critique of man.[3]

The foundation of Cassirer's critique of culture originated in a single idea borrowed from Kant and Hegel: a teleological view of humanity's progressive enlightenment, where man increasingly realized the rational basis of his own existence. With this progressive view always in the background, Cassirer proceeded to strike a balance between a Kantian logistic analysis of consciousness and a Hegelian interest in the totality of empirical and spiritual life forms. Cassirer's philosophy of symbolic forms was Kantian in so far as it sought the universal functions behind *all* types of the synthesizing activities of human reason and Hegelian when its interest in the multitude of life forms led it to stress the inherently dynamic quality of human life.

For Cassirer the main philosophical problem of the day was to transcend the conflicting demands of two different trends of thought. On the one hand, there was the dogmatic rationalist's tendency to make sweeping generalizations about the nature of knowledge and being in general. On the other hand, there was the dogmatic empiricist's inclination to limit assertions about knowledge and existence to empirically demonstrate propositions. Cassirer tried to resolve this conflict by balancing an idealist theory of human consciousness with strict empirical research. He tried to harmonize what he considered to be the most advanced theoretical view of reality with reality itself.

In constructing his philosophy of symbolic forms Cassirer made two fundamental assumptions regarding the constitution of each symbolic form and the relation of that form to the activity of human spirit. In the first instance he assumed that 'Every particular belongs from the outset to a definite *complex* and in itself expresses the rule of this complex. It is the totality of these rules that constitute the true unity of consciousness, as a unity of time, space, objective synthesis, etc.'[4] However, the unity of consciousness with its correlation between the particular and the complex culminates in a critique only when that critique 'seeks to understand and to show how every content of culture, in so far as it is more than a mere isolated content, in so far as it is grounded in a universal principle of form, presupposes an original act of the human spirit.'[5] The goal of Cassirer's critique of culture clearly rested on showing that every dimension of cultural activity (language, myth, art, and so on) was comprehensible only in so far as it revealed the creativity of human spirit. In spite of the seemingly disparate cultural activities, they could be envisioned as 'parts of a single great problem-complex.' Humanity's accomplishments through the ages could be interpreted as moving towards 'the one goal of transforming the passive world of mere *impressions*, in which the spirit seems at first imprisoned, into a world that is a pure *expression* of the human spirit.'[6] Thus, the common project of all human activity was to express the ultimate spiritual autonomy and thereby the creativity of man.

The Kantianism underlying Cassirer's symbolic conception of human culture was clear from the introduction to his critique. Cassirer himself specified that his analysis of symbolic forms was both an application and a broadening of Kant's analysis of logical form of reason onto the cultural level.[7] Further, Cassirer's entire approach rested on the Kantian belief that being itself (the noumenal realm) was unknowable, because the things in the world are perceived by man only through his own experience. These experiences were best understood as a unity of rules that regulate and constitute man's perception of the world. The unity was interpreted as functional because it unified only the rules of human perception and understanding and did not seek to posit or examine the existence of any objects or any substance beyond that rule complex.

Cassirer not only argued in favour of a Kantian, functional ideal of knowledge but he coupled that argument with a rejection of the materialist conception of knowledge. In the concluding part of his introduction to the philosophy of symbolic forms entitled 'Ideational Content of the Sign Transcending the Copy Theory of Knowledge,'[8] Cassirer specifically rejected the materialist viewpoint in terms reminiscent of F. A. Lange's critique of materialism in the 1860s. He spoke of supplanting the postulate of a unity of substance with the Kantian view of a functional unity of knowledge and existence. Materialists generally held two propositions that Cassirer could not accept: that scientific facts are the only possible objects of knowledge and that the existence and intelligibility of forces or substances does not extend beyond the facts and laws ascertained by science. Starting from the classical empiricist position that things in the world made impressions on human consciousness, which in turn gave rise to ideas that were mental images or copies of the natural world, materialists in effect held a copy theory of knowledge which reduced the human mind to passively observing and recording events.

The materialists' overdependence on the so-called hard facts of the natural world disturbed Cassirer. He believed their conception of knowledge was fundmentally incorrect because it erroneously sought the origin of knowledge in facts ('the unity of substance') rather than in the functional unity produced by human thought. Most important, the materialists failed to account for the creative role of human reason in constituting man's perception of the world around him. The issue became very important for Cassirer because in his mind the possibility and objectivity of scientific cognition were intimately bound up with the creativity of human spirit. If human reason did not actively synthesize the empirical data presented to human consciousness into a coherent set of ideas, if human reason did not create the rules for evaluating the objectivity of man's consciousness, there could be no objective criterion of knowledge. In Cassirer's mind if the error of materialism prevailed, grounded as it was in a simplistic and naive conception of the world, then only two intellectual alternatives would be available. Either one would be so overwhelmed with the complexity and eternal flux of existence that one would despair of ever making accurate mental 'copies' of it and thereby submerge oneself in the constant flux of life in an attempt to grasp the truth of being; or one would seek spiritual certainty by creating an ideal of truth where knowledge of existence was deduced from barren abstractions that descended from the heavens or from some other mystical place.

The first alternative, dogmatic empiricism, which Cassirer referred to as 'the paradise of pure immediacy,' opened the door to philosophies stressing the violent, dynamic, and evolutionary qualities of human existence. Cassirer thought the second alternative, dogmatic rationalism, to be 'the paradise of mysticism.' Here the limitations and infinite capabilities of man and of human reason would be alternatively stressed, and one would tend to fluctuate between extreme pessimism and exalted optimism. In either case, the main casualty would be scientific cognition because the middle ground on which it thrived – the understanding that true knowledge consisted in the interpenetration of pure abstractions (yielding a priori laws) and immediate experience (yielding empirical data) – would be torn apart by the competing dogmatisms. Admittedly, Cassirer's 'either/or' attitude towards materialism is not a very convincing argument. It is hard to see that the only alternatives to positivism were either dogmatic rationalism or dogmatic empiricism.

Nevertheless, Cassirer had no doubts about the validity of his dichotomy, and continued his argument on this basis. In order to avoid the paradises of 'pure immediacy' and 'mysticism' and to steer between the Scylla of extreme empiricism and the Charybdis of equally extreme rationalism, Cassirer relied on an ideal of knowledge and truth that preserved the middle ground. Here he offered his conception of the symbol to unite rules constituting pure knowledge with the basic facts of actual cultural life.

Since the 'symbol' concept was the centrepoint of Cassirer's philosophy of symbolic forms, it is useful to have a clear idea of his twofold use of the 'symbol'.[9] First, it denoted the variety of cultural forms, such as language, myth, art, religion, and science, which exemplified the realms of application of the 'symbol(ic) concept (form).' Secondly, it was applied to the categories of space, time, number, and cause, which as the most pervasive of 'symbol relations,' were thought to be the main elements comprising the symbolic forms listed under the first point. Most important, Cassirer believed that the symbol concept was the essential condition of the possibility of all true human knowledge of experience. By correlating ideas and facts the symbol concept created a framework for understanding the true nature of knowledge and human existence.

The symbol concept became the intellectual key that converted a hitherto Kantian critique of human knowledge into a critique of culture. Far from shunning life, this critique would place the direct experience of being within a rationalist scientific framework that could grasp the formative principle of human culture. In Cassirer's words:

If all culture is manifested in the creation of specific image-worlds, of specific symbolic forms, the aim of philosophy is not to go behind all these creations, but rather to understand and elucidate their basic formative principle. It is solely through the awareness of this principle that the content of life acquires its true form.[10]

Cassirer was well aware of the danger threatening his system and its harmony of teleological, logistic, and empirical tendencies. For implicit in his new critique was a tension between his logistic developmental theory of human consciousness and the empirical verification of that theory. As Cassirer himself described the dilemma:

If we hold fast to the postulate of logical unity, the universality of the logical form threatens ultimately to efface the individuality of each special province and the specificity of its principle – but if we immerse ourselves in this individuality and persevere in our examination of it, we run the risk of losing ourselves and of finding no way back to the universal.[11]

Cassirer was worried about two related problems. On the one hand, he was aware that he might be imposing an abstract theory on the course of events and thereby not rendering a true account of the facts themselves. On the other hand, he was concerned about becoming so immersed in particular details that the way back to the universal validity of the abstract concept would be forever lost.

It was essential to Cassirer to maintain a tension between the individual (concrete) and the abstract (universal) elements of knowledge, to balance the plurality of life experiences with a rationalist theory which reduced all experiences and activities to the a priori laws of reason. If this tension and harmony were not sustained, his system would regress to either dogmatic empiricism or dogmatic rationalism, the two alternatives that he wanted to avoid. So long as he maintained his intellectual equilibrium, with its tension between the individual and the universal, his system remained dynamic and creative.

LANGUAGE AND MYTH IN THE PHILOSOPHY OF SYMBOLIC FORMS

The relationship between language and myth was a very special one for Cassirer because these symbolic forms were subject to closely analogous laws of evolution.[12] What made them especially important to him was his belief that all cultural activities, like art, science, ethics, law, technology, and so on,[13] could be historically traced back to mythical consciousness and to man's linguistic attempts to express that consciousness. For Cassirer, language and myth were the primeval origins of all human culture.

Instead of measuring the content, significance, and truth of each form of human cultural activity 'by something extraneous which is supposed to be reproduced in them,'[14] the criteria for judging each form must be intrinsic to the form and based on 'its own fundamental law of formation.'[15] But what was the truth and significance of each form? For Cassirer the truth of the symbolic forms was that they were not copies but 'organs of reality,' since it was 'solely by their agency that anything real [became] an object for intellectual apprehension, and as such [was] made visible to us.'[16]

Cassirer's Kantian ideal of the true conception of knowledge emerged in relation to his understanding of symbolic forms. Human reality and perception of objects in the natural world was a product of the creative power of human consciousness.[17] This power revealed itself in the form of symbolic image worlds (symbolic forms). Since these forms were man's 'organs of reality,' Cassirer felt it unnecessary to ask what material things stood behind this reality. Rather, he focused on the fact of the creative and formative power of the human spirit. The truth and significance of the symbolic forms converged on one point: that reality as experienced by man was freely created by his own spirit.

Cassirer was always willing to acknowledge his intellectual debts. He specifically acknowledged the agreement of his own thoughts on myth with the Warburg approach to the matter,[18] and readily admitted that there was a 'pre-established harmony' linking his work to Warburg's.[19] While Cassirer's study on language relied heavily for empirical facts on the works of Meinhof, Boas, Seler, Dempwolff, Junker, Hoffmann, and Wolff,[20] his conceptual framework for analysing the development of language was part of a growing scholarly trend in Germany that dealt with art, language, and myth as integral parts of a more inclusive cultural history of man. Particularly in regard to language, there existed a line of thinkers, from the Grimm brothers to Karl Burdach and Karl Vossler, who argued that language could be used as the basis of cultural and intellectual history.[21] Cassirer and Vossler were contemporaries, and a fruitful dialogue of ideas occurred between them from 1923 to 1925. Cassirer approvingly noted Vossler's acceptance of the formula 'language = spiritual expression' which could be traced back to Wilhelm von Humboldt's conception of language,[22] a conception that Cassirer himself shared.

Much of Cassirer's analysis of language rested on Humboldt's linguistic studies. Humboldt, according to Cassirer, had created a fundamentally new approach to the problem of language when he applied the Kantian critique of reason to linguistic analysis. In the broadest sense, Humboldt understood that language was a particular example of the creative power of human consciousness. Like more formal expressions of human cognition (for example, science), language was not a barrier preventing man from apprehending the truth. Rather, it embodied a spiritual attitude that was always a crucial factor in man's objective perception of the world.[23]

As in the case of language, Cassirer tended to stress the creative aspect to mythical consciousness. He relied on Schelling's view that to unlock the secret of myth one had to understand that in the mythological process the *'powers arising within consciousness itself'*[24] moved man rather than the external objects presented in it. For example, the totemic worship of a particular plant or animal was important only because of the tribe's spiritual identification with it; the plant or animal in itself was of no importance. This principle was borne out by the fact that the object of totemic worship by members of a specific tribe had no value to members of other tribes.

At nearly every turn in his argument, Cassirer gave concrete examples to support his contention that the symbolic and cultural activities of humanity inexorably drove man to the realization that his own reason, through each of the symbolic forms, constituted reality for him. Once this point was grasped, one could understand that all human culture, from primeval to modern times, was the expression of the spiritual autonomy of man. These insights were the culmination of Cassirer's Kantian-Hegelian theory of human spirit, which he then attempted to verify empirically.

Cassirer's analysis of language and myth rested on 'the dialectical principle of progress' – the more language and myth tried to immerse themselves in the expression of sensuous things, the more effectively they contributed to the spiritual process of liberation from the sensuous (or natural) world.[25] He then subdivided this principle of progress into three stages, the mimetic, analogical, and symbolical stages,[26] and proceeded to give examples of each stage.

In the mimetic stage language and myth were still immersed in the world of sensation. Linguistic sounds and mythical images limited themselves to the limitation of sensual signs and objects and sounds. Primitive peoples tried to mimic every thing, every process, and every activity and as a consequence created linguistic and mythical forms to designate every variety of motion, process, and object in relation to one another. The Ewe had no less than thirty-three phonetic images for the verb 'to walk,' each of which specified a particular manner of walking.[27] In certain North American Indian languages the activity of washing was designated by thirteen different verbs depending on whether the verb applied to the washing of the hands, face, bowls, garments, food, and so on.[28] In the mythological hunting rites of North American Indians, the bison hunt was preceded by a bison dance, in which the capture and slaying of the beast was represented in detail.

In spite of his efforts to imitate the world around him, man realized that imitation was not sufficient for expressing what he desired. He felt the need to go beyond particular sensations in order to explain them. He then began to make analogies between different sensations. This was the second or analogical phase of the development of language and myth. Here intuitive connections made between different sights, sounds, distances, and so on, were formalized into analogies. To support this part of his theory Cassirer referred to the Sudanese and their practice of making analogies between the voice tone and distances. Thus, high-pitched words expressed long distances and rapidity, and low-pitched words articulated proximity and slowness.[29] Analogies in myth took the form of allegories, which provided a new understanding of the relation between the ideal and real worlds. Here Cassirer discussed the work of Dante as an example of a mythical (Christian) consciousness that could immerse itself in as well as withdraw from a reality that it recognized as both immediate and transcendent.[30] At this point the human spirit accepted the allegory as being analogous to events yet also a product of something else. What was this something else?

When man became aware that analogies involved something beyond the natural order of things, when he felt the need to reach behind these analogies, he entered the last and highest stage of the development of language and myth, the symbolic stage. On examining his analogies, man gradually realized that his language was really an expression of pure conceptual thought. The analogies were understood to be particular examples of abstract ideas, concepts, and classes, and these in turn were manifestations of the essential relational character of language and myth itself. To demonstrate the symbolic level of consciousness in language Cassirer pointed to those North American Indian languages where a reduplicated 'form of the verb [was] used to designate a kind of "unreality" in an action, to indicate that it [existed] only in purpose or "idea" and [was] not practically realized.'[31] In this connection, Cassirer noted the gradual evolution of other languages, such as Ural-Attaic and Melanesian, to the point where they could accept the ideal and relational bases of their respective linguistic forms.[32]

While trying to verify empirically his 'dialectical principle of human consciousness' Cassirer also provided a wealth of details to support his contention that concepts like space, time, and number were essential to the development of language and myth. He clearly showed that language and myth were saturated with varying spatial, temporal, and numerical concepts that played important roles in each symbolic form as it went through its various stages of evolution. In regard to the linguistic use of space on the analogical level Cassirer referred to the Tahitian practice of setting up a linguistic analogy between the distance of an object from the speaker and the variations in the vowels and consonants.[33] The mythical idea of space, he argued, was dominated by a basic division that permeated all levels of mythical consciousness: the division between the sacred (consecrated) and the profane (unconsecrated).[34] Accordingly, mythical perception of space established rigid spatial spheres. Each object with a specific meaning belonged to a particular place in the natural order. To give specific examples Cassirer referred to the following: the Australian Aborigines' practice of taking care to bury a deceased member of a clan 'in the spatial position and direction peculiar and essential to his clan,'[35] and the early Christian practice of turning the novice, before his baptism, 'toward the west to renounce the devil and his works, and then toward the east, toward paradise, that he might profess faith in Christ.'[36]

The concept of time tended to be very problematic for language, especially primitive languages. More often than not the same word was used to express temporal and spatial ideas. In the Klamath and Melanesian languages, for example, the word *here* merged with the word *now,* and the word for *there* was interchangeable with the word for *earlier* or *later.*[37] While language had difficulty in distinguishing the time concept from space, myth disposed of the problem by imagining time to have a divine origin. Here Cassirer noted the Vedic literature in India which made time the first of the Gods, from which all else emerged.[38]

The number concept had a special place in Cassirer's mind because it could provide the bridge over the gap separating the realm of natural events from the realm of pure spirit. In spite of the efforts of primitive languages to apprehend and classify (to 'copy') *in concreto* the multitude of different objects in a variety of temporal and spatial contexts, these languages nevertheless tended to place related or similar objects in the same name group. In Cassirer's mind 'the grouping constituted an independent logical act with a specific logical form.'[39] Once this logical stage was attained and all differentiations were subsumed under general classes, categories and groups, then the particular language was at the threshold of scientific or symbolic cognition. As an example Cassirer noted that there were no less than 5,744 names for camel in Arabic, which varied according to the camel's individual characteristics. These distinctions were further classified as male, female, adult, child, and so on. There are more subdivisions within these classes. Since Arabic has so many terms for denoting the variations in and varieties of plants and animals 'it has been cited as an example of how language study can advance our knowledge of natural history and physiology.'[40]

Once having shown that there was a logic at work in language and myth, and that these symbolic forms could be divided into distinct stages of evolution, with each stage having a particular manner of dealing with space, time, number, and so forth, it remained for Cassirer to show the end result of the evolutionary process. Not surprisingly, the process culminated in man's realization that what he saw 'out there' (in the natural world) was really the product of his own spirit. All human symbolic and cultural activities progressed towards this goal of self-understanding, and with it man achieved the realization of his own ultimate autonomy. At the end of the entire process

word and mythic image, which once confronted the human mind as hard realistic powers, have now cast off all reality and effectuality ... This liberation is achieved not because the mind throws aside the sensuous forms of word and image, but in that it uses them as organs of its own, and thereby recognizes them for what they really are: forms of its own self-revelation.[41]

Cassirer's belief that the end result of human history was man's recognition of his own creativeness and spiritual autonomy was not only predictable but also understandable in relation to his idealist liberalism. For this variety of liberalism held that all human history progressed towards the point where all men were spiritually autonomous. Hence, Cassirer's analysis of language and myth was not purely philosophical, but was full of political connotations. In effect, he made the unfolding of liberal values the central theme of his critique of human culture. It is instructive to examine how Cassirer specifically infused liberal values into his work; for such an examination will serve to underscore the point that no matter how abstract and removed from everyday practical considerations a philosophy seems to be, it nevertheless reflects the political values of its creator.

Cassirer put his facts to ideological use in two ways. First, the fate of the autonomous individual occupied the centrepoint of his analysis of mythical life and thought; throughout his discussions Cassirer constantly returned to the plight of the individual.[42] Secondly, he believed that the inherent tendency of mythical consciousness was gradually to push the individual into realizing his own autonomy.[43] Here it should be remembered that many anthropological studies had been made of primitive peoples – indeed Cassirer's volumes on language and myth rested on such studies – yet Cassirer was the first to use the theme of the individual struggling for self-consciousness as the means of making sense out of the *prima facie* irrational and senseless acts of primitive man.

In the most primitive form of mythical life, magical connections were made by primitive peoples to link their tribal existence to animals or plants, which in turn were used as the means for comprehending the whole cosmos. Thus, the Huichol Indians venerated the deer and made it the centre of their magical rites.[44] Other tribes linked the appearance of the swallow with the coming of spring; for them the swallow 'made' the spring.[45] And as Cassirer noted earlier, the 'magical' hunt of the bison by North American Indians, that is, the dances and rites preceding the 'real' hunt, was inseparable from the actual hunting and killing of the animal. Finally there was the case of the Zūni Indians, who, once having 'decided' that the cosmos was divided in a certain way, divided their clans to match the cosmic order. Following the seven major divisions of the universe, the tribal kingdom was organized into seven different zones, with each tribe representing different people or objects. Hence, there were bear people, water people, sky people, and so on.[46] In summary, at the most primitive level of mythical consciousness all life constituted a unity; no one object or person existed outside the community's perception of the world.[47]

It is evident that humanity did not remain on the level of primitive mythical consciousness, and that the individual gradually gained his spiritual autonomy. But how did this happen? Here Cassirer noted the tendency of man to personalize his gods and give them a human character. But once this humanization process began it did not stop with the gods but extended into the whole social organism until the individual ego acquired a personal life 'as opposed to the life of the tribe.'[48] Thus, Cassirer cited the Homeric epics as an example of the primitive, communal-centred consciousness giving rise to the modern conception of the free man in the image of the hero. The hero was discovered, and in him was seen the active, suffering individual: 'And with this discovery a last barrier between god and man falls away; the hero takes his place between them as an intermediary. Now the hero, the human personality, is raised to the divine sphere and the gods for their part are closely interwoven with human destiny ...'[49] Once again, Cassirer returned to the theme of the individual struggling for self-consciousness. This time it was to initiate his explanation of why humanity moved from the level of communal consciousness to the modern one where man was a self-conscious, striving individual.

While man began to think of his gods differently, he also began to act differently. Instead of relying only on the worship of a given animal or inanimate object to achieve a desired result, he began to rely more heavily on implements and on his own actions to achieve his goals. Moreover, 'as soon as man seeks to influence things not by mere image magic or name magic but through implements, he has undergone an inner crisis.'[50] The crisis was man's realization that his energetic use of implements, which he created, was crucial to the success of any enterprise. Gone was the old certainty that magical rites acting on a magically conceived cosmos were the primary means for action. Man was left with the anxiety of making his own way in the world with no assurance that the gods would intervene on his behalf. This situation represented a dramatic reversal in his attitude towards himself and the world around him. Previously man could blame the gods for his misfortunes; now the burden of blame shifted onto his own shoulders.

Cassirer's picture of a humanity confronting an indifferent universe and helped only by its own spiritual and practical abilities was a peculiarly rationalist liberal image of the human condition. Man was primitive if he had only a collective consciousness and reacted to the world in magical, that is to say, irrational, terms. Conversely, man became 'modern' in so far as he had an individual consciousness and tried to influence events by the orderly and organized, that is, rational, use of his implements in connection with given ends. Most students of civilization in Cassirer's age were content to argue that in primitive times these implements tended to be tangible items like arrowheads or farming tools and that in the modern era the implements (like mathematics or philosophy) became more intangible. However, Cassirer did not seek to draw a rigid line dividing primitive and modern man. On the contrary, and here the progressive character of his work became manifest, he tried to demonstrate conclusively that *all* humanity contributed to the understanding that man was a free agent. In every epoch of human history Cassirer found evidence that people sought to forge their own tools for comprehending the universe. Hence, he examined the diverse linguistic and mythical practices of mankind to show that man had always consciously created new ways of understanding and new tools for controlling his environment. In fact, Cassirer believed that the philosophy of symbolic forms was but one of the latest in the long series of human attempts to create the 'implements' necessary for a complete knowledge of the human condition.[51]

CASSIRER'S PHILOSOPHY AS A RESPONSE TO HIS CONTEMPORARIES

A number of people felt that Cassirer's critique of culture was an attempt to re-establish 'philosophy as a true science'[52] because it was capable of subsuming every kind of human activity, ranging from the apparently alogical activities of primitive man to the logical procedures of modern science, to specific laws of structure and development. For his own part Cassirer was not only interested in widening the horizon of philosophical science. He also wanted to prevent science, philosophy, and the rationalist ideal of knowledge and existence from being subverted. This ideal held that only through the use of his rational faculties could man both control his own destiny and realize the full extent of his freedom. After the war of 1914–18 the rationalist ideal was fiercely attacked. Spengler's *Decline of the West* was one of the most popular expressions of the new turning in European attitudes. In the early Weimar years (1919–25) Spengler was at the height of his popularity. Doubtless, Cassirer's defence of science and rationalism was directed at the whole outlook as well as the ideological sentiments expressed by Spengler and others. In Cassirer's words:

Today [December, 1924] it is openly asserted that no clear logical division can be made between myth and history and that all historical understanding is and must be permeated with mythical elements. If this thesis were sound, history itself and the entire system of the cultural sciences grounded in it would be withdrawn from the sphere of science and relegated to that of myth. Such infringements of myth on the province of science can only be prevented if we know myth in its own realm, can know its essence and what it can accomplish spiritually. We can truly overcome it only by recognizing it for what it is.[53]

Spengler was apparently a popular target for those who enlisted themselves in the defence of the Weimar Republic. Count Harry Kessler ('The Red Count'), who went on diplomatic missions for the Republic, thought Spengler was simple-minded and banal.[54] Troeltsch cited Spengler's popularity as an indication that German spirit was moving in the wrong direction; it was still holding to a romanticism that idealized the nation in mythical terms and shrank from 'the wider horizon of the parliament of man.'[55] And Sternberg, fully realizing that Spengler's mixture of naturalism and romantic symbolism was a product of the times, looked to the work of Kant and the neo-Kantians to stem the 'Spenglerian' tide.[56]

Within the context of the atmosphere pervading the early years of the Weimar Republic, the proponent of a rationalist, liberal *Weltanschauung* had two courses of action open to him. He could either ignore the growing mythical and anti-rational consciousness of many Germans or seek to situate it within his rationalist conception of man and the cosmos. Cassirer chose the latter course. Ultimately he could never admit the primacy of 'the paradise of pure immediacy' over the realm of reason, but if the finest product of human reason (scientific cognition) were to be saved, the realm of mythical consciousness had to be fully understood and its limits exposed.

Invoking Hegel's conception of science as a ladder leading from natural or naive consciousness to scientific cognition,[57] Cassirer envisioned the evolution of human spirit as the history of man's progressive achievement of the scientific standpoint. The relations between science, myth, and language had to be carefully defined and examined in great detail if an accurate picture of mankind's spiritual development were to be attained. More important, Cassirer felt that this careful examination would clarify the differences between myth and science and would therefore provide the means for preventing the former from undermining and absorbing the latter. On this last point, Cassirer presented a detailed discussion of the essential differences between exact science and myth.[58]

In accordance with his personal temperament and scholarly principles, Cassirer maintained a low-key approach to his analysis of language and myth. However, even he occasionally let the emotions motivating his defence of science erupt into his text and reveal the ideological dimension to his seemingly academic ideas. One of the ideas crucial to Cassirer's scientific critique of culture was the following: 'In defining the distinctive character of any spiritual form, it is essential to measure it by its own standards.'[59] When Cassirer encountered Steinthal's disparaging remarks about the Mandingos' primitive counting methods he quickly discarded his scholarly mien. Steinthal spoke of 'the intellectual guilt which burdens the spirit of the Negro' because he was not able to create an abstract numerical system. The Negro preferred to count with his fingers and toes and not make the imaginative leap to symbolic notation; he preferred to 'crawl around' in the natural world, as distinct from us who made the imaginative leap out of it and created symbolic numbers.[60] Cassirer belittled this argument. 'In the half-poetical, half-theological pathos of his diatribe'[61] Steinthal failed to see the obvious: that the Mandingos had in fact established a set pattern for counting things, and though this pattern was limited to the body, it was nevertheless a sure sign that this primitive tribe was on the road to establishing an abstract idea of number. Thus for Cassirer it was far more fruitful and just to evaluate the Mandingos by their own standards than on the basis of 'our fully developed concept of number.'[62]

Cassirer's severe criticism of academics who lauded the superiority of the standards of their own culture and had only contempt for the cultural achievements of others was indicative of the cosmopolitan spirit pervading his vision of human history. No one culture or nation had a greater claim than any other group to being the ultimate end of history or to possessing a standard of values so superior that it should be imposed on others. Each person, each people, each culture had its part to play in the story of human progress. As with his earlier work in *Freiheit und Form*, Cassirer's philosophy of symbolic forms stressed the harmony underlying the universe of human activities.

Again, he pushed aside a narrow nationalist framework and attempted to give every people its credit in the movement of humanity towards freedom.

Unfortunately, Cassirer's critique of culture was flawed by a conceptual dualism. It was the result of the tension between his conflicting commitments to a cultural pluralism, with its emphasis on the individual and the concrete, and a one-sided rationalism, with its interest in the abstract and universal. On the one hand Cassirer believed that every spiritual form was unique and therefore had to be measured by its own standards; and that this was the case because each spiritual (symbolic) form was progressing towards a given end and therefore had its own mode of formation and development. Cassirer made every effort to deal with the diversity of human experience and therefore account for the pluralism underlying human cultural activity. On the other hand, he believed that all of these activities were accountable to, and in fact manifestations of, universally valid laws; and that these laws were both an integral part, yet independent, of the individual symbolic form. In this connection Cassirer in effect maintained that the multitude of human activities were conformable to the logical rigour of abstract laws.

Now one either believes that human acts are essentially similar or one believes they are essentially dissimilar. If the former is accepted, then everything may be reduced to one logic of cultural development. However, if the latter position is held, then the plurality of humanity's deeds is so great that these actions can never be reduced to a single logic. In any case, our main point here is to highlight the internal stress of Cassirer's system. For while this stress proved to be fruitful between 1923 and 1925, and Cassirer was able to balance the logistic and teleological demands of his theory with the need to verify it empirically, this harmony between an abstract and universal overview of mankind and the commitment to a detailed analysis of individual cases was too precarious to last.

# 9

# The Weimar cultural milieu (1900–33)

INTRODUCTION

The activities of intellectuals in Germany, especially between 1900 and 1933, reflected national as well as Western European trends. German culture, for better or for worse, was an integral part of European developments. 'Just as the Weimar style was older than the Weimar Republic, so it was larger than Germany.'[1] Philosophical accounts of the years 1900–33 indicate that a definite shift in European philosophical interest occurred around 1900.[2] This shift began with an intellectual crisis in physics and mathematics; it was continued by the evolution of the mathematical and phenomenological ideals of scientific rigour and procedure and was accompanied by the emergence of new world views, such as irrationalism and a new realist metaphysics. The entire shift in philosophy was symptomatic of the profound disillusionment with the nineteenth century's trust in the ability of a mathematical and mechanistic ideal of science to answer all the mysteries of human and cosmic life. The sense of spiritual disenchantment carried over into other fields of cultural life as H. Stuart Hughes, Gerhard Masur, Edmund Wilson, and Werner Haftmann have shown.[3]

Political theory after 1900 was particularly hard hit by what Brecht called the rise of scientific 'value relativism': the belief that reason and science were unable to provide the criterion for choosing between the correct political values and practices.[4] While this shift towards 'value relativism' had already begun around 1900, its more widespread impact on the European, particularly the German, mind occurred only between 1918 and 1933. The scholarly consensus seems to be that European cultural activities between 1900 and 1933 may be treated as a unit, which may be called the Weimar cultural milieu.

The purpose of this chapter is to provide an overview of the Weimar cultural milieu in so far as it affected Cassirer's activities between 1923 and 1933. While before 1914 Cassirer had tried to dissolve natural entities and human activities into 'the pure functions of knowledge,' in the wake of the events of 1914–18 he attempted to broaden the epistemological basis of his critique of knowledge and existence. Between 1923 and 1926 Cassirer's reaction to contemporary events resulted in an equal partnership between theory and fact. After 1926 the partnership dissolved. He returned to a more abstract interpretation of the human condition.

For the purpose of relating Cassirer's work to the Weimar cultural milieu and observing the destabilizing effects of the latter on his intellectual equilibrium, his ideas have already in effect been divided into three levels – anthropological, philosophical, and ideological. On the anthropological level, Cassirer assumed man was a rational creature and the prime mover of history. On the philosophical level, there was the tension between his revised transcendental theory of human consciousness and human culture and a commitment to verify the theory empirically. Finally, on the ideological level, Cassirer's *Weltanschauung* predisposed him to support idealist liberal principles and the form of government that would ensure the fulfilment of those ideals by encouraging the scientific pursuit of objective knowledge.[5]

In connection with the anthropological level, I will examine Cassirer's identification with and work for the Warburg Library. But even before the appearance of Cassirer's last positive response to the cultural milieu, his study of Renaissance philosophy in 1927, his intellectual equilibrium was being undermined by developments in philosophy and political and legal theory. Regarding the philosophical situation, the works of Bergson, Sorel, Husserl and Heidegger must be discussed since they decisively affected Cassirer's system. For the ideological context of Cassirer's post-1926 ideas, the works of Gustav Radbruch, Hans Kelsen, Erich Kaufmann and Carl Schmitt, as well as the climate of opinion in the academic community during the entire Weimar period will be analysed.

## THE WARBURG LIBRARY

One of the first essays published by the Warburg Library was written by Ernst Cassirer. This essay, on the form of concepts in mythical thought, was one of the two papers of the years 1921–22 used by him to publicize the outline of his philosophy of symbolic forms. Because of the excellent personal relations between the major intellectual figures of the Library – Warburg, Panofsky, Cassirer, Saxl – and their complete identification with what they considered to be the mission of the library, each man may at various points speak for the others.[6] Thus, the tensions within Cassirer's work may represent the intellectual problems common to the entire work of those affiliated with the Warburg Library.

Cassirer's attempt to formulate a philosophy of symbolic forms complemented the Warburg conception of the unity behind cultural history. The symbolic approach of cultural activity could be applied to all fields, especially to art. Cassirer's interest in art went back to the earliest years of his life;[7] it had its first major effect on him when he was in the process of rethinking the entire German cultural heritage in 1916. Henceforth, art and philosophy were very firmly connected in Cassirer's mind; this connection was further strengthened by his affiliation with the Warburg Library, for the library itself was interested in aesthetics, especially in the images used in language, myth, and pictorial representation.

In 1919, the year Cassirer received his appointment to the philosophy faculty at the University of Hamburg, Erwin Panofsky came to the university as a *privatdozent*. Panofsky had met Aby Warburg in Rome in 1912 and since that date had become one of Warburg's closest intellectual collaborators.[8] As Panofsky was later to write, Warburg was obsessed with the relation between the rational and the irrational.[9] He carried this psychological attitude into his study of cultural history and was firmly committed to finding the rational order implicit in the seemingly irrational and random human usage of images in language, myth, and art. For Warburg, the symbol became the key to understanding the hidden meaning behind all human activity. It would provide a methodology for uncovering the rational progression behind the individually irrational activities of humanity.[10]

After Warburg's mental breakdown in 1920, Fritz Saxl was left in charge of the Warburg Library, and through his efforts it became affiliated with the University of Hamburg. In the same year Saxl managed to get someone from the philosophy faculty to visit the library. The philosopher was Ernst Cassirer. On his first visit to the library Cassirer immediately sensed the connection between his own work and materials in the library. In Cassirer's words: 'The philosophical problems involved in this library are close to my own, but the concrete historical material which Warburg has collected is overwhelming.'[11]

Cassirer's intellectual sympathy for the philosophical problems implicit in the Warburg Library collection eventually led to his becoming a constant visitor there, and he soon came into contact with Erwin Panofsky. The friendship and intellectual kinship between Cassirer and Panofsky grew throughout the 1920s. Independently of one another they had each been working towards a view of human cultural activity which not only complemented the other's but would also provide a methodology for achieving the kind of synthesis that

Warburg himself had sought. While Panofsky had tried to grasp the spiritual core of human cultural activity by focusing on the influence of classical antiquity on Western artistic experience,[12] Cassirer combined a reinterpretation of the German philosophical tradition with a growing interest in language, myth, and art so that he too might systematically comprehend the human spirit's historical development.

Beginning with the publication of the outlines for *The Philosophy of Symbolic Forms* in 1921 and 1922 in the journal of the Warburg Library and up until his departure from Germany in 1933, Cassirer increasingly agreed with Warburg's and Panofsky's ideas. His constant references to their works in his 1926 study of the Renaissance[13] and his collaboration with Panofsky at three art historical conventions in 1927, 1929, and 1931 served to underscore further Cassirer's strong indentification with the Panofsky-Warburg conception of cultural history.[14]

On his side Panofsky's work bore the indelible imprint of Cassirer's ideas. In an article published in 1924 for the Warburg Library, Panofsky expressly noted his intellectual debt to Cassirer. The title of the article, 'Die Perspektive als "Symbolische Form" ' (Perspective as 'symbolic form'), was an indication of his acceptance of Cassirer's philosophy of symbolic forms.[15] Panofsky's theory of geometric perspective in Renaissance art became a concrete demonstration of the validity of Cassirer's new philosophy of culture. Panofsky used Cassirer's analysis of space in the second volume of *The Philosophy of Symbolic Forms* as the starting point for his own argument that the use of space was not only a technical and pictorial problem but a psychological one as well.[16] In a sense, Panofsky's approach to art history was an application of Cassirer's philosophy of culture to art.[17]

While Cassirer sought to place each symbolic activity within a larger cultural context, Panofsky sought to place developments in art within the cultural *Weltanschauung* of the historical period. For example, he showed how the artistic use of human proportions changed from the Middle Ages to the Renaissance principally because of the different views of man held in each period.[18] Panofsky's methodology was similar to Cassirer's. Both proceeded from empirical evidence in art and myth and attempted to unite these facts with a transcedental theory of pure consciousness. The crucial point is that both Cassirer and Panofsky believed that every factual piece of evidence contained a spiritual and symbolic dimension. On the basis of this connection Cassirer and Panofsky could systemize the apparently random and irrational connections each epoch made between specific attitudes towards the world and the symbolic expressions of those attitudes.

Cassirer's volume *The Individual and the Cosmos in Renaissance Philosophy* was first published in 1927 as volume 10 of the Warburg Library studies – a clear indication that Cassirer's vision of the Renaissance was shared by the intellectual community revolving around the library. In his dedication letter to Warburg, dated 13 June 1926, Cassirer admitted that he could not have completed his study of the Renaissance had he 'not been able to enjoy the constant stimulation and encouragement of that group of scholars whose intellectual centre is your library.'[19] And, most important for Cassirer, in both its organization and intellectual structure 'the library embodies the idea of the methodological unity of all fields and all currents of intellectual history.'[20]

The real significance of Cassirer's Renaissance work was that he carried his critique of culture into the field of history. By examining the intellectual activities of one particular epoch, Cassirer demonstrated that his new philosophy could provide a uniform and universally valid method of understanding human cultural history. By expanding his critique of culture into history, aided by the documents and ideas of the Warburg group, he was fulfilling his own philosophical and spiritual need to create a lasting rational understanding of human history.

Cultural history for Cassirer had two principal ingredients. First, there was the idea, taken from his examination of the evolution of language and myth, that the human spirit progressed towards scientific cognition. The end of human history became synonymous with the attainment of the scientific standpoint, which for Cassirer was tantamount to accepting the primary role of reason in human affairs. Secondly, Cassirer adhered to the cosmopolitan view of history first expressed in his wartime study of German thought. Ten years later, in 1926, he still maintained that the history of a great intellectual movement could not be understood 'from a onesidedly national point of view.'[21] Finally, and this point was really an integral part of the other two, there was his commitment to factual accuracy. Every generalization had to reflect faithfully the state of affairs from which it was drawn. Cassirer applied these beliefs in his study of the Renaissance, hoping to give others a concrete example of how his new method could be profitably applied to history.

CASSIRER'S STUDY OF THE RENAISSANCE

Cassirer's general approach to the movement of thought in the fifteenth and sixteenth centuries was part of the Burckhardtian school of Renaissance interpretation.[22] Burckhardt's position rested on a double premise: that the modern world view first emerged in the Italian Renaissance, and that its major characteristic was a commitment to the total autonomy of the individual.[23] In the introduction to his Renaissance study Cassirer specifically aligned himself with Burckhardt's interpretation. However, he objected to Burckhardt's treatment of philosophy. In his 'great portrayal of Renaissance civilization' Burckhardt had 'granted no place to philosophy.'[24] For Cassirer it was precisely in the period's theoretical reflections that the attitudes and practices of the new world view were expressed in their most durable form.[25]

The originality of Cassirer's contribution to Renaissance scholarship lay in his demonstration of the unity pervading European thought from Cusanus to Galileo. A continuous chain of thought, contributed to by scientists, philosophers, and artists, linked Cusanus' partial break with the medieval world view in the fifteenth century to the emergence of the modern standpoint in Galileo's ideas in the seventeenth century. Cassirer envisioned all these men as participants in a common task: a comprehensive theoretic vision of man and the cosmos that gave rise to the modern world view.

The modern *Weltanschauung*, as first expressed by Renaissance thought, was the product of the interaction between a theory of art that sought to comprehend the natural world by reproducing its lawlike regularity and symmetry, and a new theory of science that tried to understand the natural order by combining mathematics, empirical observation, and rigorous experimentation. The natural agreement of scientific and aesthetic theory was so striking to Cassirer because it involved the modern realization that man was only capable of facing the infinite cosmos in so far as he could discover within himself those principles by which he understood the world around him.[26] Here Cassirer was extending to the historical sphere the Kantian belief that the world is knowable by virtue of the systematizing tendencies of human reason. His treatment of Renaissance thought was similar to his earlier analysis of language and myth. In each instance, language, myth, and the Renaissance, human consciousness was seen to traverse the road from simple natural perception to objective scientific cognition, from a naive or primitive vision of the world to the modern scientific viewpoint.

Cassirer's cultural and historical studies proceeded from the belief that his own critique of man was itself a product of the human spirit's progress towards scientific cognition and hence the embodiment of the modern world view. As early as 1906–7, with the appearance of the first two volumes of *Das Erkenntnisproblem*, Cassirer had stated his belief that the Kantian system was the culmination of the revolution of thought begun by Cusanus. Here again, the consistency of Cassirer's ideas over two decades (1907–27) was most striking.

As his wartime study of German thought had placed Kant and Goethe in the centre of his reflections, Cassirer made Cusanus the focal point of his discussion of the Renaissance. In Cassirer's opinion 'any study that seeks to view the philosophy of the Renaissance as a *systematic* unity must take as its point of departure the doctrines of Nicholas Cusanus.'[27] What made Cusanus' work so special to Cassirer was its modernity, its scientific and rational vision of man and the cosmos. Cusanus' idea of the *visio intellectualis* was the key to his philosophy. His vision rested on a mathematical, homogeneous conception of the cosmos. The medieval view held that the cosmos was a hierarchy with the 'higher' spiritual realm (the heavens) occupied by the angels and God and the 'lower' sensible realm (the earth) occupied by man, other creatures, and inanimate material objects. Cusanus' vision did away with this hierarchy and set up a new conception of the universe based on the activities of the human spirit, which he believed made possible a more profound understanding of God's creation.

As Cassirer saw it, in one blow Cusanus had annihilated the scholastic vision of the cosmos and set in its place 'a single universe, homogeneous within itself.'[28] The spirtual activities of the human mind had become for Cusanus the microcosm in which all the lines of the cosmic macrocosm found their most complete living expression.[29] Human reason had in a sense become the centrepoint of all human and cosmic existence. Cassirer closed his discussion of Cusanus' work with a metaphor that Cusanus himself used to summarize his *visio intellectualis*.[30] The human mind was a divine seed that comprehended in its simple essence the totality of everything knowable; but in order for this seed to blossom it had to be planted in the soil of the sensible world. Cassirer believed that this vision of man and the cosmos at once constituted the common project of the Renaissance and provided a systematic point of view of the period.

Cassirer's manner of demonstrating the unity of the activities of an historical epoch was striking. Having revealed the central theme of the period, namely the growing understanding of Renaissance man that the cosmos was an expression of humanity's inner life, he went on to trace the continuity of ideas from Cusanus to Galileo, even though few actual connections existed between the different men's ideas. He compared the ideas of various Renaissance thinkers regardless of their separation in time. For example, he argued as if Leonardo had been aware of Cusanus' ideas; yet there was no evidence to suggest that Leonardo had ever heard of Cusanus. Cassirer was well aware of this problem,[31] but did not feel that it significantly undermined his point. His belief was that an ideal unity lay at the centre of the movement of thought from the fifteenth to the seventeenth centuries, and that Cusanus' work had embodied the ideal unity. Thus, Cusanus' view of the world, even though not directly connected to the ideas of his successors, contained the major themes to be expressed by Galileo's physics, Pico's philosophical attitude towards the dignity of man, and Leonardo's view of art.[32] All in all, Cassirer's study of Renaissance thought showed how confident he was of his own historical vision and of its philosophical moorings. This is illustrated by the way in which Cassirer traced the unfolding of the Renaissance's common task in the works of Pico, Leonardo, and Galileo.

Following Burckhardt's lead Cassirer interpreted Pico's oration on the dignity of man as one of the most memorable expressions of the Renaissance spirit: '*Burckhardt* called Pico's oration one of the most noble bequests of the culture of the Renaissance. And indeed, it summarizes with grand simplicity and in pregnant form the whole intent of the Renaissance and its entire concept of knowledge.'[33] For Cassirer, Pico's idea of knowledge involved a duality of man and the world, human spirit and nature. The dualism reflected a tension between the human spirit's desire for self-elevation and for universal knowledge and the infiniteness of a cosmos that at once defied universal knowledge and threatened the human ego with complete submersion into the mysteries of cosmic existence.[34] For Cassirer Renaissance individualism emerged in Pico's thought when he confidently asserted that 'the destiny of man does not flow to him from above, from the stars, but rather arises from the ultimate depths of his innermost self.'[35] As in the case of Cusanus' *visio intellectualis*, Pico's view of man focused on universal knowledge within man's ability to create a unified vision of the cosmos in his own image.

Cassirer was very much impressed by the revolutionary quality of the Renaissance. It was an age that destroyed old ideas and established new ones. As Burckhardt succinctly put it, in the fifteenth century the Italian states produced 'the first born among the sons of modern Europe.'[36] But what was so new about the Renaissance? What ideas did the Renaissance put forth that made it seem revolutionary and therefore modern?

For Cassirer the essence of the Renaissance's claim to opening up the modern epoch lay in the importance attached to a new mathematical conception of science in comprehending man and the cosmos.[37] This conception was revolutionary from a philosophical point of view because it demanded a complete reversal of perspective and necessitated the formulation of a new theory of knowledge. Using Galileo as one of the examples of the new world view, Cassirer interpreted Galileo's scientific work as an example of the overthrow of Aristotelian physics by the modern view of the subject: 'Instead of deriving the form of activity from the dogmatic assumption of a form of being,' as was traditionally done, Galileo began 'with the empirical laws of activity, and through these indirectly gained the point of departure for the determination of being.'[38] In other words, Galileo preferred to formulate laws of nature on the basis of his own observations and mathematical calculations rather than rely on traditional religious dogma to dictate his comprehension of cosmic events.

From the church's point of view the most upsetting thing about Galileo's laws of motion lay in their confirmation of the heliocentric view of the universe. Religious dogma was committed to a specific hierarchical view of the cosmic order as established by God. The cosmic order was given a necessary and unalterable ontological status, which Christians had to accept without question. An element essential to this order was the belief that the rest of the universe revolved around the earth. If the heliocentric theory were true, then a number of other religious dogmas appeared questionable, for example, the idea that the composition of the heavens, in terms of planets, stars, planetary movements and so on, was constant. Ultimately, the entire medieval world view, along with the authority of the church, would be critically undermined. The revolutionary implications of Galileo's work were not lost on the church, which forced him to recant his heretical ideas and spend the last years of his life under house arrest.

According to Cassirer, Galileo's ideas were not an isolated phenomenon. They were the continuation of Cusanus' ideas and indicative of the major course of intellectual development in Europe since the fifteenth century. Cusanus and his successors had abolished the traditional arbitrary separation, espoused by the church, of the lower (earthly) and upper (spiritual) elements constituting the cosmos. In its place, Renaissance thinkers collectively established the primacy of the ideal of contingent existence, where nothing was certain about the cosmos except that any knowledge of it was dependent on human consciousness. The absoluteness of the theological dogma gave way to a form of 'physical relativity.' But, as Cassirer argued,

Once the relativity of all local determination is recognized in principle, we may no longer ask how we can establish fixed *points* in the universe; instead we must ask how fixed *laws* of change may be ascertained in this realm of complete material relationships and of limitless variability in which we now stand. The determination of any 'place' now presupposes, and can only be made within, a system of universal *rules* of movement.[39]

It then may be asked, who or what created these 'universal rules.' For the men of the Renaissance the answer was clear. The determination of place in accordance with fixed and universal laws of change was the product of the human spirit.[40]

Cassirer constantly returned to the Renaissance belief in the creativity of human spirit and to the idea that nature was the mirror of man's inner life. Since the speculations of practically all thinkers reflected this fundamental belief, Cassirer was able to use the 'creativity' theme as a means of passing from one man's ideas to the next. As everyone was engaged in a 'common task,' each man could speak for the others. And herein lay the reason why Cassirer found the Burckhardtian interpretation of the Renaissance so congenial. He believed that all humanity participated in the common task of advancing to the standpoint of scientific cognition and thereby to the realization that man freely created the cosmos around himself. Burckhardt's idea that in the Renaissance man emerged for the first time as a self-conscious force, as an autonomous being, and as the prime mover of history easily fitted into Cassirer's approach to the study of human culture. Furthermore, Burckhardt's historical methodology hit sympathetic vibrations in Cassirer's own critique of man.

Burckhardt treated a cultural epoch as a unit which had one theme holding it together. He saw excessive individualism, the will to complete autonomy, as the key to understanding the Renaissance in Italy.[41] On the basis of this theme he analysed attitudes towards the state, morality and religion, scholarship, art, science and social life. In other words, Burckhardt approached an epoch on the assumption that one fundamental idea could capture the essence of the cultural period and then proceeded to examine that unit idea and the culture from different points of view.[42] This was precisely the aim of Cassirer's critique of culture, but his range of interest was broader than Burckhardt's. Cassirer did not limit himself to one historical epoch: he dealt with all humanity.

The combination of his own critique of culture with a Burckhardtian vision of the Renaissance resulted in a remarkably compact and coherent discussion of Renaissance thought. Cassirer not only went with ease from philosophers like Cusanus and Pico to philosopher-scientists like Kepler and Galileo, but he also was able to harmonize their ideas with Leonardo's approach to art. Here again the creative power of the human mind was seen to prevail as it had in the scientific thought of the age. As Leonardo put it: 'Science [was] a second creation made with the understanding; painting [was] a second creation made with the imagination.'[43] It was in Leonardo that the theoretic vision of the Renaissance, with its fusion of art and science, reached its fullest expression. In Leonardo Cassirer saw the new vision of art and science united into the modern view of man, nature, and the cosmos. Regardless of whether the rational side of human spirit (the understanding) was applied to nature to yield science or man's emotional side (the imagination) was used to create a valid artistic vision of the natural world, for Leonardo, the creative power of the human spirit was the main focus of interest. Without it neither a systematic scientific view of the cosmos nor a coherent artistic vision of the natural world was possible.

For Cassirer art and science came together during the Renaissance on the fundamental insight that there was a necessity to nature, a series of laws governing all forms of existence (human or otherwise), and that Reason was the fount of all these laws.[44] Like Galileo, Leonardo pursued the rationality behind all existence. And while the former used mathematics to reproduce the natural processes in symbolic form, artists like Leonardo and Alberti drew precise geometric designs in order to grasp for artistic purposes the rational structure implicit in the laws regulating man's perception of the external world.[45] Thus, Leonardo, as the true exemplar of the Renaissance spirit in art and science, regardless of whether he examined the dynamics behind the creation of a painting or the physical principles governing the operation of a lever, always sought to uncover the 'reason' or law implicit in all the creative visions of man.[46]

To a large extent Cassirer's conception of the unity pervading European thought from Cusanus to Galileo rested on Burckhardt's vision of the Renaissance. While this point was noted earlier, its ideological dimension was not. Significantly, Cassirer never seriously questioned the validity of Burckhardt's interpretation of the Renaissance or his cosmopolitan and rationalist orientation towards human history. Cassirer based much of his own argument on Burckhardt's standpoint because he shared with Burckhardt the nineteenth-century liberal belief that the history of European man since the Renaissance was, for the most part, the story of the growth of individual freedom.

Cassirer's Renaissance study was a further example of his predisposition, first established with his wartime examination of German culture, to see the development of human freedom from a supranational or cosmopolitan standpoint. National activities only became comprehensible within the larger European cultural context. With the appearance of *The Philosophy of Symbolic Forms* Cassirer expanded his cultural context even further to include all humanity. From an ideological standpoint, Cassirer's praise of the Renaissance amounted to a defence of a cosmopolitan liberalism.

Cassirer clearly renounced the nationalist approach to history when he said that 'we cannot understand the history of a great intellectual movement [the Renaissance] ... by looking at it from a onesidedly national point of view.' Accordingly, in his discussion of the epoch Cassirer disregarded all national boundaries and treated Cusanus, Kepler, Pico, and Galileo as if they belonged to one culture. Cassirer's cosmopolitan orientation was a direct rebuff to the prevailing tendency in German intellectual circles to evaluate the Renaissance in purely national terms. In this connection, either the Renaissance was considered by men like Houston Stuart Chamberlain and Ludwig Woltmann as a manifestation of the German race's genius[47] or it was thought of as essentially non-German. The latter opinion led many, like Carl Neumann[48] and Ernst Troeltsch[49] to make a sharp division between German spirit, whose flowering occurred during the Middle Ages and the Reformation, and the Renaissance mentality. In all cases, and this point is crucial, the Renaissance was evaluated from the German national standpoint, by German rather than European standards of modernism and freedom. While Cassirer discussed the evolution of human freedom from a broad, cosmopolitan vantage point, most of his academic compatriots adhered to the separation of German culture from Anglo-French civilization. It was 1916 all over again. As in his wartime work Cassirer sought to overcome the 'limited spiritual chauvinism' of his countrymen by presenting a humanist and cosmopolitan vision of European history.

Cassirer's study of the Renaissance and the first two volumes of *The Philosophy of Symbolic Forms* represented the high-water mark of his efforts during the Weimar period to formulate a lasting liberal humanist vision of the history of human spirit. In these studies the idea that human history witnessed the triumph of reason and the emergence of the free individual was made clear. Cassirer's liberal philosophy of history remained the same from the first (in 1902) to the last (in 1932) of his major publications in Germany. The extent of his success in keeping a balance between fact and theory was discernible by his ability to unify all the relevant cultural and historical data around a central theme and to produce compact, tightly argued, and well-documented studies. By these standards the work Cassirer did in co-operation with the Warburg group from 1923 to 1926 was a success. However, his major works after 1926 had a distinctly different tone to them. While their central message remained consistent with his previous work, his focus shifted back to abstract philosophical concerns. After 1926 a renewed interest in epistemological problems began to dominate Cassirer's reflections.

THE PHILOSOPHICAL LEVEL

Cassirer's new critique of culture was caught up in the developments in science and philosophy. A movement in European thought, often referred to as the revolt against positivism,[50] seriously challenged the foundations of Cassirer's effort to verify empirically his logistic analysis of mankind's progress from primitive to modern times. Even though Cassirer was not a positivist, there was enough of a positivist tinge to his work to put him on the defen-

sive. Here we encounter a central feature of Cassirer's thought: he was by nature an eclectic thinker. He often borrowed ideas from all sides of any argument and tried to integrate them into his own work. His attempt to verify the
Kantian transcendental vision of human progress with empirical facts
smacked of positivism in the sense that he believed that empirical facts were
important objects of knowledge. They were not secondary to philosophical
theory but an equal partner in any understanding of the human condition.
Nevertheless, he was not a positivist because he believed that an over-reliance
on empirical data ignored the vital role of human reason and judgment in
making those facts intelligible to man.

In France the philosophical attack on positivism originated in Bergson's
*Introduction to Metaphysics* (1903). After the publication of *Creative Evolution*
(1907) Bergson's initial critique of positivist science became known as life philosophy. His philosophy was at the height of its popularity from 1903 to 1914.
In Germany Husserl's *Logical Investigations* (1900–1) reopened the question of
what it meant to be empirical; again positivist ideals were thoroughly analysed and rejected. Husserl and Bergson both commanded the attention of
Europe's intelligentsia. Anti-positivism became a European phenomenon and
constituted an important element of the Weimar cultural milieu.

Cassirer reacted vigorously to the anti-positivist claims of men like Bergson,
Sorel, Husserl, and Heidegger. The effect of their ideas was to erode in four
major ways the basis of Cassirer's attempt to harmonize the conflicting demands of rationalism and empiricism. First, a spontaneous intuition of the
world rather than a rational, orderly cognition of it was demanded (Bergson
and Sorel). Secondly, too much attention was devoted either to epistemological matters (Husserl) or to metphysical examinations of existence (Bergson
and Heidegger). Thirdly, the role of empirical data was either overempha-
sized (Bergson) or diminished in importance (Husserl). And fourthly, the teleological notion of man progressing towards objective cognition was under-
cut; man was either submerged in the flux of being (Bergson) or caught up in
the finitude of historical existence (Heidegger). In all four cases, Cassirer's
ideal of balancing facts and ideas was ignored in favour of a dogmatic emphasis of either rational, existential, or empirical factors as the key to comprehending the human condition.

The negative relation of life philosophy to Cassirer's own ideals was noted
by one of his close friends, Dimitry Gawronsky. In his biographical sketch of
Cassirer, Gawronsky noted that the social theories of Sorel were the background for Cassirer's philosophy of symbolic forms.[51] While it is hard to say
precisely which elements of Sorel's ideas attracted Cassirer's attention, it is
clear that a Sorelian interest in the social role played by myths was upper-

most in Cassirer's mind. The importance of myth and cultural symbolism in human affairs was further impressed upon Cassirer by the events of the years 1916 to 1923. *Mythical Thought*, the second volume of *The Philosophy of Symbolic Forms* (published in 1925), was in effect Cassirer's attempt to answer the Sorelian view that myth and history were indistinguishable. Sorel's thoughts on the use of myths and symbols in human history was inseparable from Bergson's life philosophy. In fact, Cassirer's use of the symbol concept was an attempt to establish a more refined usage of the symbol in contrast to Bergson's and Sorel's intuitionist practices.

Bergson's version of a true science of experience purported to dispense with the use of abstract mathematical symbols and substitute intuitive knowledge. Instead of logically breaking up the flux of reality into lifeless intellectual symbols, Bergson maintained that his intuitive non-symbolic knowledge of reality could immediately place one within the movement of being itself.[52] Moreover, he felt that the current disillusionment with positivism (in 1903) revealed that positivism itself had abandoned true knowledge of reality for a relativized, abstract, and symbolic view of it. And his new metaphysics of existence, far from relativizing human knowledge by submerging it into the flux of existence, would by that very submersion attain absolutely true knowledge of existence: '*What is relative is the symbolic knowledge by pre-existing concepts, which proceeds from the fixed to the moving, and not the intuitive knowledge which installs itself in that which is moving and adopts the very life of things.* This intuition attains the absolute.'[53]

While Bergson felt that his intuitive philosphy could effectuate 'the much desired union of science and metaphysics,'[54] Sorel tried to apply to the historical behaviour of groups Bergson's integral intuitive method of grasping the whole of life's eternal flux.[55] Sorel's main goal was to understand how philosophical and ideological doctrines were related to social groups. He believed that to understand a doctrine it was not sufficient to study it in an abstract manner; rather one had to find out how it had been manifested in historical groups. The social manifestations of doctrines were what Sorel called myths; they were not descriptions of things, but expressions of a determination to act. The myth became for Sorel the prime instigator of all human social action. In his discussion of myth Sorel's Bergsonianism emerged. The myth, reflecting the eternal movement of life itself, could not be analysed or refuted; it had to be taken as a living whole since it was an intuitive synthesis of both the convictions of the social groups and the expression of these convictions.[56] As Bergson argued for his spontaneous intuition of reality, Sorel similarly maintained that there could be no rational analysis of myth into individual symbolic concepts. Myth, the single most important stimulant to social action, was beyond the grasp of rationality because it reflected a human reality that itself was non-rational. In the final analysis, the Bergson-Sorelian view of science and of man willingly submerged itself into what Cassirer referred to as the 'paradise of pure immediacy.'

The ultimate result of the life philosophy conception of knowledge and existence was to denigrate all that Cassirer valued. The rational method was unacceptable to the 'life philosophers,' and they sought to replace it with a criterion that relied on the test of intuition, practice, and a vital understanding of history.[57] Cassirer's analysis of myth in the philosophy of symbolic forms attempted to refute the Bergson-Sorel conception of knowledge. Where Sorel, using Bergson's intuitionist principles, placed myth beyond the range of human rationality, Cassirer showed that mythical consciousness played an important role in the emergence of reason in human history.

He also reacted quite vigorously to the claim of life philosophers that a certain psychological distance need not be present between reality (constant flux) and the logical comprehension (the pure form) of it. For Cassirer objective knowledge of human existence presupposed the ability of human reason to raise itself conceptually above immediate life experience. By reacting so strongly to the anti-rationalist claims of the life philosophers, Cassirer closed off, at least in his own mind, the possibility of becoming a dogmatic empiricist. However, in the process of arguing against those who would trap philosophy in the paradise of pure immediacy, he perhaps went too far in the other direction and became too much of a dogmatic rationalist. In this connection his reaction to Husserl and Heidegger becomes important.

Cassirer's reaction to Husserl and Heidegger was far more ambivalent than his reaction to Bergson and Sorel. While in the latter case Cassirer had only a negative response, in the former he partially approved of Husserl's search for the 'Archimedean point' of human knowledge, although he utterly rejected Heidegger's conception of human existence. The dialogue between neo-Kantianism and Husserl dated back to 1887–8. In those years Paul Natorp produced several essays which Husserl profitably used in the early stages of his phenomenology.[58] Even though basic differences in methodology remained, for the first quarter of the twentieth century Husserl maintained a continuous correspondence with Natorp and Cassirer.[59]

Husserl's philosophy had an unsettling effect on Cassirer's work. The Husserlian interest in 'the absolute giveness of the phenomena itself,'[60] which was stripped of all empirical content, appealed to the a priori tendency in Cassirer's own thought. This appeal was negative because it pulled him away from an analysis of concrete, factual matters and thereby distracted his attention from the task of empirically verifying his transcendental vision of human progress.

Husserl's conception of philosophy as an a priori, autonomous science rested on what he believed was an unalterable cleavage between true philosphical thinking (or scientific cognition) and the human mind's natural tendencies. For philosophy to be a rigorous science, Husserl argued, it had to treat consciousness and ideas as having an existence of their own and to 'bracket' all other existence. In effect, the ideal realm of scientific knowledge was severed from the natural realm of everyday human consciousness (that is, 'the human mind's natural tendencies').

The assertion that Husserl's philosophy had the effect of undermining the empirical element in Cassirer's theory of symbolic forms may sound odd, because Husserl claimed that his phenomenological investigations were aimed at establishing a true empirical science. Indeed, if there was one problem that was never far from his mind, it was 'the cardinal methodological question of every empirical science,' that is, the 'question as to how natural, "confused" experience can become scientific experience [and] ... how one can arrive at the determination of objectively valid empirical judgments.'[61] Nevertheless, Husserl's vigorous critique of positivism pushed him into an extreme philosophical position where the study of essential or phenomenal relationships overshadowed any examination of factual (empirical) data.

Husserl's thorough critique of positivism began with the appearance of his *Logical Investigations* (1900–1). In this work he systematically criticized psychologism – the attempt to unify the insights of psychology and logic – because logic, mathematics, and philosophy are a priori sciences that deal with rational concepts and logically necessary truths while psychology deals with facts and issues, with empirical statements which new evidence may show to be inaccurate. Henceforth, philosophical (scientific) rigour would preclude any attempt to mix the insights of philosophy and the experimental natural sciences. Husserl widened the split between the a priori and natural sciences when he pressed his attack on 'scientism,' that is, the claim that statements made on the basis of experimental data are premises in philosophical argument. He specifically rejected the 'scientism' of well-known positivists like Mach and Avenarius who argued that philosophical truth depends on the truth of scientific statements.

By 1911, in the essay on 'Philosophy as Rigorous Science,' Husserl's search for the unshakeable foundation of scientific knowledge carried him to a point where the division between common, everyday experience and the experience of 'the absolute giveness of phenomena' was complete. The latter experience was an 'essential intuition,' and Husserl went to great lengths to make clear that such intuition 'is in no way "experience" in the sense of perception, recollection and equivalent acts.' Moreover, 'essential intuitions' of phenomena constitute a 'knowledge of essence [which] is by no means matter-of-fact knowledge.'[62] Husserl's interest in such matter as 'essential intuition' and the 'absolute giveness of phenomena' and his discussion in *Ideen I* (1913) of 'pure consciousness' brought him in some respects very close to the pre-1914 position of the Marburg School.

It is not surprising that Husserl's philosophical reflections, with their logical a priori approach to scientific consciousness, caused an ambivalent reaction in Cassirer. On the one hand, the Husserlian analysis was obviously attractive to his Marburg neo-Kantian sensibility, with its interest in a logistic mathematical analysis of a priori ideas. On the other hand, Husserl's rigorous separation of philosophical (scientific) thought from the human mind's natural tendencies had grave implications for Cassirer's belief that human consciousness even on its most basic level (the mimetic stage) had within it the seeds of scientific cognition.

In spite of their differences, Cassirer and Husserl could agree that science was the rational means by which man could break out of his subjective condition and transcend his limited place in being and time. The situation was quite different with Heidegger. Heidegger began as a student of Natorp's and then became the heir apparent to Husserl's phenomenological philosophy. With the publication of *Being and Time* in 1927 Heidegger broke with Husserl and continued on a path which brought him to a head-on debate with Cassirer in 1929. Just as his favourable reaction to Husserl's work served to underscore Cassirer's commitment to the primacy of reason in the comprehension of the human condition, his confrontation with Heidegger indicated how vigorous Cassirer could be in the defence of the autonomy of the individual. Heidegger's whole orientation was a negation of Cassirer's idea of individual freedom.

For Heidegger finitude was the fundamental condition of human existence. Man's limited 'existence (or being) in time' was the essential ground upon and in which man resided. In his *Being and Time* Heidegger posed the critical question 'What is it that phenomenology is to "let us see"?'[63] The rest of his phenomenology gave this answer. In order to comprehend the foundations upon which we are to erect our knowledge of humanity's 'being in time,' it is necessary to recognize that it is not for us to get out of the circle of 'being there in the world' but to comprehend the fullness of that existential circle in the true historical and philosophical manner.[64]

For Heidegger the truth of existence was to accept the primordial call of being in time: the call to be what one is in time. It is in finitude that man begins and ends his existence. Science cannot provide a way out of the circle of existential finitude because it is a manifestation of that finitude. Heidegger had decided to immerse himself in concrete historical being and to produce a structural analysis of it. The goal of using scientific cognition as the means for man to understand existence by keeping a rational distance from it was dropped. In the final analysis, Heidegger's critique of man requires us to realize that we are completely immersed in the concrete, historical world. It was precisely Heidegger's belief in the fundamental finitude of man – in the limitedness of human existence – that Cassirer was to dispute in 1929.

## THE IDEOLOGICAL LEVEL

While philosophical developments tended to weaken the theoretical underpinnings of Cassirer's liberal, humanistic *Weltanschauung*, the political side of his world view was further undermined by developments in political and legal theory. During the Weimar Republic, liberal political philosophy was linked to the fate of neo-Kantian jurisprudence and natural law. These in their turn were firmly identified in the minds of many Germans with the liberal parliamentary regime. The hallmark of neo-Kantian legal and political thought was its excessive formalism, which led it to justify laws (legal norms) independently of actual existing conditions.

In the Weimar Republic the most prominent members of the neo-Kantian school of jurisprudence were Gustav Radbruch, Hans Kelsen, and Rudolf Stammler. Starting from the neo-Kantian belief that judgments of science and value were irreducibly different, they were very careful to distinguish between a given political dogma and the scientific evaluation of that dogma. Because they believed that the selection of political goals depended on value judgments and that the validity of these judgments could not be scientifically and logically demonstrated, they avoided the formulation of concrete social policies. Truth came to represent a methodological judgment made with regard to a definite value or ideal.[65] But what was the truth? What was the ideal that all Germans should adhere to? These questions the neo-Kantians would not and could not answer.

The effect of neo-Kantian jurisprudence was to separate the scientific study of law from political and social reality. This separation was particularly evident in the writings of Stammler and Kelsen, whose analyses of legal norms tended to deprive law of all social and political content. Stammler, as noted earlier, argued that absolute validity in legal questions could be attributed to pure forms only in accordance with a uniform plan. The endeavour to formulate a universally valid law with limited (that is, particular historical, social, or political) content was completely futile. Building upon Stammler's reduction of legal questions to pure forms, Kelsen elaborated on the relation of the political and social content of the law to the law's pure form. Kelsen's statement was at once bald and startling: 'Any content whatsoever can be legal; there is no human behaviour which could not function as the content of a legal norm.'[66] Kelsen believed that there was no way to judge the value content of a law. The validity of a law depended solely on its ability to meet the requirement of pure (logical) form. When Kelsen's pure theory of law was translated into concrete political terms the state and law became identical: 'Every experience of the life of a State, *every act of State, is a legal act.*'[67]

There is no doubt that the neo-Kantian school of law completely identified itself with the Weimar Republic. In fact Radbruch had signed a petition in April 1926 with other liberal colleagues like Meinecke, which called upon other intellectuals to support 'the existing democratic-republican political order.'[68] However, the neo-Kantian support of the republic was of dubious value for two reasons. Firstly, as liberals they believed that no specific course of action could be imposed on others; accordingly, they felt that a truly liberal state had to implement its policies with great care. This attitude led to vacillation on major political issues such as the socialization bill and the school law, and this indecisiveness was severely criticized by the opponents of both the liberals and the Weimar Republic. As one critic of the government put it: 'A state that does not venture vigorous action is a mockery.'[69] Secondly, the neo-Kantian emphasis on logical standards and the omission of concrete social and political facts was so philosophically extreme that it invited an equally extreme response. Neo-Hegelians like Erich Kaufmann and Carl Schmitt radically altered the neo-Kantian procedure. They emphasized the will to power *independent* of logical procedures; they sacrificed the logical and rational consideration of values to the overwhelming presence of concrete political and social facts.[70] To the neo-Kantian pure theory of the state of law, the neo-Hegelians countered with their own power theory of the state and of international law.

Kaufmann's bitter criticism of the neo-Kantians, already noted in an earlier chapter, was carried on by Carl Schmitt. Like Kaufmann he began with the concrete political and social situation and expounded his political principles on that basis. This was in the strongest possible contrast to the neo-Kantians, who deduced their political principles from abstract, a priori concepts. In his study of the intellectual and historical background of parliamentary government at that time, Schmitt argued that the Weimar Republic had lost its social, economic, and political grounding as the result of the rise of mass democracy. The parliamentary system, Schmitt argued, rested on the concept of free and open discussion; for it was the liberals' belief that the best policy for the nation would become known through public debate. But Schmitt pointed out that the rise of the masses and of large industrial interests had made public discussion 'an empty formality.'[71] Parliamentary political parties did not frankly discuss their social and economic interests with others. Rather they bargained with the other groups to get what they could for themselves. Temporary compromises, ad hoc coalitions, and irresolute government policies were the net result of such a governing process. Thus, the liberal parliamentary system became a facade for the mastery of parties and economic interests.[72] The best interests of the nation as a whole were ignored.

Schmitt stressed the ability of a government to take effective action in the interests of the entire citizenry. Whoever and whatever was capable of making decisions and initiating effective action was the truly constitutional power of the state.[73] For Schmitt, the constitution of a state did not arise from abstract norms but from the conscious determination to act. Constitutional power could legitimize itself only by undertaking decisive political acts.[74] Further, against the liberal belief that government should reflect the diversity of political values present in the nation, Schmitt argued that social and political divisions should be neither emphasized nor encouraged. On the contrary, the nation must be unified on the basis of the complete identification of the ruler and the ruled.[75] To Schmitt's way of thinking the Weimar Republic could neither unite nor effectively govern Germany precisely because it rested on an abstract philosophy that prevented the government from taking effective action. It is not surprising that when Hitler offered the possibility of a strong, unified, and powerful Germany, Schmitt supported him.[76]

The clash between the neo-Kantians and the neo-Hegelians in the academic community was significant in two senses. First, it revealed that the theoretical disputes in the German academic community had a political dimension. Secondly, the political dimension itself provided a direct link with the political events in Germany between 1900 and 1933. The alignment of the neo-Kantians with the Republic and of the neo-Hegelians against it was striking. The a priori rationalism of the neo-Kantian position was in the strongest contrast to the neo-Hegelian demands for unity, their will to action, their antilogicism, and their submission to the claims of political expediency as dictated by day-to-day events.

There was also a distinct social dimension to the rejection by the majority of legal neo-Kantianism. Most of the German intellectuals came from the *Mittelstand*[77] – an imprecise term for a variety of middle-class groups (artisans, small businessmen, white-collar workers, state officials, lawyers, doctors, school and university teachers, and students) who tended to align themselves with the status quo. They were usually very nationalistic, anti-socialist, and anti-Semitic. The events of 1914–18, the German military defeat, and the unstable republican government that emerged from the defeat were a calamity for the *Mittelstand*. While the revolution of 1918 had destroyed the political order, the new republican government had done very little to alleviate the social and economic pressures threatening this group.

Since many of the academics came from the *Mittelstand* their philosophical and political attitudes reflected the tensions within their class. Especially after the inflation of 1923, when the savings of many middle-class people were destroyed, many academics were no longer willing to compromise with the modern world. The majority of them, like Schmitt, translated their social anxieties into a revulsion against the Weimar Republic – in practice by voting for anti-Weimar political parties and in theory by adopting an anti-liberal position. The social tensions within Germany, which they saw as the consequence of the ethical and political relativism underlying the Weimar Republic, seemed to be the result of the abstract, a priori approach to political and social problems. They therefore rejected the neo-Kantians along with the concrete embodiment of their ideals, the Republic itself.

## THE RELATION OF THE WEIMAR CULTURAL MILIEU TO CASSIRER'S POST-1926 WORK

When Hitler came to power in 1933 the neo-Kantians and their liberal allies were a completely isolated group. The net intellectual effect of the revolt against positivism and the discrediting of liberal ideals both in theory and in practice was to bring into disrepute an attitude towards man, his society, and his history with which Cassirer was closely associated. The belief in the ability of human reason to provide an adequate means for coping with the human condition was explicitly linked by people on the political right and left to liberal democratic social and political philosophy. Unfortunately, the identification of liberal parliamentarianism with rationalism became strongest precisely at a time (in the 1920s and 1930s) when intellectual currents (the revolt against positivism) and social, political, and economic developments (the general instability and ineffectiveness of parliamentary regimes after the war) placed the liberal position in the worst possible light.

On the political right, people like Spengler attributed to the left the belief that reality could be mastered by abstractions, a definition so broad that German liberals, like Cassirer, who supported the DDP, could be interpreted as left wing. Interestingly, Spengler's position was later corroborated by Karl

Mannheim, who was affiliated with the SPD. Mannheim felt that the fundamental conflict of the age was the one between the masses, who demanded economic and social equality, and the social and political elites, who wanted to retain individual autonomy and social distinctions in a world order that increasingly demanded conformity. He associated a democratic political and social viewpoint with a certain kind of intellectual activity which he called the democracy of reason. He specifically connected Kantian philosophy to a democratic political stance.[79]

The very abstract nature of the Kantian democracy of reason made all points of view appear to be equal to one another and dependent on an activist, autonomous individual.[80] One view of politics, ethics, or philosophy was as good as the other so long as each view successfully met the requirements of logical form. Now, for Cassirer and other idealist liberals it was precisely the rigid adherence to logic which in their minds guaranteed the objectivity and universality of their own position. Nevertheless, the vast majority of educated Germans linked relativism to the abstract, a priori formalism of the liberals and of their form of government, the unpopular Weimar Republic.[81] Unfortunately, the liberals' opponents had a valid point. Something did seem to be missing from the liberal argument, namely, the ability to deal with concrete situations. In this regard the tendencies of Cassirer's work suffered along with the general liberal position.

Cassirer's own writings and those of other pro-republican intellectuals had virtually nothing to say about ethics – a striking omission in Cassirer's case because he had written on so many different topics. However, his neglect of ethics was not accidental. As a Kantian possessing an abstract and formalistic view of law and politics, he felt it was not within his competence to prescribe in concrete terms what was right or wrong for other people; he could only suggest the formal rules circumscribing all human activities. This attitude was not at all palatable to most Germans, especially after the economic collapse of the Western industrial system in 1929–33, when definitive social and economic policies were needed to alleviate the misery of the general populace.

In political terms the liberals were caught between the right and the left. Where the former saw the liberals as potential allies of the socialists, and hence as abetters of social unrest, the latter viewed them as indecisive reformers who would not fulfil their promises. While the liberals' fear of the masses put a limit on how far they would co-operate with the socialists, there was no corresponding limit to their movement towards the right, that is, their inclination to place middle-class economic interests and elitist sentiments above compromise with the socialists. Consequently, when the liberal electorate started to desert the liberal cause, they shifted to the political right (to the nationalists, the economic and state parties, and the national socialists). The flight of the electorate from the centre to the political right and left started in June 1920. The shift in liberal ranks to the right from the centre DDP to the anti-socialist DVP was evident in the elections of 1920. While in 1919 the DDP received about 80 per cent of the liberal vote as opposed to 20 per cent for the DVP, in 1920 the DDP's portion dropped to 37 per cent and the DVP's rose to 63 per cent. Furthermore, the total liberal vote declined by 800,000. Interestingly, if the net losses of the DDP and DVP are compared to the gains of the nationalist and economic parties in Breslau, Liegnitz, Magdeburg, and Frankfurt (Oder),[82] it is obvious that the liberals losses became the right wing's gains. While the movement to the right was slowed from 1924 to 1928, in September 1930 it began again in earnest and did not stop until Hitler gained power in January 1933. The German electorate's rightward movement did not leave Cassirer unaffected. From 1930 he voted for the State Party, which itself moved moderately to the right by abandoning the DDP's emphasis on social co-operation, especially with the socialists, and emphasizing the need for strong and effective leadership.

As a Kantian, a rationalist, and a liberal Cassirer saw the intellectual and political consequences of the revolt against the democracy of reason.[83] He realized that either reason or unreason prevailed in political and academic activities. Either one accepted a cosmopolitan and rational view of man and the cosmos, or one would surrender to a limited spiritual chauvinism. One believed that man ultimately understood himself in so far as he was part of humanity in general, or one would deny the universal humanity in each man in the name of the nation-state. As always, Cassirer strongly opposed the one-sided nationalist approach. For the truth of existence and the truth of knowledge was comprehensible only if one accepted the most universal standpoint: the standpoint of reason. Only on the basis of the rationalist world view could the fundamental equality of all men be fully realized. However, in order to defend the primacy of reason in human affairs in the context of the cultural situation of 1900–33, Cassirer yielded to the pressures of the times in becoming a dogmatist of one sort or another. He inclined towards an intellectual extreme he had always wanted to avoid. In this respect the course of his work from 1927 to 1933 represented a resurgence of the logical apriorism of the Marburg School.

# 10

# Cassirer's final defence
of reason in Germany (1927–33)

INTRODUCTION

After 1926 Cassirer shifted his priorities. He became more interested in purely theoretical issues, like the logical content and preconditions of human consciousness, and less concerned with empirical facts themselves. This is not to say that after 1926 Cassirer completely ignored facts in his arguments; rather, the extent of the influence of empirical data on the development of his arguments was lessened. In Cassirer's later Weimar thought there is a shift of nuance in the relation between a transcendental critique of human culture and the attempt to verify that critique empirically.

A certain rigidity seems to have crept into Cassirer's work between 1927 and 1929 and hardened into dogmatism after 1929, indicating how much his own thought was succumbing to the pressures of the times. Between 1927 and 1933 the tone of Cassirer's argument became more mechanical. He tended to rely on repeated affirmations of his own central articles of faith: that reason was important because it opened the way for an understanding of the universal basis of human freedom; and that each man was free in so far as humanity as a whole was capable of achieving freedom. In a word, after 1927, Cassirer was intellectually on the defensive.

While tending his intellectual defences Cassirer also came out in public in defence of the Weimar Republic. Beginning with his speech of 11 August 1928 at the ninth anniversary celebration of the Weimar constitution, Cassirer apparently felt obliged to display his pro-republican sentiments.[1] His timing was reminiscent of his earlier protest against the effects of the war on German society in 1916. Unfortunately, as in 1916, his public stance after 1928 was too late to have any decisive impact on the opinions of others; he was merely reaffirming the sentiments of a politically isolated group.

In political terms Cassirer was responding to the decline of liberalism in Germany. The theoretical decline of idealist liberalism has already been discussed in the context of the disputes between the neo-Kantians' and neo-Hegelians' legal and political philosophies. The practical decline of idealist liberalism in Germany was further accentuated by the DDP's losses in the election of 20 May 1928, in which its percentage of the popular vote declined to 4.9, and the number of deputies elected diminished from thirty-two to twenty-five. These meagre results were a far cry from the original DDP success on 19 January 1919, where it captured 18.6 per cent of the vote and elected seventy-five deputies to the Reichstag. While Cassirer himself reacted in August 1928 to political developments, his uncle, Max Cassirer, a prominent Berliner, in June 1928 had participated in the meetings of the Liberal Union in order to see what could be done to prevent the further erosion of liberal support. Max Cassirer, along with liberal notables like Friedrich Meinecke and Gerhard Anschütz, signed a statement urging all liberals to unite and forget their differences, as otherwise liberalism would cease to be a significant factor in German politics.[2]

The electoral results of May 1928 were very disappointing and even alarming to many supporters of the DDP because it was felt that the last few years of prosperity would have provided a suitable economic backdrop for a liberal resurgence. If the DDP could not win under these favourable conditions, it was unlikely to preserve its support among the electorate if things got even slightly worse. In 1928 many liberal democrats intuitively recognized the danger threatening their political position. Not only was the future of the DDP placed under a cloud but the future of the Republic as well. For the Republic was largely the creation of liberal democrats, like Hugo Preuss and Max Weber, who were instrumental in drafting the Weimar constitution. Cassirer undoubtedly had in mind the declining popularity of liberalism on 11 August 1928 when he asked Germany to display more enthusiasm for liberal republican sentiments.[3]

CASSIRER'S NEW FORMALISM: *THE PHILOSOPHY OF SYMBOLIC FORMS VOLUME 3 AND ITS SIGNIFICANCE*

The defensive posture of German liberalism was the major factor in the ideological environment surrounding Cassirer's later works. In the two years preceeding the liberal setback of 1928, Cassirer's own work had reached a turning point, which was to be further aggravated by the decline in liberal fortunes. The third volume of *The Philosophy of Symbolic Forms, The Phenomenology of Knowledge,* completed in 1927, presents an interesting example of

Cassirer at an intellectual crossroads. As might be expected, his disaffection with current events was most fully expressed on the philosophical level. Throughout the mid-1920s he increasingly felt the need to produce a lasting intellectual synthesis, and the third volume of *The Philosophy of Symbolic Forms* was intended to achieve this.[4] Consequently, he returned to his earliest works so that he could rethink his entire position.[5] Cassirer himself considered the first two volumes of *The Philosophy of Symbolic Forms* to be steps in the direction of his new synthesis. But did he accomplish what he set out to do? Or did he vacillate between his old Marburg apriorism and the ideas of the Weimar cultural milieu?

Cassirer's introduction to the third volume seemed straightforward enough. Language, myth, and art were designated as symbolic forms. He then argued that the philosophy of symbolic forms aspired to know the special qualities of these forms and 'to understand each one according to its nature and the laws of its structure.'[6] Significantly, Cassirer held that each symbolic form was not to be analysed in terms of its 'empirical' aspects, but rather in terms of its 'pure content.' He explained his shift of interest from the empirical to the 'ideal' or 'pure' aspect of philosophy as follows:

The Philosophy of Symbolic Forms in general inquires not into the empirical source or consciousness but into its pure content. Instead of pursuing its temporal, generating causes, The Philosophy of Symbolic Forms is oriented solely toward what 'is in it' – toward apprehending and describing its structural forms. Language, myth and theoretical knowledge are all taken as fundamental forms of the objective spirit, whose being it must be possible to disclose and understand purely as such independently of the question of its becoming.[7]

In these lines Cassirer was ostensibly discussing the general nature of the philosophy of symbolic forms to date; in fact, he was revealing his new orientation. In contradiction to his assertion that *The Philosophy of Symbolic Forms* inquired into the pure content and not the empirical source of human consciousness, his own studies of language and myth, particularly the latter, had concentrated on the empirical, temporal generating causes of these particular symbolic forms. Accordingly, he had devoted nearly a third of his study of myth to discussing a few of the historical (that is, temporal) conditions supporting various mythical practices.

On the surface the third volume seemed to complement the two earlier works, where the latter traced the emergence of the scientific standpoint in the collective efforts of all mankind, the former tried to perceive the same movement in individual consciousness. But even though the third volume was itself given a tripartite division – that is, individual consciousness was divided into the perceptive, intuitive, and cognitive levels to parallel the mimetic, analogical, and symbolic levels in language and myth[8] – there was still something quite distinct about his phenomenology of knowledge which separated it from his previous analyses of the linguistic and mythical forms.

The distinction hinged on his professed interest in the pure content as opposed to the empirical source of consciousness. From 1916 to 1926, Cassirer had moved towards a more realistic, empirical, and broader conception of man; from 1927 to 1933, he increasingly returned to the abstract, logical apriorism of his pre-1914 ideas. In the third volume of *The Philosophy of Symbolic Forms* he decided to comprehend the evolution of human consciousness by a primarily logistic approach. He intended to produce an analysis of the different formations of human thought which would clearly disclose the formal, abstract 'conditions of their possibility.'[9] Cassirer had indeed returned to his pre-1914 formalistic Kantian orientation. The phrase 'the conditions of their possibility' was his admission that he was returning to the Kantian task of showing that the conditions of the possibility of experience in general were also the conditions of the possibility of the objects of experience. Cassirer explicitly admitted his return to Marburg Kantian concerns when he said that the third volume represented 'a return to the investigations with which I began my work in systematic philosophy two decades ago.'[10]

While in philosophical terms Cassirer's post-1927 work marked an admirable return to earlier theoretical concerns, this turning in his thought was still disappointing. The third volume was not a philosophically intriguing conclusion to his earlier work. No new theoretical ground was broken in relation to either the first or second volumes or to *Substance and Function*. Cassirer's return to his pre-1914 interest in purely epistemological matters may be understood as a relapse in the sense that he did not continue his post-1917 advance into the humanities. Instead of continuing his expansion of Kantian thought into the realm of common experience, Cassirer turned back to the realm of pure forms.

The marked difference in content between the third and the preceding two volumes of *The Philosophy of Symbolic Forms* tells the tale. In the first two volumes Cassirer usually cited factual evidence to support his arguments; in the third volume he spent a good deal of time arguing with other philosophers. The text was filled with philosophical discussion in relation to the work of other thinkers of the Weimar cultural milieu like Heidegger, Bergson, and Husserl.[11] In fact, Cassirer's conception of phenomenology reflected Husserl's belief that phenomenological science required the examination of the structures of objective knowledge 'without concern for the "reality" of their objects.'[12] Instead of considering the evolution of the world view of reason and exact knowledge primarily in its factuality, as he had done with language and myth, in the third volume of *The Philosophy of Symbolic Forms* he would attempt to comprehend this world view 'in its necessary intellectual mediations.'[13] This shift of emphasis away from empirical factuality was essentially an acceptance of the Husserlian analysis of pure phenomena as well as a return to a Kantian interest in epistemology.

Cassirer's admiration for Husserl had been growing since the early 1920s. By 1925 he considered Husserl one of the foremost advocates of scientific philosophy in Germany. Cassirer's warm support for Husserl was not surprising, as the latter's phenomenology dealt with many issues that the Marburg neo-Kantians had considered before the first world war. Husserl's study of 'pure consciousness' and 'the absolute giveness of phenomena' was of great interest to a man who after 1926 sought to apprehend the world by reducing man's cognition of it to 'necessary intellectual mediations.'

Cassirer's logical a priori tendency reasserted itself especially when he envisioned the use of a structural analysis of consciousness and of its necessary intellectual mediations as the means of apprehending 'the original substance of all reality' through an 'analysis of consciousness.'[14] If anything Cassirer's new interest was a mixture of Hegel and Husserl, with emphasis on the latter's thought. For though Hegel wanted to discover the whole truth of existence through an analysis of the progressive, rational unfolding of human consciousness, it was Husserl who argued that the basis of scientific truth necessitated the apprehension of 'pure consciousness.'

A number of conflicting tendencies were apparent in Cassirer's response to Husserl. Initially, his interest in analysing the conditions of the possibility of experience was Kantian. However, he felt that in order to accomplish this analysis he had to go beyond Kant. This entailed a 'structural analysis of consciousness' (Kantian again), but Cassirer's assertion that the analysis could reveal 'the original substance of all reality' was a move in the direction of accepting that 'reality in itself' was knowable. This Kant would not have said, though Hegel might have. Further, Cassirer's analysis of the phenomenology of knowledge, his assertions to the contrary notwithstanding, was at least as much Husserlian as it was Hegelian. In his own phenomenology Hegel always sustained the belief that existence and knowledge were ultimately a unity. And it was Husserl, following Kant to some extent, who tried to show the necessary connection between the phenomenal world of consciousness and pure relations. In effect, existence depended on consciousness; the two were not a unity. Cassirer's rethinking of Kant was done with Husserl's work in mind. Its result was a phenomenology of knowledge which was Kantian in so far as it stressed 'pure relations' and un-Kantian in its quest for reality itself. It was Hegelian in so far as it presupposed a certain progression towards scientific cognition and un-Hegelian in that it abjured Hegel's empiricism, that is, his interest in the totality of 'concrete spiritual life forms.'

When taken as a whole Cassirer's renewed emphasis of purely epistemological concerns indicated that his own reflections were turning towards an abstract structural analysis of pure thought. The excessive formalism inherent in neo-Kantianism gained the upper hand in his work. As if to confirm deliberately the new formalist direction of his studies, Cassirer made a distinction between the three levels of his analysis that he had not made before. In his earlier studies of symbolic forms he did not sharply differentiate the first two steps of his triadic analysis from the third. In the first two volumes the progression from the mimetic to the analogical and finally to the symbolic stage of consciousness was gradual and continuous. This did not happen in volume three. The perceptive and intuitive levels of consciousness were subsumed under the natural world concept,[15] and this in turn was rigidly separated from the cognitive level of consciousness, the level where the building up of scientific knowledge occurred. In effect, Cassirer accepted Husserl's basic division of scientific, philosophical consciousness from the mind's natural tendencies.

In defending his rigid separation of the natural and scientific levels of human consciousness Cassirer relied on the belief 'that theory can achieve the desired closeness to reality only by placing a certain distance between itself and reality.'[16] With this kind of claim Cassirer unwittingly revealed how far the life philosophers' arguments had pushed him onto his old epistemological track. He was so concerned with preserving the integrity of science and preventing it from being submerged in pure immediacy that he placed scientific cognition in its own ethereal realm. Science no longer emerged gradually from the natural world and from naive consciousness, rather it suddenly appeared on the highest (that is, cognitive) level of human perception of the world in the form of a strictly theoretical concept. After having made his leap onto the cognitive level, Cassirer tended to restrict his analysis to abstract philosophical matters. His loss of desire to achieve a balanced, as distinct from a philosophically one-sided, view of man was evident. An analysis of theoretical knowledge had replaced the desire to find the relation between man and his natural environment.

The last third of volume three was devoted to elaborating the same point Cassirer had made in *Substance and Function* in 1910: 'We do not need to know the objectivity of absolute things, but we do require the objective determinacy of the way of experience itself.'[17] The symbol concept and symbolic thinking were, according to Cassirer, the only means for grasping the objective determinacy of experience; or, to use Kantian language, the only means for understanding the conditions of the possibility of both experience and the objects of experience. Only through the symbol could the intellect transform 'the succession of the steps of thought' into 'a pure simultaneity of synopsis.'[18] Cassirer then discussed this synopsis in relation to the development of mathematics and physics. Here again his analysis was a disappointing rehash of his prewar thoughts on the subject. There may be a clue in all this as to why Cassirer's philosphy had a limited appeal in Germany. In spite of his advance beyond neo-Kantianism after 1916, he always seemed to be consolidating philosophical ground that was already largely laid out by Kant, Hermann Cohen, and Paul Natorp, while philosophers like Husserl and Heidegger appeared to be embarking on new philosophical paths.

Cassirer finally published the third volume of *The Philosophy of Symbolic Forms* in the summer of 1929. Several months later, in November 1929, on the occasion of his becoming the rector of the University of Hamburg, he gave a speech on the changing nature of philosophical concepts of truth. In this speech he summarized his 'new' theoretical orientation and affirmed his commitment to the primacy of the functional ideal (or coherence theory) of truth over the substantialist (or correspondence) conception of truth.[19] He repeatedly emphasized the 'pure' logical aspect of his functional ideal of truth. 'The bare extensive criterion of knowledge' could in his eyes no longer be justified. It had to be replaced by 'an intensive criterion,'[20] which was grounded solely in human cognition, not in the material world of objects. Here again Cassirer revealed that the equilibrium between fact and theory, between concrete empirical data and conceptual abstractions, in his system of symbolic forms had been upset in favour of the abstract, a priori approach.

In summary, Cassirer's attempt to preserve what he considered to be the middle ground between dogmatic empiricism, which dissolved all concepts into empirically given objects, and dogmatic rationalism, which reduced 'every datum to the form of its conceptual determination.'[21] had failed because he let the latter absorb the former. His own symbolic conception of knowledge had itself lapsed into a one-sided rationalism.

## THE CASSIRER-HEIDEGGER DEBATE

The big philosophical event in Germany in 1927 was the publication of Heidegger's *Being and Time*. Although Cassirer had completed his chapters on space and time in the third volume of *The Philosophy of Symbolic Forms* before the appearance of Heidegger's work, he felt compelled to distinguish his own position from Heidegger's. He summed up the difference between himself and Heidegger as follows:

The Philosophy of Symbolic Forms does not question this temporality which Heidegger discloses as the ultimate foundation of existentiality and attempts to explain in its diverse factors. But our inquiry begins *beyond* this sphere, at precisely the point where a transition is effected from this existential temporality to the *form* of time.[22]

Cassirer clearly recognized that he and Heidegger were not talking about the same thing. He spoke of his own philosophy as beginning 'beyond' Heidegger's sphere of inquiry. Toni Cassirer made the revealing remark that her husband found the atmosphere and writing style of Heidegger's work uncongenial to his sensibilities.[23] Apparently, Cassirer's disagreement with Heidegger went beyond a philosophical difference of opinion. The true dimension of the differences separating the two men became clear in the personal debate between them.

In the same year that Cassirer published the final volume of *The Philosophy of Symbolic Forms* and delivered his speech on the functional ideal of truth, he had also debated Heidegger at Davos, Switzerland. The Cassirer-Heidegger discussions between 17 March and 6 April 1929, as well as the articles they wrote as a consequence of those discussions, represented at the highest intellectual level the ideological divisions of Weimar Germany. The political dimension to the debate was also revealed in their respective attitudes towards the Republic, which Cassirer supported while Heidegger did not.

The Cassirer-Heidegger confrontation was also interesting because it showed how even the most technical philosophical disagreements were never far removed from fundamental political and cultural values. The confrontation may be divided into three levels. On the philosophical level, Cassirer and Heidegger were debating the meaning and significance of Kant's work. Soon it became apparent that their debate involved two different conceptions of man (anthropological level). Finally, these different conceptions of man were associated with different political ideologies.

Generally, the difference between Heidegger and Cassirer was that while the former stressed the ontological (or existential) dimension to Kant's philosophy and criticized the Marburg reduction of knowledge to the pure functions of intellect,[24] Cassirer emphasized the logical side of Kant's critique and its opening up of the possibility of human freedom. He also criticized Heidegger's underestimation of the independent and lifelike quality of thought.[25]

Technically, the difference between Cassirer and Heidegger rested on their conflicting views of the relation between reason and existence. Heidegger placed the transcendental imagination and intuition at the centre of Kant's critique. Pure reason was assigned a secondary position with respect to the imagination and the intuitions which came from it. Heidegger argued that it was incorrect to maintain, as the Marburg neo-Kantians had, that the pure concepts of reason could be derived by logical analysis,[26] for reason was not separate from the imagination, which itself was rooted in the sensible, living world. Reason was therefore not susceptible to logical constraint since logic pertained only to the realm of abstract ideas. Further, Heidegger argued that reason in fact was a 'sensible reason.'[27] It was not, as the Marburg neo-Kantians thought, independent and prior to the finite temporality of actual historical existence.

Cassirer severely criticized Heidegger on this last point. He argued that Heidegger's 'sensible reason' would have made no sense to Kant. Reason by its very nature was supersensuous and supertemporal. In this instance Heidegger was not speaking as a commentator but as a usurper of Kant's ideas.[28] Cassirer then pressed his attack on Heidegger's central thesis: that all the conditions of knowledge and reason rested on the transcendental imagination. According to Cassirer, Heidegger had misconstrued the relation between pure reason and existence and had failed to recognize the independent character of thought in Kant's philosophy. For in Kant's system reason was independent of sensuous intuition and of the imagination. Reason went beyond the conditioned phenomenal realm of actual existence.[29]

Underlying Heidegger's conception of a 'sensible reason' was the conviction that reason itself was an integral part of the essential finitude of man. Cassirer's attack on Heidegger's belief in a 'sensible reason' was therefore inseparable from a critique of Heidegger's concept of man. Cassirer argued that Heidegger misunderstood Kant's idea of humanity when he interpreted man in terms of *Dasein*.[30] *Dasein* – meaning literally, 'being there' in the finite, temporal historical world – permeated every turn of Heidegger's argument. There was no way out, Heidegger argued, of the essential finiteness of human existence; human thought could reflect only the essential finitude of man. As Heidegger put it: 'The comprehension of Being itself is the innermost essence of finitude,'[31] or expressed another way, 'finitude resides in the essential structure of knowledge itself.'[32] Since man could not avoid the essential fact that he was thrown (Heidegger's notion of *Geworfenheit*) into finite existence (*Dasein*), human reason was misled and even deluded if it thought that it could avoid the anxiety inherent in man's comprehension that he was finite and not essentially free.[33]

Cassirer's response to Heidegger's view of man was predictable. He envisioned philosophy as the means of liberating man from his fear of the finitude of existence.[34] When asked by which road man could reach the infinite and transcend his finite, anxiety-ridden existence, Cassirer responded that it was only through the realm of spiritual form that man himself becomes infinite. Further, this 'realm of spirit' was not metaphysical in the sense that it was imposed on man by the very nature of his existence; rather it was a 'spiritual world which he has created himself. It is the very hallmark of his infinity that he could, and can, build it up.'[35]

In a very profound sense, Cassirer and Heidegger were talking past each other. Heidegger himself noted 'that what I call *Dasein* is not translatable into Cassirer's vocabulary.'[36] *Dasein* and the existential anxiety of being in time were specifically excluded from philosophy by Cassirer. As far as he was concerned, philosophy was the very means of overcoming that anxiety. For him Kant always remained a thinker of the Enlightenment who strove for illumination even when he thought about the deepest and most hidden grounds of human existence.[37] Heidegger possessed an altogether different conception of knowledge and human existence. Heidegger's world was the world of Kierkegaard, where anxiety, finitude, and the whirlpool of primordial questioning extinguished the rays of light of reason.

The philosophical and anthropological differences separating Cassirer and Heidegger extended into the political realm and were dramatically highlighted in May 1933. In the very month that Cassirer fled from Germany because of the Nazi regime's anti-liberal, anti-Semitic policies, Heidegger accepted the rectorship of Freiburg University with a speech praising the new regime.[38] While he later withdrew his support from the regime his initially favourable reaction to it was no accident.

In his study of several anti-republican and pro-Nazi intellectuals, C. G. von Krockow tried to show that the presuppositions and consequences of their common world outlook could be understood only in relation to a given legal and political standpoint.[39] The works of Schmitt and Heidegger were interpreted as being complementary to one another. We have already seen that Schmitt stressed the primacy of political will in the legal constitution of a state. His decisionism was complemented by Heidegger's determination 'to stand with being,' and with the destiny of the German people. Heidegger developed his conception of being (*Dasein*) in a violence-filled vision of national existence. The spiritual world of a people was for him synonymous with 'the strength of the profoundest preservation of its [the people's] earthly and racial forces' and an expression of 'the power of the innermost agitation and the most penetrating convulsions of its being.'[40] Instead of a universal human nature, which people like Cassirer stressed, the unique 'volkisch' substance of a nation was extolled. On the basis of this new national substance arose the belief that all laws emanated from the living law of the people.[41] With this thought the cosmopolitan, supranational view of man, politics, and law was rejected. Each people had its own historical mission to fulfil. For Heidegger this was particularly true of the German people, whose destiny was embodied in the life and deeds of the Führer, Adolf Hitler.[42] Thus Heidegger aligned his philosophy with a regime that completed on the national and political level the intellectuals' revolt against the liberal, cosmopolitan *Weltanschauung* associated with the Weimar Republic.[43]

## CASSIRER'S DEFENCE OF THE REPUBLIC AND HIS NEO-KANTIAN SENSE OF LAW

Cassirer neither wavered in his support of the Republic nor had any illusions about the results of a political regime headed by a charismatic leader of the people.[44] Between 1928 and 1930 he made his strongest statements in support of the Republic. On the ninth anniversary of the promulgation of the republican constitution on 11 August 1928, he said in a speech that the republican idea of government as such was not foreign to German intellectual history; on the contrary, it came from German idealism itself.[45] It was typical of Cassirer not to give the credit for specific ideas to one nation. Republican ideals were the result of a genuine interchange of ideas between Wolff, Leibniz, Blackstone, Rousseau, and Kant.[46] All of these thinkers worked towards the formulation of the basic liberal, humanitarian idea that the individual as such and humanity as a whole possessed basic inalienable rights. As a consequence, and in contrast to Heidegger's position, Cassirer stressed that humanity as a whole and not only one national people was the proper scope of political theory.[47]

Cassirer's speech is interesting not only because it characterizes his political orientation at a specific point in time, but because it reveals both the consistency of his thought and his anomalous relation to German society in general. His argument that a genuine interchange of ideas occurred between Germany, France, and England, specifically his passages dealing with the relation between Wolff, Blackstone, and the ideas of the French Revolution, were literally a transcription of passages from *Freiheit und Form*. In other words, Cassirer's political philosophical orientation had remained virtually unchanged since 1916. Yet Cassirer and his listeners knew how little popular support there was in Germany for the liberal democratic ideals of the seventeenth and eighteenth centuries. German thinkers may well have made major philosophical contributions to republican political ideals, but very few people in Germany in 1928 were interested in this theoretical dimension of the Weimar Republic's origins.[48]

Cassirer's defence of liberalism might as well have been delivered in a vacuum. Outside his immediate audience, his words fell on deaf ears. His political isolation was not only a personal problem; it was an historical reality for all German liberals, especially if they were Jews. The Jews were thought of as cultural aliens, as was made clear by Othmar Spann's attack on Cassirer and Marburg neo-Kantianism.[49] In March 1929 Spann, a leading conservative writer, published an article dealing with the contemporary cultural crisis. He complained that foreigners like Cohen and Cassirer, with their defective Kantianism, had played so important a part in the last sixty years of Kantian interpretation; it was time for Germans to interpret Kant for themselves.[50] Spann also saw the spread of liberal democracy as an integral part of the cultural crisis; in his mind democracy would inevitably lead to anarchy.[51] The breakdown of German culture by a foreign form of thinking (Marburg Kantianism) was part of the spread of democracy in Europe. Spann, like Spengler and Mannheim, firmly linked contemporary German Kantianism to the spread of liberal democratic ideals.

The association in German public opinion of liberalism, democracy, and anarchy with neo-Kantianism highlights the dilemma of German liberalism after 1918. Liberals like Cassirer were obliged to formulate their ideas in a nation where the climate of opinion and the political situation put constraints on the range of action and argument. Ever since the signing of the Versailles Treaty in June 1919 the Weimar Republic had at best been tolerated by the majority of Germans. Its inability to maintain domestic peace from 1918 to 1923 or to stop the disastrous inflation of 1923 left most Germans disgusted with the ineffectiveness of the regime, and as the depression worsened after 1929 all public confidence vanished. In fact, after September 1930 the Republic kept itself in power by issuing presidential decrees. Liberal democracy had clearly failed in Germany. Within this context fervent liberals could not do much for their government. Cassirer's predisposition to stay out of active politics might be seen as a personal matter, but even if he had wanted to do more for his country, as a Jew and a liberal, he would not have been accepted. Here his personal limitations acquired a larger social and ideological dimension. The only public activity open to Cassirer was to defend liberal democracy through public speaking engagements.

One of these was a speech remarkable because it was delivered on 18 January 1930, the day commemorating the founding of the Reich in 1871, which for many Germans had become a substitute for 11 August as a day for national celebration. Whereas the former date signified the unification of Germany by victory in the military and political fields, the latter was associated with the shame of Germany's defeat in 1918 and the ineffectiveness of the Weimar Republic. January 18 was therefore a day on which many Germans gave full vent to their anti-republican sentiments, yet Cassirer chose it as an occasion to speak forcefully of the Weimar constitution of 11 August 1919 as giving a new confirmation as well as a new vigour to the original unification of Germany.[52] Cassirer's statement was symptomatic of the inclination of many liberals to envision the Republic as a continuation of the Reich. In fact, his position was very similar to Hugo Preuss' earlier statement of 1923, which subsequently became very popular in liberal ranks, that the German Reich could only be continued as a republic.[53]

Cassirer's most fascinating political statement was delivered on 30 June 1930 in a speech on the changes in conceptions and theories of state in German intellectual history. It was revealing both for what it said and for what it omitted. Cassirer's analysis of the state characteristically remained on the level of ideas; the harsh realities of the time, particularly the growing impact of the depression on Germany, were ignored. He was still analysing Germany from the vantage point of 'German spirit';[54] hence, his speech focused on 'ways of thinking' and 'theories of state' in the history of German thought. He could not come down to the level of concrete political and economic realities. In this connection, Cassirer showed himself unwilling to correct one of Kant's errors. In his speech of 11 August 1928 he had ruefully admitted that Kant's substitution of an examination of the categorical imperative for the study of concrete historical facts had the unfortunate effect of throwing German philosophical reflection of political and historical events back into the realm of pure ideas.[55] Yet even though he was witnessing the ineffectiveness of neo-Kantian legal and political thought in dealing with Germany's problems, he still could not force himself to break out of the Kantian spell.

Just as Heidegger and the neo-Hegelian legal philosophers like Schmitt were all too willing to dwell on the immediate needs of the German people and to demand forceful political leadership, Cassirer adopted the neo-Kantian philosophy of law and stressed the need for abstract and absolutely valid legal norms in order to sustain the fundamental unity of the state – a state rooted in a common consciousness and not in purely material concerns:

The idea of the State rests upon the idea of law – but this last idea cannot be derived from positive ordinances [that is, laws passed by men in a specific historical context], rather they represent an *absolutely, universally valid norm* which is first grounded ... in the communty of reason ... All particular lawful norms are ultimately legitimized in universal legal principles; *all actual circumstances proceed from a pure ideal, all temporal bonds and conditions return to an unconditioned value norm. There could be no real foundation of law and no true foundation of society and state, if this were not the case.*[56]

This passage has been quoted at length because it clearly shows where Cassirer's functional ideal of truth and knowledge was translated into a specific view of politics. His interest in absolutely, universally valid norms, his contention that all facts proceed from pure ideals, together with his belief that the foundations of laws, societies, and nations were rooted in these abstract norms, clearly demonstrated Cassirer's adherence to the neo-Kantian formalistic view of man and society. As in his phenomenology of knowledge, he tended to stress the formal conditions of the possibility of (political) experience. Hence, he placed the absolutely, universally valid norms at the base of politics in the same way he envisioned 'the pure development of thought' as the foundation of all knowledge. In both instances, philosophical and political, Cassirer retreated from empirical reality, that is, he preferred to deal with abstract ideas rather than with facts.

There were, however, practical reasons for Cassirer's new stance. He feared that too much involvement in the immediate reality of world affairs would endanger the pursuit of truth. Hence, in his speech Cassirer advised German universities to stay out of politics; the universities should serve the state by pursuing the truth and not by permitting themselves to become another political battlefield.[57] He intuitively felt that an overconcern with immediate realities was inconsistent with true philosophical activity. We can now see the contemporary aspect to Cassirer's philosophical differences with Heidegger. From Cassirer's viewpoint, Heidegger's obsession with 'being in time,' with the essential historicity and finitude of human existence, indicated a surrender to the immediacy of historical being. Such a surrender, according to Cassirer, would only pervert the pursuit of truth and ultimately prevent man's transcendence of his own limitations.[58]

While it is true that after 1926 Cassirer's analysis of man became more abstract, he still maintained his cosmopolitan and humanistic overview of history and with it tried to hold the middle ground. As in 1916 when he was trying to salvage the remains of German *Geist,* he turned to Goethe. In his mind, to stand with Goethe was to stand with what was best in Germany.[59] Thus, Cassirer used Goethe's thoughts on education as the jumping-off point for his own reflections on contemporary Germany. Goethe's conception of education, according to Cassirer, began with the idea that while prophets stood either on the left or the right, mankind as a whole stood in the middle.[60] Goethe's educational goal was to bring about the liberation of a humanity that was the middle in so far as it united within itself the extremes of a concrete, finite existence with the possibility of a universal, infinite existence. Man was universal only in so far as he comprehended the bond linking him with the rest of humanity; with this realization each man could attain his true individuality.[61] It therefore became imperative to Cassirer to make clear to his contemporaries that a true and total conception of man was possible only when that conception rested on a cosmopolitan, supranational vision of man.

The ideological overtone to Cassirer's use of Goethe becomes clearer especially when one focuses on the idea of liberation. Goethe wanted to be remembered as the liberator of his people,[62] as the man who helped Germany overcome the one-sidedness of its own national existence. This argument was first made in 1916 in *Freiheit und Form*. When Cassirer's resurrection of this argument in 1932 is seen against the backdrop of rising nationalism coupled with the collapse of the middle classes as a viable economic social and political group, his own defensive posture becomes more obvious.

In 1932 Cassirer again turned to a discussion of political philosophy. His article on the nature and development of natural law was the third time in four years that he had dealt with political philosophy per se. His defence of natural law was most understandable because the presuppositions of his cosmopolitan conception of humanity grew out of the same body of thought that natural law did.[63] Natural law was based on a cosmopolitan view of man, that is, the view that man, regardless of his place in space and time, was always subject to the same universally valid laws. A law which purported to be eternally valid by logical necessity had to be independent of a specific time and place, otherwise it could not be valid for all times and places.

Cassirer was very sensitive to the criticism that natural law was lifeless and abstract. In his speech he specifically tried to answer this charge and maintained that natural law was tied to the life process itself.[64] But was this last point correct? Unfortunately, Cassirer's conception of the philosophy of law was very abstract; it was another variation of the neo-Kantian view that law was an abstract norm. Cassirer saw legal philosophy as dealing with pure definitions and logical proofs, not with factual situations.[65] His inability and that of the neo-Kantian legal philosophers to deal with laws and ethics in other than abstract terms opened them to the charge of being political and ethical relativists. From the perspectives of their left- and right-wing opponents, their abstract formalism prohibited the neo-Kantians from translating their ideals into concrete policies which would help the nation and unify it. Ironically, what the neo-Kantians felt to be their strongest point – that is, their logical conception of universally valid legal norms which encompassed all humanity – was precisely what their opponents most violently criticized. Their concern with humanity in general estranged them from their more nationalist compatriots.

## CASSIRER'S STUDY OF THE ENLIGHTENMENT

Cassirer's study of the Enlightenment was his final attempt to produce a systematic view of philosophy and history before he was forced to flee Germany in 1933. In the preface (dated October 1932) to *The Philosophy of the Enlightenment* Cassirer expressly made the connection between his prior work, his present study of the Enlightenment, and contemporary events in Germany. He saw the Enlightenment as a special part 'of that whole intellectual development through which modern philosophic thought gained its characteristic self-confidence and self-consciousness.'[66] It was in the realm of science that Enlightenment philosophy had achieved its first victory. In this respect the age of reason completed what the Renaissance had begun: 'It marked off a definite field for rational knowledge within which there was to be no more restraint and authoritative coercion but free movement in all directions. By virtue of this freedom philosophy could attain to full self-knowledge and to knowledge of its inherent forces.'[67] The ultimate result of this movement of thought was the emergence of the belief in the fundamental autonomy of reason. For on the foundation of this autonomy could be erected a view of knowledge and existence which might reveal the secrets of man and the cosmos.

While he reaffirmed the continuity in Western thought from the Renaissance to the twentieth century, Cassirer had his fears about the fate of rationality in the modern era. The age which venerated 'reason and science as man's highest faculties' and upheld the 'autonomy of reason' must not, Cassirer argued, 'be lost even for us.'[68] On the contrary, the time was ripe for reapplying the Enlightenment's ideals and 'its self-criticism to the present age.'[69] There was a note of desperation in Cassirer's defence of the Enlightenment. On reading the preface one gets the impression that his study of the seventeenth and eighteenth centuries was more than a philosophical exercise. He was defending a whole way of thinking rather than just explaining the achievements of a bygone era.

Not surprisingly, Cassirer's view of the Enlightenment was identical with Kant's own slogan summarizing the era: 'Dare to Know! Have the courage to use your own reason.' The eighteenth century was 'imbued with the belief in the unity and immutability of reason.' Reason was 'the same for all thinking subjects, all nations, all epochs and all cultures.'[70] For the men of the Enlightenment, all the various energies of the mind are ... held together in a common center of force. Variety and diversity of shapes are simply the full unfolding of an essentially homogeneous formative power. When the eighteenth century wants to characterize this power in a single word, it calls it 'reason.' 'Reason' becomes the unifying and central point of this century, expressing all that it longs and strives for, and all that it achieves.[71]

The methodological resemblance between Cassirer's previous study of the Renaissance and his present analysis of the Enlightenment was remarkable. As in the Renaissance study Cassirer assumed that there was a unity to the period, that it was engaged in one project. After deciding on the central aim and basic characteristics of the project, he subdivided the activities of the period into various categories to show that at every cultural level the thought of the epoch was moving in one direction. He also retained his cosmopolitan overview of historical events. Descartes, Leibniz, Locke, Hume, d'Alembert, and others were treated as if they belonged to one culture and shared the same goal: to give men the courage to use their reason. While Cassirer sought to deepen his own understanding of the epoch by dealing with more figures, he combined his new research with an inclination to avoid re-evaluating his earlier work on the subject. Consequently, he repeated his earlier thoughts on various philosophers like Galileo, Newton, and Condillac, instead of rethinking his own understanding of them. His numerous cross references to his earlier work, the first two volumes of *Das Erkenntnisproblem,* in which he examined their ideas,[72] was a clear sign that he was reiterating old ideas rather than expounding new ones.

Cassirer's resurrection of old ideas was not as surprising as the fact that Kant was almost completely omitted from his study. For a man of Cassirer's convictions the achievements of Kant and the Enlightenment were synonymous. Why then did he virtually ignore Kant? After all he believed that the critical philosophy was the grand synthesis of everything that came before it. Kant was certainly worth at least one chapter of solid discussion, rather than the fleeting references Cassirer actually made to him.

Furthermore, if European events of the years 1900 to 1933 required one thing, it was a total re-evaluation of the power and limits of reason. Clearly, the significance of Kant's work had to be reassessed because he was one of the greatest modern proponents of the power of human reason. However, a reassessment of Kant implied a re-evaluation of the movement of thought summarized by his philosophy. And Cassirer was unwilling to go beyond a certain point in his re-evaluation of Kant and the age of reason.

Even in the wake of his debate with Heidegger, Cassirer never seriously questioned the grounds of his own philosophy. When Heidegger's radically new views of Kant and the nature of human reason were published in 1927, instead of re-evaluating his own thoughts on the subject, Cassirer merely reiterated his position in relation to Heidegger's. In a vital sense Cassirer sharply separated his discussions with Heidegger from a possible rethinking of Kant's basic ideas.

When it was necessary to discuss Kant in relation to the Enlightenment, in view of Heidegger's reinterpretation of Kant, Cassirer could have done one of three things: re-evaluate Kant and the nature of reason itself; rephrase his earlier ideas on Kant; or ignore the implications of the new vision of Kant and of the era he embodied. Cassirer chose the latter course. One may argue that he was simply dodging the fundamental issues, but on the other hand it is possible that his reluctance to re-evaluate his position signified something beyond his own philosophy. Perhaps there were political implications to this philosophical dispute that he was either unable or unwilling to accept.

Cassirer's intellectual position must be understood within the historical context of Germany in the early 1930s. The nation was reeling under the impact of the economic depression. The triumph of political extremism in the rising popularity of the Nazis and Communists had paralyzed the political system. Many German intellectuals were pandering to the nationalist political parties (especially the Nazis). The atmosphere in the universities was oppressive. As the rector of the University of Hamburg from November 1929 to November 1930 Cassirer was directly exposed to the fanatical nationalism and anti-republicanism spreading in the German universities after 1929.[73] Moreover as the first Jewish rector of a university in Germany he had to be especially aware of the pitfalls of university politics because anti-Semitism went hand in hand with the anti-republican sentiments of many students and professors. In April 1930 Cassirer's relations with the nationalists became so strained because of the plans for the next constitutional celebrations (August 1930), which they opposed, that he confided to his wife that he wished his rectorship would be terminated.[74] When seen in this context, Cassirer's constant reaffirmation of the primacy and autonomy of reason and its cosmopolitan orientation took on distinct political overtones. The defence of reason against a one-sided nationalist view of man became Cassirer's main task. For this view degraded and enslaved man because it denied his humanity; it submerged him in the finitude of immediate national existence and denied the ability of reason to help man transcend his limitations; on the contrary, those limitations were exalted as being the highest virtues. Under these circumstances Cassirer undoubtedly felt that to re-examine the nature of reason would only further undermine the cause of human freedom.

In equating human freedom with the courage to use one's reason independent of all external authority, and by using an a priori conception of reason to comprehend knowledge and existence, Cassirer had unwittingly yielded to the polarizing tendencies of his age. His defence of reason had driven him to an extreme, that is, to an abstract, conception of man as espoused in his phenomenology of knowledge. While many of his compatriots had surrendered to the spirit of the times by submerging themselves in 'the paradise of immediate historical experience,' he went to the other extreme of grounding everything in 'the pure functions of reason.'

Understandably, Cassirer's renewed commitment to the primacy of pure reason in human affairs found its way into his study of the law, state, and society in Enlightenment thought. For people like Leibniz and Grotius the apriority of law was the main thing. If law were to be universally valid it had to be pure, that is, independent of transitory empirical and temporal qualities. In this respect law was like pure mathematics. Accordingly, the Enlightenment's doctrine of natural law looked 'upon law and mathematics as the best evidence of the autonomy and spontaneity of the intellect.'[75] It was precisely this idea of law that became an integral part of German idealism from Leibniz onwards.[76] Moreover, Cassirer praised the Enlightenment's, and particularly Rousseau's, enthusiasm for the force and dignity of natural law. This was important for Cassirer because it was the basis of the social contract. Without the majestic force of natural law to reinforce in political life the spiritual autonomy of the individual, the social contract between free men could not survive; in fact, it would give way to lawlessness. Since these words were written in the Germany of 1932, which was increasingly under the sway of political and legal lawlessness, the motive behind Cassirer's argument could hardly be more obvious.

In the last months of the Weimar Republic's existence, Cassirer and many of his like-minded colleagues were reduced to reminding their compatriots not to abandon themselves to the irrational. In a sense, Cassirer's last major work in Germany had been a challenge to the German people to live up to the high standard of their philosophical tradition. When he fled Germany it became apparent that they had failed collectively to take up the challenge because they lacked the inner courage to use their reason. Instead they had turned to follow the champions of a new Dark Age.

# 11

# Epilogue and conclusion

When Cassirer left Germany in 1933 he was no longer a German liberal reacting to his national environment. His thoughts and actions became a part
of the Western world's struggle against Hitler. Thus, our narrative has,
strictly speaking, carried us beyond the scope of our study, namely, the dilemma of a liberal intellectual in Germany since 1914. However, between his
departure from Germany in May 1933 and his death on 13 April 1945,
Cassirer's ideas began to turn in a new direction. While his death cut short
this development, a brief discussion of it may throw light on his ideas of
1899–1933.

When Cassirer left Germany in 1933 he had not resolved the dilemma facing the liberal intellectual. The greater his effort to construct a durable rational and liberal world view, the greater his estrangement from the majority
of his countrymen. Alternatively, the more he tried to compromise with the
extreme ideas of his contemporaries, the greater his infidelity to his liberal
world view. When in the last years of the Weimar Republic Cassirer tried
more vigorously to make clear to his compatriots the overwhelming importance of preserving the autonomy of the rational individual, he went about
this undertaking in such a way as to undermine his own position. By overem-
phasizing the logical, a priori dimension to human existence and totally ig-
noring the insecurity and anxiety experienced by most Germans since 1918,
Cassirer unwittingly revealed the shortcomings of a liberalism that could
plead for faith in the power of human reason to solve all problems in principle but could not offer specific solutions for Germany's immediate problems.
Unfortunately, it was only after being on the difficult road of exile for a number of years that Cassirer slowly stumbled upon the inadequacy of his own

naive faith in the power and influence of human reason in history. It now remains to trace briefly his growing realization of the frailty of human reason
and culture.

After Hitler came to power in January 1933 the new government imple-
mented the first phase of the now famous 'co-ordination policy,'[1] in which all
undesirable people were removed from government and key economic and
social positions and ultimately isolated from the rest of German society. Jews
were among those groups of people singled out for immediate expulsion from
government jobs. Since university professors in Germany were civil servants
and subject to summary dismissal by the federal and local governments, Cassirer resigned his university post in April 1933. In May he left Germany for
ever.

The circumstances of Cassirer's resignation and his reaction to the worsen-
ing situation of Jews in Germany since the first Nazi electoral triumph of
September 1930 revealed the true quality of the man. When he read in several newspapers that he had resigned for 'personal reasons' Cassirer sent a
sharp letter to the Department of Higher Education, clearly affirming that he
had resigned on principle and not on private grounds; as a Jew he could no
longer remain a part of an educational system which discriminated against
Jews. For Cassirer education was a co-operative affair in which everyone had
a role to play. Once the co-operative spirit was lost, once whole groups of people either for political or racial reasons were excluded from the educational
process, he felt obliged to repudiate the new state of affairs. Both as a Jew and
as a liberal he was dismayed about the future of the Jews in Germany.[2]

Once Cassirer entered a world whose academic and political traditions
were very different from those in Germany, he could no longer take his own
philosophical presuppositions for granted or assume that his readers were well
acquainted with, let alone accepted, the basic principles of German idealism.
After 1933 Cassirer found himself in different cultural environments, where
his intellectual frame of reference was open to grave doubts. He first settled in
England and remained in Oxford until 1935, but he was not really content
there and moved to Sweden. He stayed there from 1935 to May 1941, when,
with Hitler's armies all around him, he left for the United States. He died in
New York City on 13 April 1945.

In the midst of his travels, and largely in reaction to the events of 1933 to
1945, Cassirer had to confront history, man, and the limits of rationalism in a
way that he had never done before. Before 1933, an optimism permeated his
work; after that year, and particularly after 1942, a sombre and pessimistic
tone crept into his writings. For the first time, and largely as a consequence of
the events of 1933–45, Cassirer began to have doubts about the durability of

human culture. In his last major publication, *The Myth of the State* (published posthumously in 1946), Cassirer used these words to summarize the major lesson of the last twelve years:

What we have learned in the hard school of our modern political life is the fact that human culture is by no means the firmly established thing that we once supposed it to be. The great thinkers, the scientists, the poets, and the artists who laid the foundations of our Western civilization were often convinced that they had built for eternity ... It seems, however, that we have to look upon the great master works of human culture in a much humbler way. They are not eternal nor unassailable. Our science, our poetry, our art, and our religion are only the upper layer of a much older stratum that reaches down to a great depth. We must always be prepared for violent concussions that may shake our cultural world and our social order to its very foundations.[3]

Here we have the first and perhaps the only clear admission by Cassirer that the continued existence of human culture was not absolutely certain. Since his entire pre-1933 orientation rested on the belief that human culture was the product of a free and essentially rational humanity, his confession of uncertainty raised some doubt in his own mind that man was a rational creature. For who else was threatening 'our cultural world' and 'our social order' but man himself? With this question Cassirer had to confront a new problem, namely the nature of man. In the context of post-1933 events the absolute fact upon which he constructed his earlier critique of culture had become an unknown variable. In short, man had become the fundamental problem.

Once Cassirer could no longer assume that man was a free and rational creature who was comprehensible through his symbolic, cultural creations, his pre-1933 philosophical system was found wanting. Indeed, when Cassirer was asked in 1944 to translate his *Philosophie der Symbolischen Formen* into English he declined. He decided that his perspective of the subject had changed so completely that it would be best to write a new book. His former abstract approach to the problem was no longer satisfactory, even to himself.[4] The extent of Cassirer's dissatisfaction with his former work can be seen in the title of his new study of human culture – *An Essay on Man*. Man, not symbolic forms, became the centre of Cassirer's attention. He devoted the first six chapters of his essay to formulating a definition of man.[5] To be sure, he never abandoned the belief that man and the cosmos were ultimately rational and subject to an all-inclusive logic of development, but the fact that after his departure from Germany he increasingly reflected on the problem of man indicated that he was less inclined to accept his old ideas without reservation.

For a time after his self-imposed exile, Cassirer was in a state of personal and intellectual shock, so these new thoughts about the problematic nature of human reason remained in the background. In fact for the first eight years of exile, 1933–41, he continued his old interest in epistemological matters. In 1936 he updated his 1910 study of modern science, *Substance and Function*, by publishing *Determinism and Indeterminism in Modern Physics*. Here he incorporated developments in physics between 1910 and 1935 into his earlier epistemological analysis of the subject.[6] From 1937 to 1939 Cassirer turned his attention back to Descartes and Leibniz, whose works he had first studied in detail between 1896 and 1902. His book on Descartes, which appeared in 1939, was a replay of his study of German intellectual history in *Freiheit und Form*. This time Cassirer was examining Descartes' place in the French Enlightenment. As in his earlier work, where he saw in the works of Goethe and Kant the thoughts and sentiments of a whole epoch, so he used Descartes and Corneille to embody the major characteristics of the Enlightenment in France.[7] And finally, from 1940 to 1941 he elaborated on two other old themes of his work. First, he completed the fourth volume of his series on *The Problem of Knowledge* and brought it up to the present day. Secondly, in his book *The Logic of the Humanities* he dealt with the ideas of men like Burckhardt, Rickert, and Simmel that had formed the background of his own previous thoughts on cultural history.

By 1942 Cassirer had worked dry his old intellectual mines. During the next two years the Nazi crimes against humanity began to preoccupy his thought[8] and temporarily change his optimism about man into a sombre pessimism about the human condition. It is precisely during these years, 1942–44, that the declining curve of Cassirer's optimism intersected with the rising curve of his rejection of an abstract overview of man and his relation to the cosmos. The net result of this intellectual development was that Cassirer no longer took for granted the primacy of reason in human affairs. Once he entertained doubts about the viability of human reason he was able to see the flaw which made his work from 1914 to 1933 seem so alien to many of his compatriots. Simply put, Cassirer realized that his philosophy of symbolic forms had overintellectualized man's achievements; that by trying to understand man, his history, and his culture in symbolic terms, he had in fact reduced them to a mere play of abstract, dehumanized symbolic forms.

By 1944 Cassirer was at least aware that there was an existential anxiety problem (*Angst*) confronting modern man because he had lost his spiritual bearings.[9] Before he left Germany he had never understood this as a problem, which was one reason why he never understood the reasons for Hitler's appeal to the German people. For Cassirer Hitler was foreign to Germany,[10] an historical aberration, and not the expression of the anti-modernist, anti-liberal, and anti-capitalist currents present in Germany since the mid-nineteenth century. In spite of his own political misconceptions, Cassirer began to admit that philosophy was partially responsible for the contemporary spiritual malaise and ethical bankruptcy of twentieth-century European man. When he accused philosophy in general of becoming a stranger to the world, he was also in retrospect criticizing his own previous estrangement from German society in the 1920s and 1930s:

In spite of all its learning philosophy had become a stranger to the world and the problems of life which occupied man and the whole thought of the age had no part in its activities. It philosophized about everything except civilization. 'So little did philosophy philosophize about civilization that it did not even notice that it itself and the age along with it were losing more and more of it. In the hour of peril, the watchman who ought to have kept us awake was himself asleep and the result was that we put up no fight at all on behalf of our civilization.'

That is one of the gravest and most serious charges made against our contemporary philosophy; but if we look at the development of our social and political life in these last decades we can hardly say that this charge was unjust.[11]

Cassirer clearly blamed himself and twentieth-century philosophy generally for failing to address the crucial problems facing modern man.

Even though Cassirer began to doubt the viability of modern philosophy and of the role of rationalism in human existence, he nevertheless remained a thinker of the Enlightenment, a man of the age of reason. He aspired towards light and clarity even when reflecting on the depths of human existence. *Angst* never became a fundamental part of his work. To the end he retained his optimism. He did not live to confront the emotions and uncertainties that might have given him a deeper insight into the anxiety-ridden existence of twentieth-century man and might perhaps have provided him with a means for resolving the liberal dilemma.

CONCLUSION

Ever since the Paris Commune of 1871 defenders of the status quo have become increasingly aware of the connection between national defeat and social revolution. The spectacle of bitter class conflict in the streets of Paris after the collapse of national resistance to the Germans was not soon forgotten by the propertied classes of Europe. The lesson was of particular interest to the Germans, who had after all decisively beaten the French. What was accomplished by military victory could be undone by defeat. Military victory led to the political unification of Germany. The other side of that victory, the French defeat, led to a violent assault on the bastions of private property. What if the national roles were reversed?

In 1918 the Germans were the vanquished. Like the French in 1871, Germans were confronted with the spectre of social revolution. However, the situation was more ominous, because Communist Russia was eager to help anyone in Germany and in other countries overthrow capitalism. In the aftermath of defeat German liberals were caught between hammer and anvil; they had to choose between the forces of revolution demanding the reorganization of society and the inertia of an established order which sought to minimize most if not all changes.

In November 1918 German liberals were presented with the opportunity to adjust their ideals to twentieth-century realities. Their plight – symbolized for us in the person of Ernst Cassirer – is important because we feel that they represent the first chance for middle classes of a highly industrialized society to respond positively to a peculiarly twentieth-century challenge – that of balancing a rapid increase in the demands for the reorganization of society in the name of social equality with their desire to preserve individual liberty. German liberals failed to strike a balance between the two and in the process permitted events to undermine their ideals.

What are the enduring values of liberalism? In 1935 John Dewey argued that 'these values [were] liberty; the development of the inherent capacities of individuals made possible through liberty, and the central role of free intelligence in inquiry, discussion and expression.'[12] Dewey not only pinpointed the most durable liberal values, he had also revealed the centrepoint of any liberal's concern. If liberalism stands for anything it is a commitment to 'the development of the inherent capacities of individuals.' The primacy of the individual in the development of his capacities is the *sine qua non* of liberalism. This assumption was the starting point of Ernst Cassirer's reflections on the human condition. Throughout his philosophical career he never doubted that humanity in general and man in particular were free, and that the continuation of this freedom depended on the use of reason. It was the courage to use one's own reason, together with his belief in human freedom, that Cassirer sought to pass onto his contemporaries.

Cassirer's difficulties were symptomatic of the crisis confronting all liberals in the early twentieth century. The industrialization of Europe and the political and social disarray caused by the first world war had decisively changed the rules of the game. The standards of successful political behaviour had changed almost overnight for all political groups. Liberals were especially hard hit by the change. In the nineteenth century liberals believed, with good reason, that the separate, competing economic actions of individuals were the best method of preserving the autonomy of the individual and hence of maximizing social well-being. In the twentieth century, particularly after the wartime success of government planning in achieving specific economic goals, the idea grew that a socially regulated economy might be the best way of providing the economic basis for the development of the inherent capacities of *all* individuals. For many liberals a socially controlled economy was indistinguishable from the tyranny of the majority.

Liberalism reached the great divide. Circumstances forced it to choose between progress and reaction. The middle classes had to choose between a new (social) liberalism which saw the state as a friend capable of directing the social action necessary to keep individuals free or the old (individualist, *laissez-faire*) liberalism which saw the state as an enemy ever ready to deprive the individual of his liberty. Should the liberals go to the left, favouring social progress and the extension of economic benefits to all, or should they move to the right, thereby reacting negatively to the rising clamour for equality and favouring the preservation of social perogatives restricted to a small minority of the people? Liberals as a group procrastinated in making a decision.

As in the case of a geographical fault, German liberals had a fatal flaw running beneath their intellectual landscape. They loved to conceive of concrete problems in abstract terms – an inclination that may be called the formalist error. These liberals talked a great deal about their concern for the whole German people and for the rights of man. They spoke as if their interest extended to all humanity and then acted in accordance with the imperatives of middle-class politics.

The intellectual dimension of this clash between the universal sweep of their humanistic theory and their narrowly based middle-class political behaviour is well illustrated in the works of Ernst Cassirer. His commitment to maintain the autonomy of the individual rested on an ethical ideal which he, like many other German liberals, got from Immanuel Kant. In the tradition of Kantian ethics Cassirer believed that each individual should always be treated as a rational being who was an end in himself, rather than as a means to an end. Only if this attitude were adopted would the individual have the opportunity to develop his 'inherent capacities.'

Cassirer's inclination to envision particular events as expressions of abstract, universal laws (or relations) was inseparable from his neo-Kantian epistemology. This particular theory of knowledge argued that abstract, a priori, and universally valid relations were indispensable for making the world intelligible to man. Cassirer's conception of knowledge committed him to a procedure whereby every concrete fact was transformed into abstract relations of facts and values. Thus, when he turned his attention to legal and political matters, Cassirer supported the belief that the study of law focused on definitions and logical proofs, not on particular individual and historical facts.

Every benefit has a cost. The major benefit of the Kantian defence of individual freedom was a coherent overview of the role of human rationality in maintaining liberty. The cost of the formalist error was political irrelevancy. While there may have been good philosophical reasons for adopting a formalist approach to politics, this mode of argument was a lamentable relapse to the outdated ideals of nineteenth-century (individualist) liberalism that avoided any consideration of the social and economic obstacles to individual freedom. Cassirer and other liberals were not unaware of this problem, yet they persisted in keeping their politics in the realm of pure ideas.

While the enduring values of liberalism were noble, they rested on questionable assumptions – the beliefs that all people were rational and that they were able and willing to develop their inherent capacities. The problem with Cassirer's type of DDP liberalism is that instead of these assumptions being questioned, they became dogma, which required little or no factual confirmation. It is hard to decide whether these liberals were conscious or only half conscious of the fact that their assumptions needed re-examination. The orgy of European self-destruction during 1914–18 and the domestic chaos in Germany from 1918 to 1923 and 1930 to 1933 led Cassirer to worry about the evil effects of nationalism on the German spirit, but he never doubted the validity of his liberal assumptions.

The assumption of human rationality was so dear to these liberals that they adopted a mode of argument that buttressed their rationalist principles, but at the cost of losing the support of their countrymen and undermining their own goals. Their solutions always remained on the level of generalities. One vainly seeks a prescription of how the individual or the state should act in a particular case. Even from 1930 to 1932, when the economic depression was tightening its grip on Germany, when the extreme right and left were fighting pitched battles in the streets, and when parliamentary government was replaced by a presidential dictatorship, Cassirer persistently remained on the level of theory and discussed such matters as different conceptions of the state and the ideal basis of law. The effect of this kind of argument was to preserve the autonomy of the individual in theory and to permit economic and political events to destroy that autonomy in fact.

Liberal democrats were caught in a dialectic of self-destruction. The more they argued for individual liberty, the more they conceived of that liberty in abstract terms and made it meaningless to those who might have supported the enduring values of liberalism. Liberals should have offered bread instead of precious stones. But could they have done this? Here the reason for the DDP's vacillation on political issues is made clear. The members of the DDP never seriously tried to define their liberalism in relation to their historical and social environment, because the majority of the rank and file never intended to put into practice basic liberal principles in which they only half believed. Their traditional fear of the masses further undermined the liberals' commitment to such principles. The poverty of liberalism was never more obvious than when it feigned interest in social matters while in reality it was concerned only with its own class interests.

The failure of liberal democracy in Germany from 1912 to 1932 was as much a product of its own inability to translate its ideals into practice as the result of finding itself in a national environment which was neither willing nor able to give it a chance of success. Confronted with a difficult situation liberals might have asked themselves a very hard question. Was it possible to make the enduring values of liberalism relevant in a world that increasingly showed such values to be incorrect and irrelevant? Cassirer's answer was a curious mixture of acute realism and naive idealism. He and liberals like him decided to preserve the ideal of a free, rational, self-developing individual by placing that individual in a social and historical vacuum. What could not be achieved in reality was at least preserved in the hermetically sealed world of pure theory.

In dealing with Cassirer's response to his age we encounter the inevitable strengths and weaknesses of the intellectual's life style and manner of responding to world events. Intellectuals try to make themselves into men of action by defining action in terms of an intellectual struggle between faith and doubt, between knowledge and uncertainty. This struggle is really an inner one, waged within an individual. It may be related to and even caused by social, economic, or political events, but it is primarily a struggle of ideas. Nevertheless, on the intellectual level, solutions to problems often emerge which though of no use to one era may be very useful to another. This is the legacy that Cassirer left us in his writings. It is a vision of a free humanity that has the courage to use its reason as well as the inner certainty that while the voice of reason may be ignored in certain ages this voice will not rest until it has gained a hearing.

# Notes

Full bibliographical information on works cited here may be found in the bibliography.

CHAPTER 1

1 Ernst Cassirer *The Individual and the Cosmos in Renaissance Philosophy* (1927) 40
2 Fritz K. Ringer *The Decline of the German Mandarins* 3
3 Ibid. 89
4 Dimitry Gawronsky 'Ernst Cassirer: His Life and His Work' 4
5 Ibid. 6
6 Georg Simmel *The Sociology of Georg Simmel* 59
7 See Benedetto Croce *History of Europe in the Nineteenth Century* chap. 1 passim.
8 See Leonard Krieger *The German Idea of Freedom* 86-7.
9 See comment by Ernst Cassirer's wife, Toni, that before the first world war neither of them were political (Toni Cassirer *Aus meinem Leben mit Ernst Cassirer* 97).
10 Ibid. 27–8
11 Friedrich Paulsen *Die deutschen Universitäten und das Universitätsstudium* 195
12 Alexander Busch *Die Geschichte des Privatdozenten* 160
13 Ibid.
14 Gawronsky 'Ernst Cassirer' 17, Toni Cassirer *Aus meinem Leben* 66–7
15 Ludwig Elm *Zwischen Fortschritt und Reaktion* 262
16 Krieger *The German Idea of Freedom* 86
17 Ernst Cassirer *Kants Leben und Lehre* (1918) 435
18 Günter Fischenberg 'Der deutsche Liberalismus und die Entstehung der Weimarer Republik' 32, 180
19 For a detailed examination of how the diverse social composition of the liberals' supporters complicated liberal political efforts in the early years of the Weimar

Republic see Lothar Albertin *Liberalismus und Demokratie am Anfang der Weimarer Republik* chap. 2 passim.

20 For an account of Barth's fruitless search for liberal socialist unity see Konstanze Wegner *Theodor Barth und die freisinnige Vereinigung* vii, 111–21.
21 Carl E. Schorske *German Social Democracy 1905–1917* 233–4
22 Ralph Dahrendorf *Society and Democracy in Germany* 45
23 Schorske *Social Democracy* 5–6
24 L.E. Jones ' "The Dying Middle": Weimar Germany and the Fragmentation of Bourgeois Politics' 24
25 Ernst Cassirer *Das Erkenntnisproblem in der Philosophie und Wissenschaft der neueren Zeit* (1907) 2: 762
26 Ernst Cassirer 'Vom Wesen und Werden des Naturrechts' (1932) 2
27 Otto Butz *Modern German Political Theory* 15
28 Guido de Ruggiero *The History of European Liberalism* 257
29 William Ebenstein *The Pure Theory of Law* 23
30 Siegfried Marck *Substanz- und Funktionsbegriff in der Rechtsphilosophie* foreword
31 Arnold Brecht *Political Theory* 218–20
32 John H. Hallowell *The Decline of Liberalism as an Ideology* 92
33 Erich Kaufmann *Kritik der neukantischen Rechtsphilosophie* 10; on the neo-Kantian disdain for apples, animals, dollars, and cents see Ebenstein *Pure Theory of Law* 37.
34 Wolfgang Hartenstein *Die Anfänge der deutschen Volkspartei 1918–1920* 37
35 Lothar Albertin 'German Liberalism and the Foundation of the Weimar Republic: A Missed Opportunity?' in A. Nicholls and E. Matthias, eds. *German Democracy and the Triumph of Hitler* 41
36 Ernst Cassirer *Die Idee der republikanischen Verfassung* (1928) 31
37 For summaries of the liberals' vacillation between progress and reaction see Elm *Zwischen Fortschritt und Reaktion* 276–82, Fischenberg 'Der deutsche Liberalismus' 180–3

CHAPTER 2

1 Immanuel Kant *The Critique of Judgement* part 2, 92–100
2 Georg W.F. Hegel *The Phenomenology of Mind* 144
3 Friedrich Überweg *Grundriss der Geschichte der Philosophie* 4: 310
4 Friedrich A. Lange *History of Materialism* 3: 335–6
5 Albert Görland 'Hermann Cohens systematische Arbeit im Dienst des kritischen Idealismus' 232–4; cf. Hermann Cohen *Das Prinzip der Infinitesimal–Methode und seine Geschichte.*
6 Hermann Cohen *Kants Theorie der Erfahrung* 69
7 Ibid. 538

8 Paul Natorp *Die logischen Grundlagen der exakten Wissenschaften* 39
9 Henri Dussort *L'École de Marbourg* 53
10 George L. Mosse *Germans and Jews* 177; also see Georg G. Iggers *The German Conception of History* 146.
11 Hermann Lübbe *Politische Philosophie in Deutschland* 103–5
12 Ibid. 123–4; cf. Bernstein's futile efforts to convince his Marxist colleagues that Kant's ideas were relevant to contemporary socialism in Peter Gay *The Dilemma of Democratic Socialism* 151–60.
13 Cassirer *Das Erkenntnisproblem in der Philosophie und Wissenschaft der neueren Zeit* (1907) 2:762
14 Ibid. 371–2
15 Immanuel Kant *The Critique of Pure Reason* 194
16 Ibid. 175
17 Ernst Cassirer *Substance and Function* (1910) and *Einstein's Theory of Relativity* (1921) 175
18 Ernst Cassirer *Leibniz' System in seinen wissenschaftlichen Grundlagen* (1902) 1
19 Ibid. 71
20 Ibid. 29
21 Ibid. 5
22 Ibid. 102
23 Ibid. 379
24 Florian Kalbeck 'Die Philosophie Systematik Ernst Cassirers' 15
25 Cassirer *Leibniz' System* 397–8
26 Ibid. 399
27 Ibid. 440
28 Ibid. 446
29 Cassirer *Erkenntnisproblem* 1: vii
30 Ibid. 55
31 Ibid. 321–2
32 Ibid. 330–3
33 Ibid. 408–9
34 Ibid. 10–11
35 Cohen as quoted by Gawronsky 'Ernst Cassirer' 21
36 See O. Ewald 'Die deutsche Philosophie im Jahre 1909' 421–4, 436–8.
37 Cassirer *Substance and Function* 203–20
38 Ibid. 220
39 Ibid. 227–8
40 See ibid. 261.
41 Cassirer 'Die Grundprobleme der Kantischen Methodik und ihr Verhältnis zur Nachkantischen Spekulation' (1914) 814

42 Ibid. 815
43 Ibid. 813
44 Kant *Critique of Pure Reason* 93
45 Cassirer *Freiheit und Form* (1916) xi
46 Cassirer, personal letter to Natorp, 11 August 1903, Natorp Personal Papers, Ms. 831:617 (reference made by permission of Marburg University Library)

CHAPTER 3

1 See Cassirer *Das Erkenntnisproblem in der Philosophie und Wissenchaft der neueren Zeit* (1907) 2: 733–62.
2 See Elie Halévy *The Era of Tyrannies* 215–16.
3 Plenge as quoted by Fritz K. Ringer *The Decline of the German Mandarins* 181
4 Ibid. 189
5 See Hermann Cohen *Deutschtum und Judentum* 36–43, 46–7.
6 Egmont Zechlin *Die deutsche Politik und die Juden im ersten Weltkrieg* 86–9
7 Ibid. 92; also see Toni Cassirer *Aus meinem Leben mit Ernst Cassirer* 99.
8 Zechlin *Die deutsche Politik* 89
9 Ibid. 99–100
10 T. Cassirer *Aus meinem Leben* 95
11 Cassirer *Freiheit und Form* (1916) xvi
12 T. Cassirer *Aus meinem Leben* 65, 86
13 *Neue Deutsche Biographie* 3: 167–8
14 Dimitry Gawronsky *Ernst Cassirer* 22
15 Ringer *The German Mandarins* 183
16 See Thomas Mann *Betrachtungen eines Unpolitischen* 21–3, 576
17 Cassirer *Kants Leben und Lehre* 293
18 Ibid. 384
19 Ibid. 397–8
20 Ibid. 367
21 Ibid. 366
22 Ibid. 306
23 Ibid 398; cf. Cassirer *Freiheit und Form* 326–7.
24 *Kants Leben und Lehre* 238
25 Ibid; cf. Kant *The Critique of Judgement* part 2, 96.
26 See Ralph Dahrendorf *Society and Democracy in Germany* 120–3; Ringer *The German Mandarins* 164–7.
27 See Mann *Betrachtungen*; Ernst Troeltsch 'Die deutsche Idee von der Freiheit' in *Deutscher Geist und Westeuropa*; Werner Sombart *Händler und Helden*.
28 Cassirer *Freiheit und Form* 18–19

29 Ibid. 327
30 Ibid.
31 Krieger *The German Idea of Freedom* 460
32 Friedrich Meinecke 'Der Weltkrieg' passim
33 Troeltsch *Deutscher Geist und Westeuropa* 84
34 Ibid. 88–90
35 Ibid. 94
36 See Krieger *The German Idea of Freedom* 86–125.
37 Cassirer *Kants Leben und Lehre* 242
38 Ibid. 242–3
39 Ringer *The German Mandarins* 84
40 See Ernst Cassirer *The Philosophy of the Enlightenment* (1932) chap. 1, passim.
41 Krieger *The German Idea of Freedom* 86–7
42 Ibid. 97
43 Cassirer *Kants Leben und Lehre* 366
44 Ibid. 391
45 Krieger *The German Idea of Freedom* 105
46 T. Cassirer *Aus meinem Leben* 101
47 Ibid. 99
48 Friedrich Meinecke *Werke* 236

CHAPTER 4

1 T. Cassirer *Aus meinem Leben* 100
2 Gawronsky *Ernst Cassirer* 23
3 T. Cassirer *Aus meinem Leben* 100
4 See Ralph Dahrendorf *Society and Democracy in Germany* 266–81.
5 Cassirer *Freiheit und Form* (1916) xvi
6 Jacob P. Mayer *Max Weber and German Politics* 74
7 Bethmann Hollweg as quoted by Fritz Fischer *Germany's Aims in the First World War* 636–7
8 Ringer *The German Mandarins* 199
9 Ismar Schorsch *Jewish Reactions to German Anti-Semitism 1870–1914* 137
10 See Egmont Zechlin *Die deutsche Politik und die Juden im ersten Weltkrieg* 516–67 passim.
11 S. Friedländer 'Die politische Veränderung der Kriegzeit und ihre Auswirkungen auf die Judenfrage' in Werner Mosse and Arnold Paucker, eds. *Deutsches Judentum in Krieg und Revolution 1916–1923* 36
12 Cassirer, personal letter to Natorp, 26 November 1916, Natorp Personal Papers, Ms. 831:657 (reference made by permission of Marburg University Library)

13 H. Liebeschütz 'Jewish Thought in its German Background' 229
14 Ibid. 230
15 T. Cassirer *Aus meinem Leben* 76
16 Cassirer, personal letter to Natorp, 26 November 1916, Natorp Personal Papers, Ms. 831:657, quoted by permission of Marburg University Library
17 Cassirer *Freiheit und Form* xi (italics mine)
18 Ibid. xii
19 Ibid. xi
20 Ibid. 7
21 Ibid. 18
22 See Cassirer 'Deutschland und Westeuropa im Spiegel der Geistesgeschichte' (1931).
23 Wilhelm Windelband, as quoted by Wallace K. Ferguson *The Renaissance in Historical Thought* 284
24 Liebeschütz 'Jewish Thought in its German Background' 231
25 Troeltsch 'Humanismus und Nationalismus in unserem Bildungswesen' in *Deutscher Geist und Westeuropa* 232
26 Ibid.
27 Fritz Stern *The Failure of Illiberalism* 20–1
28 For a definition of illiberalism see ibid. xvii–xviii.
29 Mann *Betrachtungen* 23
30 Ibid. 39–40
31 Ibid. 32
32 Ibid. 267
33 Ibid. 576
34 Cassirer *Freiheit und Form* xii
35 Ibid. 115
36 Ibid. 28
37 Ibid. 82 (italics mine)
38 Ibid. 61
39 Ibid. 115
40 Ibid. 28
41 Ibid. 312–16
42 See Cassirer *Substance and Function* (1910); for numbers, 27–67 and for chemistry, 203–20.
43 See Cassirer *Freiheit und Form* xiii–xv, 323–7, 336–7.
44 Ibid. 126; cf. Cassirer *The Philosophy of Symbolic Forms* (1925) 2: 107.
45 For a detailed examination of the growing interrelation of philosophy and art history see E. Utitz 'Aesthetik und allgemeine Kunstwissenschaft' passim and his 'Aesthetik und Philosophie der Kunst' passim.

46 See Karl Vossler 'Das Verhältnis von Sprachgeschichte und Literaturgeschichte.'
47 Fritz Medicus 'Philosophie und Dichtung' 45
48 Cassirer *The Philosophy of the Enlightenment* (1932) xii
49 In one of his few wartime references to Goethe, Mann used the poet's work to attack the French Revolution; see Mann *Betrachtungen* 458.
50 See Thomas Mann 'Goethe as Representative of the Bourgeois Age' in *Essays of Three Decades* 66–92, passim.
51 T. Cassirer *Aus meinem Leben* 66–7
52 See Peter Gay *Weimar Culture* 1–2, 87–8.
53 Cassirer *Freiheit und Form* 249–50
54 Ibid. 142
55 Ibid. 170
56 Ibid. 268
57 Ibid. 257
58 Ibid. 265
59 Ibid. 310
60 Ibid. 309
61 Friedrich Meinecke *Cosmopolitanism and the National State* 21
62 Cassirer *Freiheit und Form* 326–7
63 Ibid. 342
64 Ibid. 313
65 For an incisive contemporary analysis of why natural law acquired negative connotations in Germany see Ernst Troeltsch's speech 'The Ideas of Natural Law and Humanity in World Politics' (delivered in October 1922).
66 Cassirer *Freiheit und Form* 314–15
67 See Cassirer *Die Idee der republikanischen Verfassung* (1928) 16–17, 31.
68 On Cohen's lifelong estrangement from the mainstream of German academic life see H. Liebeschütz 'Hermann Cohen and his Historical Background' 19–20.
69 Cassirer 'Hermann Cohen: Worte gesprochen an seinem Grabe am 7 April 1918' 350

CHAPTER 5

1 Toni Cassirer *Aus meinem Leben mit Ernst Cassirer* 101
2 Ibid. 102
3 Heinrich Hannover and Elisabeth Hannover-Drück *Politische Justiz* 63–8
4 See Robert G.L. Waite *Vanguard of Nazism* 87–93.
5 W.T. Angress 'Juden im politischen Leben der Revolutionszeit' in Werner Mosse and Arnold Paucker, eds. *Deutsches Judentum in Krieg und Revolution 1916–23* 297
6 Werner Becker 'Die Rolle der liberalen Press' in ibid. 69

7 Dimitry Gawronsky 'Ernst Cassirer: His Life and His Work' 25
8 See Cassirer *Das Erkenntnisproblem in der Philosophie und Wissenschaft der neueren Zeit* (1920) 3: 371; also see Cassirer *Freiheit und Form* (1916) 160.
9 This intellectual continuum was particularly obvious to Cassirer; see Georg Lasson 'Kritischer und spekulativer Idealismus' 8–17 and 49–51 passim.
10 Cassirer *Erkenntnisproblem* 3: 328
11 Ibid. 327
12 Ibid. 325
13 See Georg W.F. Hegel *Hegel's Lectures on the Philosophy of History* 1–36.
14 See Georg W.F. Hegel *The Phenomenology of Mind* 140–4.
15 Georg W.F. Hegel *The Logic of Hegel* 148
16 Hegel *The Phenomenology of Mind* 144–5
17 Cassirer *Freiheit und Form* 365
18 Ibid. 366
19 Ibid. 368
20 For an example of Cassirer's applying the moment concept to his study of the works of famous German cultural figures, see ibid. 299–300.
21 Ibid. 115
22 To see how Leibniz was treated in this manner, see ibid. 48–61, 313–14, 368.
23 Cassirer 'Hölderlin und der deutsche Idealismus' in *Idee und Gestalt* (1924) 155
24 Ibid. 151
25 Ibid. 136
26 Cassirer 'Heinrich von Kleist und die Kantische Philosophie' in ibid. 160
27 Cassirer 'Hölderlin und der deutsche Idealismus' 121
28 Cassirer 'Goethes Pandora' in ibid. 27
29 Cassirer *Erkenntnisproblem* 3: viii
30 Crane Brinton *Nietzsche* chap. 7 passim
31 Cassirer *Erkenntnisproblem* 3: viii
32 For one striking example of a virulent nationalism in the universities, see an excerpt of the citation presented to Ludendorff by the School of Medicine of the University of Königsberg when he was granted an honourary degree in 1919, cited in Hans Kohn *The Mind of Germany* 309.
33 Cassirer *Erkenntnisproblem* 3: 482
34 Ibid. 369

CHAPTER 6

1 See S. Friedländer, 'Die politischen Veränderung der Kriegszeit und ihre Auswirkung auf die Judenfrage' in Werner Mosse and Arnold Paucker, eds. *Deutsches Judentun in Krieg und Revolution 1916–1923* 53–7 passim.

2 Golo Mann, as quoted by Friedländer in ibid. 49

3 Toni Cassirer *Aus meinem Leben mit Ernst Cassirer* 104

4 W. Jochmann 'Die Ausbreitung des Antisemitismus' in Mosse *Deutsches Judentum* 458, 475

5 T. Cassirer *Aus meinem Leben* 114

6 Jochmann 'Die Ausbreitung des Antisemitismus' in Mosse *Deutsches Judentum* 467

7 T. Cassirer *Aus meinem Leben* 111–12

8 Esra Bennathan 'Die demographische und wirtschaftliche Struktur der Juden' in Mosse *Deutsches Judentum* 91

9 Henry M. Pachter, personal letter to author, New York City, May 1973

10 Werner Mosse 'Der Niedergang der Weimarer Republik und die Juden' in Werner Mosse, ed. *Entscheidungsjahr 1932* 33

11 Jochmann 'Die Ausbreitung des Antisemitismus' in Mosse *Deutsches Judentum* 445–6

12 Fritz Saxl 'Ernst Cassirer' in Paul A. Schilpp, ed. *The Philosophy of Ernst Cassirer* 47

13 Fritz Saxl in Erich H. Gombrich *Aby Warburg: An Intellectual Biography* 326

14 For Weber's idea of the proper environment for scientific study, see Max Weber 'Science as a Vocation' 136–52 passim.

15 Friedrich Meinecke 'Drei Generationen deutscher Gelehrtenpolitik' 270

16 Peter Gay *Weimar Culture* 30–1

17 See Fritz Stern *The Politics of Cultural Despair* 1–22, 352–61.

18 See Ernst Troeltsch 'Der historische Entwicklungsbegriff in der modernen Geistes- und Lebensphilosophie' part 1, 377–8; also see Troeltsch 'The Ideas of Natural Law and Humanity in World Politics' 202–4, 210–12.

19 Troeltsch 'Der historische Entwicklungsbegriff' part 2, 395; Troeltsch's rejection of Cassirer's one-sided rationalism was a part of Troeltsch's general criticism of the neo-Kantian tendency to reduce all human reality (especially historical reality) to abstract concepts; see Georg G. Iggers *The German Conception of History* 193.

20 Erwin C. Schrödinger *Science, Theory and Man* 54; cf. 68.

21 George L. Mosse *The Culture of Western Europe* 286

22 Cassirer *Substance and Function* (1910) and *Einstein's Theory of Relativity* (1921) 357

23 Ibid. 358

24 Ibid. 386 (italics mine)

25 Ibid. 427 (italics mine)

26 Ibid. 447

27 Ibid.

28 The first essay, 'Der Begriff der symbolischen Form im Aufbau der Geisteswissenschaften' (hereafter referred to in the text as the 'symbolic form' essay), originally appeared in *Vorträge der Bibliothek Warburg* (1921–2); the second, 'Die Begriffsform im mythischen Denken' (hereafter referred to in the text as the

186 Notes to pages 93–103

'mythical thought' essay), originally appeared in *Studien der Bibliothek Warburg* I (1922); the two essays will be cited from Cassirer *Wesen und Wirkung des Symbolbegriffs* (1969).

29 Cassirer 'Mythischen Denken' 3
30 See above, page 25.
31 Cassirer 'Symbolischen Form' 171–2 (italics mine)
32 'Mythischen Denken' 10
33 'Symbolischen Form' 177 (italics mine)
34 'Mythischen Denken' 7
35 Ibid. 18
36 'Symbolischen Form' 180–3
37 'Mythischen Denken' 11
38 Ibid. 53
39 'Symbolischen Form' 182–3
40 Ibid. 174
41 Ibid.
42 Wilhelm Sauer 'Neukantianismus und Rechtswissenschaft in Herbst' 162; also see Arnold Brecht *Political Theory* 216–31 passim.
43 Cassirer 'Mythischen Denken' 27–8
44 Ibid. 28; also see 64–7.
45 Wilhelm Sauer *Lehrbuch der Rechts- und Sozialphilosophie* 54–5
46 See Kelsen's admission that Cohen's interpretation of Kant was crucial to his own philosophy of law in Hans Kelsen *Hauptprobleme der Staatslehre* xvii.
47 For Stammler's logicism see R. Pound 'Fifty Years of Jurisprudence' 448; though acknowledging the work of the Marburgers, Radbruch was decisively influenced by Windelband and Rickert; see Anton-Hermann Chroust 'The Philosophy of Law of Gustav Radbruch' 24–5.
48 Erich Kaufmann *Kritik der neukantischen Rechtsphilosophie* 10; also see his criticism of the Baden and Marburg Schools, 35–6.
49 Ibid. 12
50 Kurt Sontheimer *Antidemokratisches Denken in der Weimarer Republik* 84–5, 108–9
51 See Jëno Kurucz *Struktur und Funktion der Intelligenz während der Weimarer Republik* 90–2 chap. 6, passim.

CHAPTER 7

1 Fritz K. Ringer *The Decline of the German Mandarins* 128–43; the following discussion of the orthodox-modernist controversy is derived from these pages.
2 Spengler as quoted by Hans H. Knütter *Die Juden und die deutsche Linke in der Weimarer Republik 1918–1933* 12
3 See Hans Kohn *The Mind of Germany* 335, Klemens von Klemperer *Germany's New*

*Conservatism* 175, and H. Stuart Hughes *Consciousness and Society* 377–8.

4 See Max Weber 'Science as a Vocation' 145–51.

5 Cassirer *Philosophy of Symbolic Forms* (1925) 2: 147–8

6 Ringer *The German Mandarins* 277–8; for Cassirer's complete neglect of Natorp's political ideas see Cassirer 'Paul Natorp' (1925) passim.

7 See Cassirer *Philosophy of Symbolic Forms* (1923) 1: 85–93.

8 Henry M. Pachter 'The Intellectuals and the State of Weimar' 239

9 Arnold Paucker *Der jüdischen Abwehrkampf gegen Antisemitismus und Nationalismus in den letzten Jahren der Weimarer Republik* 94

10 Ibid. 84–5

11 Karl D. Bracher *Die Auflösung der Weimarer Republik* 21–7

12 M. Stürmer 'Parliamentary Government in Weimar Germany, 1924–1928' in A. Nicholls and E. Matthias, eds. *German Democracy and the Triumph of Hitler* 77

13 For a discussion of how the DDP was damaged by the tension between its conservative and anti-socialist supporters (who incidentally made large contributions to the DDP campaign of 1919) and the more democratic (and less anti-socialist) elements in the party, see Lothar Albertin 'German Liberalism and the Foundation of the Weimar Republic: A Missed Opportunity?' in ibid. 37–42.

14 Ibid. 41–2

15 Günter Fischenberg 'Der deutsche Liberalismus und die Enstehung der Weimarer Republik' 52, 62 – 72 passim

16 Thomas Mann 'Von deutscher Republik' in *Reden und Aufsätze* 21–2, 40

17 Richard W. Sterling *Ethics in a World of Power* 174

18 Fischenberg 'Der deutsche Liberalismus' 32

19 See Carl Schmitt *Die geistesgeschichtliche Lage des heutigen Parlamentarismus* 10, 13, 62.

20 Otto Butz *Modern German Political Theory* 15

21 Francois Gény *Méthode d'interprétation et sources en droit privé positif* 366

22 Wilhelm Sauer *Lehrbuch der Rechts- und Sozialphilosophie* 24–5

23 Kurt Sontheimer *Antidemokratisches Denken in der Weimarer Republik* 108–9

24 Rudolf Stammler as quoted by John H. Hallowell *The Decline of Liberalism as an Ideology* 92–3

25 Ernst Troeltsch 'The Ideas of Natural Law and Humanity in World Politics' 202

26 Ibid. 203–6

27 Ibid. 210

28 Cassirer 'Vom Wesen und Werden des Naturrechts' (1932) 1–13 passim

29 Toni Cassirer *Aus meinem Leben* 127

CHAPTER 8

1 Carl H. Hamburg *Symbol and Reality* 41

2 Cassirer *Language and Myth* (1925) x

3 See Max Scheler *Die Wissenformen und die Gesellschaft* (Bern, Franke 1960) 10, 201, M. Frischeisen-Köhler 'Die Philosophie der Gegenwart' in Max Dessoir, ed. *Die Geschichte der Philosophie* (Berlin, Ullstein 1925) 585–6, Ernst von Aster 'Zur Philosophie der Gegenwart' *Die Neue Rundschau* (August 1925): 793, 801–2.

4 Cassirer *The Philosophy of Symbolic Forms* (1923) 1: 102

5 Ibid. 80

6 Ibid. 80–1

7 Ibid. 79–80

8 Ibid. 105–14

9 Carl H. Hamburg 'Cassirer's Conception of Philosophy' in Paul A. Schilpp, ed. *Philosophy of Ernst Cassirer* 77

10 Cassirer *Philosophy of Symbolic Forms* 1: 113

11 Ibid. 84; see J.H. Randall 'Cassirer's Theory of History' in Schilpp, ed. *Philosophy of Ernst Cassirer* 726–7 for his summary of the tensions and polarities in Cassirer's historical vision.

12 Cassirer *Language and Myth* 84; cf. Cassirer *The Philosophy of Symbolic Forms* (1925) 2: 237–9

13 *Philosophy of Symbolic Forms* 2: xiv

14 *Language and Myth* 8

15 *Philosophy of Symbolic Forms* 1: 177

16 *Language and Myth* 8

17 *Philosophy of Symbolic Forms* 2: 29

18 Ibid. xviii

19 Cassirer, personal letter to Saxl, 24 March 1923, Private Papers of the Warburg Institute, London, England (used by permission of the Warburg Institute)

20 *Philosophy of Symbolic Forms* 1: 72

21 H. Naumann 'Versuch einer Geschichte der deutschen Sprache als Geschichte des deutschen Geistes' 139–43

22 *Philosophy of Symbolic Forms* 1: 174–5

23 Ibid. 158

24 Ibid. 2: 8

25 Ibid. 1: 228 and 2: 237–9

26 Ibid. 1: 190 and 2: 237

27 Ibid. 1: 190

28 Ibid. 289

29 Ibid. 194

30 Ibid. 2: 256–7

31 Ibid. 1: 196

32 Ibid. 311–12

33 Ibid. 202

34 Ibid. 2: 79
35 Ibid. 93
36 Ibid. 102
37 Ibid. 1: 216
38 Ibid. 2: 116
39 Ibid. 1: 294
40 Ibid. 290
41 *Language and Myth* 99
42 See *Philosophy of Symbolic Forms* 1: 249–77 passim and 2: 155–231 passim.
43 Ibid. 2: 175
44 Ibid. 182
45 Ibid.
46 Cassirer 'Mythischen Denken' (1922) 65
47 Cassirer *Philosophy of Symbolic Forms* 2: 198
48 Ibid. 199
49 Ibid. 197
50 Ibid. 214
51 Ibid. 216–18
52 See K. Sternberg's review of the second volume of *The Philosophy of Symbolic Forms*.
53 Cassirer *Philosophy of Symbolic Forms* 2: xvii
54 Harry Graf Kessler *Aus den Tagebüchern* ed. W. Pfeiffer-Belli (Munich, Deutscher Taschenbuch Verlag 1965) 258
55 Ernst Troeltsch 'The Ideas of Natural Law and Humanity in World Politics' 220
56 K. Sternberg 'Die philosophischen Grundlagen in Spenglers "Untergang des Abendlandes" ' 134–5
57 Cassirer *Philosophy of Symbolic Forms* 2: xvi
58 Ibid. 46–70 passim
59 Ibid. 1: 177
60 Ibid. 231
61 Ibid.
62 Ibid.

CHAPTER 9

1 Peter Gay *Weimar Culture* 6
2 See Friedrich Überweg *Grundriss der Geschichte der Philosophie* 313; also see I.M. Bochenski *Contemporary German Philosophy* 11.
3 See H. Stuart Hughes *Consciousness and Society* chap. 2 passim, Gerhard Masur *Prophets of Yesterday* chap. 4 passim, Edmund Wilson *Axel's Castle* chaps. 1 and 5 passim, Werner Haftmann *Painting in the Twentieth Century* 2: 18–19.

4 Arnold Brecht *Political Theory* (Princeton, Princeton University Press 1959) 3–10
5 On the parallel between ideas of truth and forms of government see Ralph Dahrendorf *Society and Democracy in Germany* chap. 10 passim.
6 On the co-operation between Cassirer, Saxl, and Warburg see F. Saxl, personal letter to Warburg, 7 May 1923 (used by permission of the Warburg Institute); cf. Cassirer's favourable view of Warburg's work, Cassirer, personal letter to Saxl, 25 May 1921 (used by permission of the Warburg Institute).
7 Dimitry Gawronsky 'Ernst Cassirer: His Life and His Work' 4
8 Erich H. Gombrich *Aby Warburg: An Intellectual Biography* 316
9 Gay *Weimar Culture* 31
10 Gombrich *Aby Warburg* 260–1
11 Fritz Saxl 'Ernst Cassirer' in Paul A. Schilpp, ed. *The Philosophy of Ernst Cassirer* 48
12 See especially Panofsky's 'Albrecht Dürer and Classical Antiquity' in Erwin Panofsky *Meaning in the Visual Arts* 236–85 passim. Note Panofsky's constant reference to Warburg; it was yet another indication of the intellectual harmony pervading the work of the Warburg group.
13 See Cassirer *The Individual and the Cosmos in Renaissance Philosophy* (1927); for references to Warburg, 75–7, 105, 169; for references to Panofsky, 31, 101, 114, 163, 165, 182; also see F. Saxl, personal letter to Warburg, 19 May 1923, where Saxl praised the harmony in the Warburg Library (used by permission of the Warburg Institute).
14 See E. Utitz's comment that Cassirer and Panofsky together formed one centre of philosophical and historical art research in Germany in Utitz 'Aesthetik und Philosophie der Kunst' 314; also see F. Saxl, private letters to Warburg of 2 and 9 January 1929, where Saxl wrote about Cassirer's and Warburg's united front at the scholarly congress on aesthetics (used by permission of the Warburg Institute).
15 Erwin Panofsky 'Die Perspektive als "Symbolische Form" ' 268
16 Ibid. 260–1
17 K. Gilbert 'Cassirer's Placement of Art' in Schilpp *Philosophy of Ernst Cassirer* 624
18 See Panofsky 'The History and the Theory of Human Proportions as a Reflection of the History of Styles' in *Meaning in the Visual Arts* 72–107 passim.
19 Cassirer *Renaissance Philosophy* xiii
20 Ibid.; see Cassirer, personal letter to Warburg, Saxl, and Bing, 21 September 1927, where Cassirer said that his own study of the Renaissance was a true work of the Warburg Library (letter used by permission of Warburg Institute).
21 Cassirer *Renaissance Philosophy* 47
22 On the Burckhardtian tradition see Wallace K. Ferguson *The Renaissance in Historical Thought* 195–252, especially 218–25 regarding Cassirer's own position in the tradition.
23 Ibid. 188–94

24  Cassirer *Renaissance Philosophy* 3
25  Ibid. 4–6
26  Ibid. 190–1
27  Ibid. 7
28  Ibid. 26
29  Ibid. 40
30  Ibid. 45
31  See ibid. 46–50.
32  Ibid. 54, 84–5
33  Ibid. 86
34  Ibid. 86–7, 190
35  Ibid. 120
36  Jacob Burckhardt *The Civilization of the Renaissance in Italy* 121
37  Ferguson *Renaissance* 218
38  Cassirer *Renaissance Philosophy* 183
39  Ibid. 178
40  Ibid. 180
41  Burckhardt *Renaissance in Italy* 320
42  Ferguson *Renaissance* 185
43  Leonardo as quoted by Cassirer *Renaissance Philosophy* 161
44  Ibid. 156
45  See especially Leon Battista Alberti *On Painting* 43–59.
46  Cassirer *Renaissance Philosophy* 162–3 171
47  Ferguson *Renaissance* 323–5
48  Ibid. 326–7
49  Ibid. 288–9
50  H. Stuart Hughes has been the primary popularizer of the idea that European
    thought from 1890 to 1930 could, generally speaking, be conceived as originating
    from a 'revolt against positivism'; see Hughes *Consciousness and Society* 37.
51  Gawronsky 'Ernst Cassirer' 25
52  Henri Bergson *An Introduction to Metaphysics* 23–4
53  Ibid. 53
54  Ibid. 54
55  See Georges Sorel *Reflections on Violence* 46-53, 122–3.
56  Ibid. 50
57  Bochenski *Contemporary German Philosophy* 101
58  F. Kaufmann 'Cassirer, Neo-Kantianism and Phenomenology' in Schilpp
    *Philosophy of Ernst Cassirer* 801–2
59  See Iso Kern *Husserl und Kant* 28–32; also see Herbert Spiegelberg *The
    Phenomenological Movement* 1: 110–11.

192 Notes to pages 140–51

60 Edmund Husserl *The Idea of Phenomenology* 35

61 Edmund Husserl 'Philosophy as Rigorous Science' 99–100

63 Martin Heidegger *Being and Time* 59

64 Ibid. 195

65 Anton-Hermann Chroust 'The Philosophy of Law of Gustav Radbruch' 25

66 Kelsen as quoted by John H. Hallowell *The Decline of Liberalism as an Ideology* 98

67 Ibid.

68 See the resolution of the pro-Weimar university professors in *Recht und Staat* 44 (1926): 38–9.

69 Wilhelm Stapel as quoted by Kurt Sontheimer *Antidemokratisches Denken in der Weimarer Republik* 233

70 Hallowell *German Liberalism* 100

71 Carl Schmitt *Die geistesgeschichtliche Lage des heutigen Parlamentarismus* 11

72 Ibid. 28–9

73 Hallowell *Decline of Liberalism* 105

74 Schmitt as quoted by Horst Ehmke *Grenzen der Verfassungsänderung* 43

75 Schmitt *Parlamentarismus* 35

76 Hallowell *Decline of Liberalism* 104–5

77 See Jëno Kurucz *Struktur und Funktion der Intelligenz während der Weimarer Republik* 110–20

78 Herman Lebovics *Social Conservatism and the Middle Classes in Germany 1914–1933* 12

79 Karl Mannheim 'The Democratization of Culture' 189

80 Ibid. 188

81 The idea that relativism was an integral part of liberalism was a generally held belief; for one example see Gerhard Leibholz *Die Auflösung der liberalen Demokratie in Deutschland und das autoritäre Staatsbild* 35

82 Lothar Albertin *Liberalismus und Demokratie am Anfang der Weimarer Republik* 164–5

83 See Toni Cassirer *Aus meinem Leben mit Ernst Cassirer* 172, 184–6.

CHAPTER 10

1 Toni Cassirer *Aus meinem Leben mit Ernst Cassirer* 157–9

2 See Manifesto of the 'Liberalen Vereinigung' circulated to the public in June 1928. Photocopy provided by Modris Eksteins.

3 Cassirer *Die Idee der republikanischen Verfassung* 31

4 Some scholars have argued that the third volume of *The Philosophy of Symbolic Forms* (1929) was the high point of Cassirer's entire philosophy. See Donald Verene 'Cassirer's Concept of Symbolic Form and Human Creativity' 6; also see Hendel 'Introductory Note' to Cassirer *Philosophy of Symbolic Forms* (1929) 3: ix.

5 *Philosophy of Symbolic Forms* 3: xiii

6 Ibid. 1

7 Ibid. 49

8 See Donald Verene 'Kant, Hegel and Cassirer: The Origins of the Philosophy of Symbolic Forms'; in these pages Verene discussed Cassirer's tripartite division in regard to Hegel's *Phenomenology of Mind*.

9 Cassirer *Philosophy of Symbolic Forms* 3: 57

10 Ibid. xiii

11 See ibid.: for Heidegger 149, 163, 189; for Bergson 38–9, 184–90; for Husserl 196–9.

12 Ibid. 2 (1925): 12

13 Ibid. 3: xiv

14 *Philosophy of Symbolic Forms* 3: 23

15 Ibid. 281

16 Ibid. 283

17 Ibid. 476

18 Ibid. 388–9

19 Cassirer 'Formen und Verwandlungen des philosophischen Wahrheitsbegriffs' 34

20 Ibid.

21 Cassirer *Philosophy of Symbolic Forms* 3: 414

22 Ibid. 163

23 Toni Cassirer *Aus meinem Leben mit Ernst Cassirer* 165

24 C.O. Schrag 'Heidegger and Cassirer on Kant' 95

25 Ibid. 97

26 Ibid. 92

27 Martin Heidegger *Kant and the Problem of Metaphysics* 177–8

28 Cassirer 'Kant and the Problem of Metaphysics' (1931) 149

29 Schrag 'Heidegger and Cassirer' 97

30 Ibid 98

31 Heidegger *Kant and the Problem of Metaphysics* 237

32 Schrag 'Heidegger and Cassirer' 89; cf. Cassirer 'Kant and the Problem of Metaphysics' 136–7.

33 Carl H. Hamburg 'A Cassirer-Heidegger Seminar' 217

34 Ibid. 218

35 Ibid.

36 Ibid. 219

37 Cassirer 'Kant and the Problem of Metaphysics' 155–6

38 Karl D. Bracher *The German Dictatorship* 268

39 Christian Graf von Krockow *Die Entscheidung* 1

40 Martin Heidegger *Die Selbstbehauptung der deutschen Universitäten* 13

41 Von Krockow *Die Entscheidung* 104
42 Bracher *The German Dictatorship* 268
43 Heidegger clearly placed his faith in the *Volk* rather than in any constitution; see Heidegger *Die Selbstbehauptung* 6–7, 15–16.
44 T. Cassirer *Aus meinem Leben* 172
45 Cassirer *Die Idee der republikanischen Verfassung* 31
46 Ibid. 16–17, 20–4
47 Ibid. 20–1
48 See T. Cassirer *Aus meinem Leben* 159.
49 Othmar Spann 'Die Kulturkrise der Gegenwart' 33–5
50 John Haag 'The Spann Circle and the Jewish Question' 104
51 Spann 'Die Kulturkrise der Gegenwart' 42
52 Cassirer 'Ansprache zur Reichsgründungsfeier der Hamburgischen Universität am 18 January 1930' 2, used by permission of the Yale University Library
53 Hugo Preuss *Deutschlands republikanische Reichsverfassung* 12, 39–40; Preuss was one of the prominent spokesmen of the DDP and the chief architect of the Weimar constitution.
54 Cassirer 'Wandlungen der Staatsgesinnung und der Staatstheorie in der deutschen Geistesgeschichte' passim, used by permission of the Yale University Library.
55 Cassirer *Die Idee der republikanische Verfassung* 24
56 Cassirer 'Wandlungen der Staatsgesinnung' (1930) 4–5 (italics mine) quoted by permission of the Yale University Library
57 Ibid. 26
58 See Von Krockow 58–9 on Fascism's aversion to objectivity.
59 See Carl von Ossietzky's remark that 'official Germany' (in 1932) celebrated Goethe 'not as a poet or prophet, but above all as opium,' as quoted by Gay *Weimar Culture* 88.
60 Ernst Cassirer 'Goethes Idee der Bildung und Erziehung' 342
61 Ibid. 358
62 Ernst Cassirer *Goethe und die geschichtliche Welt* (1932) 52
63 Cassirer 'Vom Wesen und Werden des Naturrechts' (1932) passim
64 Ibid. 13–14
65 Ibid. 2
66 Cassirer *The Philosophy of the Enlightenment* (1932) vi
67 Ibid. 49
68 Ibid. xi
69 Ibid.
70 Ibid. 6
71 Ibid. 5
72 Ibid. 42 (for Galileo), 52 (for Newton), 117 (for Condillac)

73 See Karl D. Bracher *Die Auflösung der Weimarer Republik* 146–9.
74 T. Cassirer *Aus meinem Leben* 162–3
75 Cassirer *Enlightenment* 238
76 Ibid. 249

CHAPTER 11

1 Karl D. Bracher *The German Dictatorship* 247–59
2 Toni Cassirer *Aus meinem Leben* 185
3 Cassirer *The Myth of the State* (1946) 297
4 Cassirer *An Essay on Man* (1944) vii
5 Ibid. 1–71 passim
6 Cassirer *Determinism and Indeterminism in Modern Physics* (1936) xxi–xxiv
7 Cassirer *Descartes* (1939) 76–81, 116–17
8 See especially Cassirer 'Judaism and the Modern Political Myths' (1944) passim.
9 See Cassirer *Essay on Man* 1–26.
10 Henry Pachter, personal letter to author, New York, May 1973
11 Cassirer lecture delivered at Yale University, 3 April 1944, last page, quoted by permission of Yale University Library
12 John Dewey *Liberalism and Social Action* 32

# Bibliography

THE WORKS OF ERNST CASSIRER

Listed below in chronological order of original publication or completion are those works of Ernst Cassirer which I consider most relevant to an understanding of his thought.

1899–1914

*Leibniz' System in seinen wissenschaftlichen Grundlagen* Hildesheim, Georg Olms 1962 (1902)

*Das Erkenntnisproblem in der Philosophie und Wissenschaft der neueren Zeit* vols. 1–2. Berlin, Bruno Cassirer, 1922 (vol. 1 1906, vol. 2 1907)

*Substance and Function* and *Einstein's Theory of Relativity* Translated by W.C. Swabey and M.C. Swabey. New York, Dover Publications 1953 (*Substance and Function* 1910)

'Hermann Cohen und die Erneuerung der Kantischen Philosophie' *Kant-Studien* 17 (1912): 252–73

'Erkenntnistheorie nebst den Grenzfragen der Logik' *Jahrbücher der Philosophie* 1 (1913): 1–59

'Die Grundprobleme der Kantischen Methodik und ihr Verhältnis zur Nachkantischen Spekulation' *Die Geisteswissenschaften* 1 (1914): 784–7, 812–15

1914–22

*Freiheit und Form* Darmstadt, Wissenschaftliche Buchgesellschaft 1961 (1916)

*Kants Leben und Lehre* Berlin, Bruno Cassirer 1921 (1918; manuscript ready in 1916)

*Idee und Gestalt* 2nd edition. Berlin, Bruno Cassirer 1924; reprint edition Darmstadt, Wissenschaftliche Buchgesellschaft 1973 (essays in this collection published 1917–21)

'Hermann Cohen: Worte gesprochen an seinem Grabe am 7. April 1918' *Neue jüdische Monatshefte* no. 15–16 (1918): 347–52

*Das Erkenntnisproblem in der Philosophie und Wissenschaft der neueren Zeit* vol. 3, Berlin, Bruno Cassirer 1923 (1920)

*Substance and Function* and *Einstein's Theory of Relativity*. Translated by W.C. Swabey and M.C. Swabey. New York, Dover Publications 1953 (*Einstein's Theory of Relativity* 1921)

*Wesen und Wirkung des Symbolbegriffs* Darmstadt, Wissenschaftliche Buchgesellschaft 1969 (the two essays used from this collection published 1921–22)


1923–32

*The Philosophy of Symbolic Forms* 3 vols. Translated by R. Manheim, with an introduction and preface by C.W. Hendel. New Haven, Yale University Press 1953–7 (vol. 1 1923, vol. 2 1925, vol. 3 1929)

'Die Kantischen Elemente in Wilhelm von Humboldts Sprachphilosophie' in *Festschrift für Paul Hensel* 105–27. Greiz i.V., Ohag 1923 (1923)

*Language and Myth* Translated and introduced by S.K. Langer. Toronto, Harper and Brothers 1946; reprint edition New York, Dover Publications 1953 (1925)

'Paul Natorp' *Kant-Studien* 30 (1925): 273–98

*The Individual and the Cosmos in Renaissance Philosophy* Translated by M. Domandi. New York, Harper and Row, Harper Torchbooks 1964 (1927)

'Erkenntnistheorie nebst den Grenzfragen der Logik und Denkpsychologie' *Jahrbücher der Philosophie* 3 (1927): 31–92

'Das Symbolproblem und seine Stellung im System der Philosophie' *Zeitschrift für Aesthetik und allgemeine Kunstwissenschaft* 21 (1927): 191–208

*Die Idee der republikanischen Verfassung* Speech delivered at the Constitutional Celebrations of 11 August 1928. Hamburg, Friederichsen 1929 (1928)

'Formen und Verwandlungen des philosophischen Wahrheitsbegriffs' in *Hamburger Universitäts-Reden* Hamburg, n. p. 1931, 17–36 (1929)

'Ansprache zur Reichsgründungsfeier der Hamburgischen Universität am 18 Januar 1930' 18 January 1930. Yale University, Beinecke Manuscript Library (1930)

'Wandlungen der Staatsgesinnung und der Staatstheorie in der deutschen Geistesgeschichte' Speech delivered 30 June 1930. Yale University, Beinecke Manuscript Library (1930)

' "Geist" und "Leben" in der Philosophie der Gegenwart' *Die Neue Rundschau* 41, no. 1 (1930): 244–64

'Form und Technik' in *Kunst und Technik* edited by L. Kestenberg. Berlin, Wegweiser 1930, 15–61 (1930)

'Kant and the Problem of Metaphysics' in *Kant: Disputed Questions*. Translated and edited by Moltke S. Gram. Chicago, Quadrangle Books 1967, 131–57 (1931)

'Deutschland und Westeuropa im Spiegel der Geistesgeschichte' *Inter-Nationes* 1
(1931), no. 3: 57–9 and no. 4: 83–5
*The Philosophy of the Enlightenment* Translated and edited by F.C.A. Koelln and J.P.
Pettegrove. Boston, Beacon Press 1966 (1932)
*Goethe und die geschichtliche Welt* Berlin, Bruno Cassirer 1932 (1932)
'Goethes Idee der Bildung und Erziehung' *Pädagogisches Zentralblatt* 12 (1932): 340–58
'Vom Wesen und Werden des Naturrechts' *Zeitschrift für Rechtsphilosophie in Lehre und
Praxis* 6 (1932): 1–27


1933–45
*Determinism and Indeterminism in Modern Physics* Translated by O.T. Benfey, with a
preface by H. Margenau. New Haven, Yale University Press 1966 (1936)
*Descartes* Stockholm, Bermann-Fischer 1939 (1939)
*The Problem of Knowledge* Translated by W.H. Woglom and C.W. Hendel, with a
preface by C.W. Hendel, New Haven, Yale University Press 1950; Yale paperback
1969 (1940)
*The Logic of the Humanities* Translated by C.S. Howe. New Haven, Yale University
Press 1960; Yale paperback 1967 (1939–42)
'Some Remarks on the Question of the Originality of the Renaissance' *Journal of the
History of Ideas* 4 (1943): 49–46
'Hermann Cohen, 1842–1918' *Social Research* 10 (1943): 219–32
*An Essay on Man* New Haven, Yale University Press 1944; Yale paperback 1964 (1944)
'Remarks on the English edition of Jacob Burckhardt's Reflections on History'
*American Scholar* 13 (1944): 407–17
'Judaism and the Modern Political Myths' *Contemporary Jewish Record* 7 (1944): 115–26
Lecture delivered at Yale University 3 April 1944. Yale University, Beinecke
Manuscript Library (1944)
*The Myth of the State* Edited and with a foreword by C.W. Hendel. New Haven, Yale
University Press 1946; Yale paperback 1969 (1946)

BIOGRAPHIES, DIARIES, AND PERSONAL DOCUMENTS

The sources listed in this section are not very numerous. Many potential private
sources revealing the personal life of Cassirer were either lost or destroyed between
1933 and 1945 or are still not available to the public.

Cassirer, Ernst  Personal letters to Paul Natorp. Natorp Personal Papers, University of
Marburg, Marburg, West Germany
– Personal letters to Warburg, Saxl, and Panofsky. Private Papers of the Warburg
Institute, London, England

Cassirer, Toni *Aus meinem Leben mit Ernst Cassirer* New York, privately published 1950
Gawronsky, Dimitry 'Ernst Cassirer: His Life and His Work' in Paul A. Schilpp, ed. *The Philosophy of Ernst Cassirer* New York, Tudor Publishing 1958
Kessler, Harry Graf *Aus den Tagbüchern* Edited by W. Pfeiffer-Bell. Munich, Deutscher Taschenbuch 1965
Manifesto of the 'Liberalen Vereinigung' with list of signatories circulated to the public in June 1928. Photocopy provided by Modris Eksteins
Meinecke, Friedrich *Werke* vol. 8: *Autobiographische Schriften* Edited by E. Kessel. Stuttgart, K.F. Koehler 1969
*Neue Deutsche Biographie* vol. 3. Berlin, Duncker und Humblot 1956
Pachter, Henry Personal letter to author, New York, May 1973

POLITICS AND LAW

These are the most useful sources dealing with liberal legal and political ideas and with their connection to contemporary events.

Albertin, Lothar *Liberalismus und Demokratie am Anfang der Weimarer Republik* Dusseldorf, Droste 1972
Brecht, Arnold *Political Theory* Princeton, Princeton University Press 1959
Butz, Otto *Modern German Political Theory* Garden City, N.Y., Doubleday 1955
Chroust, Anton-Hermann 'The Philosophy of Law of Gustav Radbruch' *Philosophical Review* 53 (1944): 23–45
Ebenstein, William *The Pure Theory of Law* Madison, Wisconsin, University of Wisconsin Press 1945
Ehmke, Horst *Grenzen der Verfassungsänderung* Berlin, Duncker und Humblot 1953
Elm, Ludwig *Zwischen Fortschritt und Reaktion* Berlin, Akademie-Verlag 1968
Fischenberg, Günter 'Der deutsche Liberalismus und die Entstehung der Weimarer Republik' Unpublished dissertation, Münster 1958
Gény, François *Méthode d'interprétation et sources en droit privé positif* 2nd ed. Translated by J. Mayda. St Paul, West Publishing 1954
Hallowell, John H. *The Decline of Liberalism as an Ideology* Berkeley, University of California Press 1943
Hartenstein, Wolfgang *Die Anfänge der deutschen Volkspartei 1918–1920* Düsseldorf, Droste Verlag 1962
Jones, L.E. ' "The Dying Middle": Weimar Germany and the Fragmentation of Bourgeois Politics' *Central European History* 5 (1972): 23–54
Kaufmann, Erich *Kritik der neukantischen Rechtsphilosophie* Tübingen, Neudruck der Ausgabe Tübingen 1921; reprint edition Tübingen, Scientia Verlag Aalen 1964
Kelsen, Hans *Hauptprobleme der Staatslehre* Tübingen, J.C.B. Mohr 1923

Krieger, Leonard *The German Idea of Freedom* Chicago, Chicago University Press 1957; reprint edition Chicago Phoenix Books 1972

Leibholz, Gerhard *Die Auflösung der liberalen Demokratie in Deutschland und das autoritäre Staatsbild* Munich, Duncker und Humblot 1933

Lübbe, Hermann *Politische Philosophie in Deutschland* Basel, Benno Schwabe 1963

Mann, Thomas *Reden und Aufsätze* vol. 2. Oldenburg, S. Fischer 1965

Marck, Siegfried *Substanz- und Funktionsbegriff in der Rechtsphilosophie* Tubingen, J.C.B. Mohr 1925

Meinecke, Friedrich 'Der Weltkrieg' *Die Neue Rundschau* (1914), vol. 2: 1615–27

– *Werke* vol. 2: *Politische Schriften und Reden* Edited by G. Kotowski. Darmstadt, S. Toeche-Mittler 1966

Pound, R. 'Fifty Years of Jurisprudence' Part 3. *Harvard Law Review* 51 (1937–8): 444–72

Preuss, Hugo *Deutschlands republikanische Reichsverfassung* Berlin, Neuer Staat 1923

Sauer, Wilhelm *Lehrbuch der Rechts- und Sozialphilosophie* Berlin, W. Rothschild 1929

– 'Neukantianismus und Rechtswissenschaft in Herbst' *Logos* 10 (1921–2): 162–94

Schmitt, Carl *Die geistesgeschichtliche Lage des heutigen Parlamentarismus* 3rd edition. Berlin, Duncker und Humblot 1961

Schorske, Carl E. *German Social Democracy 1905–1917* Cambridge, Mass., Science Editions 1965

Schwabe, K. 'Zur politischen Haltung der deutschen Professoren im ersten Weltkrieg' *Historische Zeitschrift* 193 (1961): 601–34

Sell, Friedrich C. *Die Tragödie des deutschen Liberalismus* Stuttgart, Deutsche Verlags-Anstalt 1953

Sorel, Georges *Reflections on Violence* Translated by T.E. Hulme, with an introduction by E.A. Shils. New York, Free Press 1950; Collier Books 1970

Troeltsch, Ernst 'The Ideas of Natural Law and Humanity in World Politics' in Otto F. von Gierke *Natural Law and the Theory of Society.* Translated and with an introduction by Ernest Barker. Cambridge, Cambridge University Press 1958

Wegner, Konstanze *Theodor Barth und die freisinnige Vereinigung* Tübingen, J.C.B. Mohr 1968

Zechlin, Egmont *Die deutsche Politik und die Juden im ersten Weltkrieg* Göttingen, Vandenhoeck und Ruprecht 1969

PHILOSOPHY AND CULTURE

These are the most useful primary and secondary sources on the philosophical and cultural context of the work of Cassirer and the neo-Kantians.

Alberti, Leon Battista *On Painting* Translated, with notes and an introduction by J.R.

Spencer. New Haven, Yale University Press 1956; Yale paperback 1966

Bergson, Henri *An Introduction to Metaphysics* Translated by T.E. Hulme, with an introduction by T.A. Goudge. Indianapolis, Bobbs-Merrill 1949; Library of Liberal Arts 1955

Bochenski, I.M. *Contemporary German Philosophy* Translated by D. Nicholl and K. Aschenbrenner. Berkeley, University of California Press 1966

Cohen, Hermann *Deutschtum und Judentum* Giessen, A. Topelmann 1916

– *Kants Theorie der Erfahrung* Berlin, Bruno Cassirer, 1925. Originally published in Berlin 1871

– *Logik der reinen Erkenntnis* Berlin, Bruno Cassirer 1902

– *Das Prinzip der Infinitesimal-Methode und seine Geschichte* Frankfurt a.M., Suhrkamp 1968. Originally published in Berlin, F. Dümmlers 1883

Copelston, Frederic *A History of Philosophy* vol. 7, part 2. Garden City, N.Y., Doubleday Image Books 1965

Dussort, Henri *L'École de Marbourg* Paris, Presses Universitaires de France 1963

Ewald, O. 'Die deutsche Philosophie im Jahre 1909' *Kant-Studien* 15 (1910): 421–58

Findlay, John N. *The Philosophy of Hegel* New York, Collier Books 1966

Gay, Peter 'The Social History of Ideas: Ernst Cassirer and After' in K.H. Wolff and B. Moore, Jr., eds. *The Critical Spirit* Boston, Beacon Press 1967

Geis, R. 'Hermann Cohen und die deutsche Reformation' *Yearbook of the Leo Baeck Institute* 4 (1959): 81–91

Görland, Albert 'Hermann Cohens systematische Arbeit im Dienst des kritischen Idealismus' *Kant-Studien* 17 (1912): 222–51

Haag, John 'The Spann Circle and the Jewish Question' *Yearbook of the Leo Baeck Institute* 18 (1973): 93–126

Hamburg, Carl H. *Symbol and Reality* The Hague, Martinus Nijhoff 1956

– 'A Cassirer-Heidegger Seminar' *Philosophy and Phenomenological Research* 25 (1964): 208–22

Hegel, Georg W.F. *The Phenomenology of Mind* Translated with an introduction and notes by J.B. Baillie. London, George Allen and Unwin 1931; reprint edition, with an introduction by G. Lichtheim, New York, Harper Torchbooks 1967

– *Hegel's Lectures on the Philosophy of History* vol. 1. Translated by E.S. Haldane. London, Routledge and Kegan Paul 1955

– *The Logic of Hegel* Translated by W. Wallace, 2nd ed. London, Oxford University Press 1968

Heidegger, Martin *Die Selbstbehauptung der deutschen Universitäten* Rectoral speech, 27 May 1933. Breslau, Wilh. Gottl. Korn 1934

– *Being and Time* Translated by J. Macquarrie and E. Robinson. New York, Harper and Row 1962

– *Kant and the Problem of Metaphysics* Translated by J.C. Churchill, with a foreword by

T. Langan. Bloomington, Indiana University Press 1962

Husserl, Edmund 'Philosophy as Rigorous Science' in *Phenomenology and the Crisis of Philosophy* Translated with an introduction by Quentin Lauer. New York, Harper Torchbooks 1965

- *The Idea of Phenomenology* Translated by W.P. Alston and G. Nakhnikian, with an introduction by G. Nakhnikian. The Hague, Martinus Nijhoff 1970

Itzkoff, Seymor W. *Ernst Cassirer: Scientific Knowledge and the Concept of Man.* Notre Dame, Indiana, University of Notre Dame Press 1971

Kalbeck, Florian 'Die Philosophie Systematik Ernst Cassirers' Unpublished dissertation, Vienna 1951

Kant, Immanuel *The Critique of Pure Reason* Translated by Norman Kemp Smith. London, Macmillan 1958

- 'What is Enlightenment?' in Lewis W. Beck, ed. *On History* Indianapolis, Bobbs-Merrill 1963; Library of Liberal Arts edition 1963

- *The Critique of Judgement* Translated by J.C. Meredith. Oxford, Clarendon Press 1964

Kern, Iso *Husserl und Kant* The Hague, Martinus Nijhoff 1964

Klibansky, R. and H.J. Paton, eds. *Philosophy and History: Essays Presented to Ernst Cassirer* 2nd ed. New York, Harper Torchbooks 1963

Körner, S. *Kant* Harmondsworth, England, Penguin Paperbacks 1970

Krockow, Christian, Graf von *Die Entscheidung* Stuttgart, Enke 1958

Lange, Friedrich A. *History of Materialism* 3 vols. Translated by E.C. Thomas, with an introduction by Bertrand Russell. London, Routledge and Kegan Paul 1950

Lasson, Georg 'Kritischer und spekulativer Idealismus' *Kant-Studien* 27 (1922): 1–58

Liebeschutz, H. 'Hermann Cohen and his Historical Background' *Year Book of the Leo Baeck Institute* 13 (1968): 3–33

Löwith, Karl *From Hegel to Nietzsche* Translated by D.E. Green. Garden City, N.Y., Anchor Books 1967

Mandelbaum, Maurice H. *The Problem of Historical Knowledge* New York, Liveright 1938

Mann, Thomas *Betrachtungen eines Unpolitischen* Frankfurt a.M., S. Fischer 1956

Mannheim, Karl 'The Democratization of Culture' in *Essays on the Sociology of Culture.* E. Mannheim and P. Kecskemeti, eds. London, Routledge and Kegan Paul 1967

Medicus, Fritz 'Philosophie und Dichtung' *Logos* 4 (1913): 36–45

Meinecke, Friedrich 'Drei Generationen deutscher Gelehrtenpolitik' *Historische Zeitschrift* 125 (1922): 248–83

Natorp, Paul *Die logischen Grundlagen der exakten Wissenschaften* Leipzig, Teubner 1910

Naumann, H. 'Versuch einer Geschichte der deutschen Sprache als Geschichte des deutschen Geistes' *Deutsche Vierteljahrsschrift für Literaturwissenschaft und Geistesgeschichte* 1 (1923): 139–60

Panofsky, Erwin 'Die Perspektive als "Symbolische Form" ' *Vorträge Bibliothek Warburg* 4 (1924–5): 258–330
- *Meaning in the Visual Arts* Garden City, N.Y., Anchor Books 1955
Schilpp, Paul A., ed. *The Philosophy of Ernst Cassirer* New York, Tudor Publishing 1958
Schrag, C.O. 'Heidegger and Cassirer on Kant' *Kant-Studien* 58 (1967): 87–100
Schrödinger, Erwin C. *Science, Theory and Man* New York, Dover Publications 1957
Simmel, Georg 'Goethes Individualismus' *Logos* 3 (1912): 251–74
- *The Sociology of Georg Simmel* Translated and edited by K.H. Wolff. New York, Free Press paperback 1964
Sombart, Werner *Händler und Helden* Munich, Duncker und Humblot 1915
Spann, Othmar 'Die Kulturkrise der Gegenwart' *Mitteilungen des Kampfbundes für deutsche Kultur* 1 (1929): 33–44
Spiegelberg, Herbert *The Phenomenological Movement* vol. 1. The Hague, Martinus Nijhoff 1960
Sternberg, K. 'Die philosophischen Grundlagen in Spenglers "Untergang des Abendlandes" ' *Kant-Studien* 27 (1922): 101–37
- Review of the second volume of *The Philosophy of Symbolic Forms* in *Kant-Studien* 30 (1925): 194–5
Troeltsch, Ernst 'Der historische Entwicklungsbegriff in der modernen Geistes- und Lebensphilosophie' parts 1 and 2 *Historische Zeitschrift* 122 (1920): 377–453 and 124 (1921): 377–447
- *Deutscher Geist und Westeuropa* Edited by H. Baron. Tübingen, Neudruck der Ausgabe Tübingen 1925; reprint edition Darmstadt, Scientia Verlag Aalen 1966
Überweg, Friedrich *Grundriss der Geschichte der Philosophie* vol. 4. Berlin, E.S. Mittler und Sohn 1923
Utitz, E. 'Aesthetik und allegemeine Kunstwissenschaft' *Jahrbücher der Philosophie* 1 (1913): 322–64
- 'Aesthetik und Philosophie der Kunst' *Jahrbücher der Philosophie* 3 (1927): 306–32
Verene, Donald 'Kant, Hegel and Cassirer: The Origins of the Philosophy of Symbolic Forms' *Journal of the History of Ideas* 30 (1969): 38–46
- 'Cassirer's Concept of Symbolic Form and Human Creativity' Paper delivered at the Society for Philosophy of Creativity. Boston, 27 December 1972
Vossler, Karl 'Das Verhältnis von Sprachgeschichte und Literaturgeschichte *Logos* 2 (1911–12): 167–78
- *The Spirit of Language in Civilization* Translated by O. Oeser. London, Kegan Paul, Trench and Trubner 1932
Weber, Max 'Science as a Vocation,' in *From Max Weber.* Translated, edited, and introduced by H.H. Gerth and C. Wright Mills. New York, Oxford University Press paperback 1970
Wind, E. 'Contemporary German Philosophy' *Journal of Philosophy* 22 (1925): 477–93

GENERAL ACCOUNTS

Benda, Julien *The Treason of the Intellectuals* Translated by R. Aldington. New York,
W.W. Norton 1969; Norton Library paperback 1969

Bracher, Karl D. *Die Auflösung der Weimarer Republik* With an introduction by H.
Herzfeld. Villingen/Schwarzwald, Ring 1964

– *The German Dictatorship* Translated by J. Steinberg, with an introduction by P. Gay.
New York, Praeger 1970

Brinton, Crane *Nietzsche* New York, Harper and Row 1965

Burckhardt, Jacob *The Civilization of the Renaissance in Italy* Translated by S.G.C.
Middlemore, revised and edited by I. Gordon. New York, The New American
Library 1960; Mentor Books 1961

Busch, Alexander *Die Geschichte des Privatdozenten* Stuttgart, Ferdinand Enke 1959

Croce, Benedetto *History of Europe in the Nineteenth Century*. Translated by H. Furst.
London, Unwin University Books 1965

Dahrendorf, Ralph *Society and Democracy in Germany* Garden City, N.Y., Anchor Books
1969

Dewey, John *Liberalism and Social Action* New York, Capricorn Books 1963

Ferguson, Wallace K. *The Renaissance in Historical Thought* Cambridge, Mass.,
Houghton Mifflin 1948

Fischer, Fritz *Germany's Aims in the First World War*. Translation with an introduction
by James Joll. London, Chatto and Windus 1967

Gay, Peter *The Dilemma of Democratic Socialism* New York, Collier Books 1962

– *Weimar Culture* New York, Harper and Row 1968; Harper Torchbooks 1970

Gombrich, Erich H. *Aby Warburg: An Intellectual Biography* London, The Warburg
Institute 1970

Haftmann, Werner *Painting in the Twentieth Century* vol. 2. Translated by J. Seligman.
New York, Praeger 1965

Halévy, Elie *The Era of Tyrannies* Translated by R.K. Webb, with a note by F. Stern.
Garden City, N.Y., Anchor Books 1965

Hannover, Heinrich and Elisabeth Hannover-Drück *Politische Justiz*. With an
introduction by Karl D. Bracher. Frankfurt a.M., Fischer Bücherei 1966

Hughes, H. Stuart *Consciousness and Society* New York, Vintage Paperbacks 1958

Iggers, Georg G. *The German Conception of History* Middletown, Connecticut, Wesleyan
University Press 1968

Klemperer, Klemens von *Germany's New Conservatism* With a foreword by S.
Neumann. Princeton, Princeton University Press paperback 1968

Knütter, Hans H. *Die Juden und die deutsche Linke in der Weimarer Republik 1918–1933*
Düsseldorf, Droste 1971

Kohn, Hans *The Mind of Germany* New York, Harper and Row 1965; Harper
Torchbooks 1965

Kuhn, Thomas *The Structure of Scientific Revolutions* Chicago, University of Chicago Press 1962; Phoenix Books 1969

Kurucz, Jëno *Struktur und Funktion der Intelligenz während der Weimarer Republik* Cologne, Grote 1967

Lebovics, Herman *Social Conservatism and the Middle Classes in Germany 1914–1933* Princeton, Princeton University Press 1969

Liebeschütz, H. 'Jewish Thought in its German Background' *Yearbook of the Leo Baeck Institute* 1 (1956): 217–36

Mann, Thomas *Essays of Three Decades* Translated by H.T. Lowe-Porter. New York, Alfred A. Knopf 1947

Masur, Gerhard *Prophets of Yesterday* New York, Harper and Row 1961; Harper Colophon paperback 1966

– *Imperial Berlin* New York, Basic Books 1971

Mayer, Jacob P. *Max Weber and German Politics* London, Faber and Faber 1956

Meinecke, Friedrich *Cosmopolitanism and the National State* With an introduction by F. Gilbert, translated by R.B. Kimber. Princeton, Princeton University Press 1970

Mosse, George L. *The Culture of Western Europe.* U.S.A., Rand McNally 1965

– *Germans and Jews* New York, H. Fertig 1970

Mosse, Werner, ed. *Entscheidungsjahr 1932* Tübingen, J.C.B. Mohr 1965

Mosse, Werner and Arnold Paucker, eds. *Deutsches Judentum in Krieg und Revolution 1916–1923* Tübingen, J.C.B. Mohr 1971

Nicholls, A., and E. Matthias, eds. *German Democracy and the Triumph of Hitler* London, George Allen and Unwin 1971

Nolte, Ernst *Three Faces of Fascism* Translated by L. Vennewitz. New York, Mentor Books 1969

Pachter, Henry M. 'On Being in Exile' *Salmagundi* (1969–70): 12–51

– 'The Intellectuals and the State of Weimar' *Social Research* 39 (1972): 228–53

Paucker, Arnold *Der jüdischen Abwehrkampf gegen Antisemitismus und Nationalismus in den letzten Jahren der Weimarer Republik* Hamburg, Leibniz 1969

Paulsen, Friedrich *Die deutschen Universitäten und das Universitätsstudium* Hildesheim, Georg Olms 1966

Polanyi, Karl *The Great Transformation* With an introduction by R.M. MacIver. Boston, Beacon Press 1968

Ringer, Fritz K. *The Decline of the German Mandarins* Cambridge, Mass., Harvard University Press 1969

Ruggiero, Guido de *The History of European Liberalism* Translated by R.G. Collingwood. Boston, Beacon Press 1959

Schorsch, Ismar *Jewish Reactions to German Anti-Semitism 1870–1914* New York, Columbia University Press 1972

Sontheimer, Kurt *Antidemokratisches Denken in der Weimarer Republik* Munich, Nymphenburger 1972

Sterling, Richard W. *Ethics in a World of Power* Princeton, Princeton University Press 1958

Stern, Fritz *The Politics of Cultural Despair* Garden City, N.Y. Anchor Books 1965

– *The Failure of Illiberalism* New York, Alfred A. Knopf 1972

Waite, Robert G.L. *Vanguard of Nazism* New York, W.W. Norton 1969; Norton Library paperback 1969

Wilson, Edmund *Axel's Castle* New York, Charles Scribner's Sons paperback 1959

# Index